India
Before
the
Ambanis

India
Before
the
Ambanis

A History *of* Indian Business, Money *and* Economy

LAKSHMI SUBRAMANIAN

PENGUIN
BUSINESS

An imprint of Penguin Random House

PENGUIN BUSINESS

Penguin Business is an imprint of the Penguin Random House group of companies
whose addresses can be found at global.penguinrandomhouse.com

Published by Penguin Random House India Pvt. Ltd
4th Floor, Capital Tower 1, MG Road,
Gurugram 122 002, Haryana, India

First published in Penguin Business by Penguin Random House India 2024

ISBN 9780670098576

Typeset in Adobe Garamond Pro by MAP Systems, Bengaluru, India
Printed at Manipal Technologies Limited, Manipal

www.penguin.co.in

For my students of F375, BITS Pilani, Goa

Contents

Acknowledgements

The idea for writing a brief history of Indian business between the eighteenth and twentieth centuries was largely informed by the enthusiasm shown by my students at BITS Pilani—Goa for a course I ran on business and politics over a couple of semesters (2022–23). I realized how little we actually knew about business history in India and how much of our contemporary imagination and understanding of India's industrial experience was formed by hearsay and anecdotal information passed on by fathers and uncles who happened to work in MNCs or in public sector establishments. Business history was barely accommodated in standard history syllabi, and there were hardly any handy and accessible books on the subject. There were very few visual representations of India's businessmen, the film *Guru* being the only exception. Furthermore, with the rise of the IT industry, the glamour of old-world business establishments receded, appearing to be almost antediluvian. Yet, in retrospect, one acutely realized how so many of our contemporary perceptions, tastes and aspirations have been formed by the culture of manufacture and marketing, which has a history and which I felt was worth telling. Personally, as I looked back on my own experience, from the vantage point of historical inquiry, I appreciated many processes: for example, the ubiquity of industrial objects in our lives, such as the Godrej Storwel, the crippling tax regime that many of our fathers had to deal with and the overall shortages that characterized the Indian economy in the 1960s, as well as the appeal of 'foreign' objects for us at that time. I vividly recall how excited I was when my uncle, after a visit to Thailand and Southeast Asia, picked up a couple of polyester crimped pleated skirts that were a novelty and deeply coveted. Little did I realize then that the craze for polyester had found roots in India and that it persuaded men like Dhirubhai Ambani to think ahead and find an object that was worthy of mass consumption.

Researching business experience was thus an exercise in past forward and gave me deep personal pleasure as I braided memory with history and used a personal and biographical approach to the exercise of reconstructing historical events. I relied on extensive secondary material such as the archival holdings that I had access to, especially Godrej Archives, digital material on the house of Bajaj, business biographies and autobiographies, and contemporary business publications and newspapers. I am grateful to all those who extended their support in making these materials available, particularly Vrunda Pathare and her colleagues at Godrej Archives. I also use this occasion to express my appreciation of students who opted for my F375 course on business and politics, asked probing questions and enjoyed participating in the course as much as I enjoyed teaching it.

Lakshmi Subramanian
Goa, 2024

Introduction

My readers may legitimately question the purpose of another book on the history of Indian business and entrepreneurship. In defence and anticipation, I suggest that it engages with several issues thrown up by earlier histories of business, mainly dealing with matter and method. It does not offer a prescription on what business history is or should look like; instead, it focuses on stories of individual enterprise, talent and vision to reflect on the larger milieu and context of business activity. Yet it does not follow the line or tone adopted by recent biographical sketches, which is to pitch either the 'rags to riches' story or the success and resilience of business dynasts drawn from traditional mercantile communities. Rather, it foregrounds the context in which businessmen operated, planned and toiled, and within it, it plots the tales of individuals who, in their personas, manifest what American biographer Debby Applegate calls 'historical forces'.[1] The book takes its cue from several pioneering studies on business and economic history, especially of India, to put together a narrative that is as much about individuals with fire in their belly as it is about the larger context in which they laboured, innovated and dared to dream big. It tries to capture that intangible element of creativity, of the risk-taking propensity and single-minded pursuit of success, by a selection of case studies over a period of two centuries and more from about the latter decades of the eighteenth century. These two centuries straddled the colonial and post-colonial regime with its attendant challenges and opportunities for business groups to experiment with not merely money-making but with the act of entrepreneurship, an act that Peter Drucker defined as something that endowed resources with a new capacity to create wealth or her ability to respond to change, and this was what amounts to innovation. In the case of India, for example, the ability to respond was not unrelated to structure and context, especially under conditions of colonial rule. Capital was always scarce, and the resources available to generate wealth were restricted. Labour, on the other hand, was plentiful and cheap, inhibiting merchants from experiment with innovation or technology and achieving a breakthrough. Yet, some individuals and communities were able to overcome this lack to initiate ventures that were dynamic, competitive, original and sustainable, enabling Indian business to emerge as a force in its own right and not simply a derivative of colonial patronage. Our protagonists were aware of the emancipatory dimensions of business and entrepreneurship, which they pursued with single-minded zeal. We will see this in the careers of businessmen across time, from Jamsetjee Jeejeebhoy and Dwarkanath Tagore in the mid-nineteenth century, both of whom saw enterprise as a conduit to modernity, to later Parsi industrialists such as Jamshedji Nusserwanji Tata (J.N. Tata) and Ardeshir Godrej, who found it possible to translate the ideals of Swaraj and Swadeshi into their business, to the flamboyant Dhirubhai Ambani, who, as we shall see, gave innovation a new meaning altogether. This included gaining the confidence of small investors and raising capital for his ventures.

Implicit in such a description of individual entrepreneurs is an adherence to a biographical approach to the understanding of business experience. How does such a perspective enrich and expand the field of business history? To answer this, we will need to review what business history is and the extent to which this subfield has enjoyed traction in the Indian context. This is important because business history is of recent provenance and also because business history, like most fields of history, has a double life and profile. One, which is part of a larger academic discipline informed by method and writing protocols, and the other, which is more public and generally expressed in the form of business biographies of which there are now quite a few. While conventional business history would plot the rise and fall of firms and place their operations in context, public and popular histories of business would be anecdotal and foreground individual achievements, occasionally even uncritically. As a discipline, business history was initially associated with developments in business studies in the United States from about the 1920s, with Alfred Chandler stepping in to carve a clear niche for the subject. For Chandler, the development of managerial enterprise stood out as the distinguishing mark of business history.[2] However, critical voices emerged thereafter, and there was a clear move to move beyond large-scale enterprise to reimagine the discipline and also consider different geographies for studying business and not simply confine it to the modern west.[3] The critique described his focus as being too narrow and his methodology restrictive. It was argued that it was not enough to study big companies and corporations; it was important to look at individuals, their context and the evolution of ideas and culture.[4] Arthur Cole made the point that the identification of business history with company history was far too narrow, it was like identifying one architectural style with architecture.[5] With new questions emerging to command the attention of business history pandits, there were concerns about methodology and about the approaches to be used in understanding the world of modern business. Per Hansen's interventions in this regard were especially compelling. He argued that a cultural and narrative perspective could enrich the discipline and expand its contours.[6] Hansen recommended this approach as a means of expanding the database for business history; in his words, 'a cultural approach could therefore lead us to use new kinds of sources and to use traditional sources for new purposes'.[7] At the same time, new lines of research on entrepreneurship and enterprise helped expand the remit of business history since the 1980s, when entrepreneurship emerged as a major topic of interest for scholars.[8] According to Jones and Wadhwani, entrepreneurship played a decisive role in the emergence of business history as a discipline and withstood the challenges of Chandlerian emphasis on organizational structures. Entrepreneurs emerged as agents of historical change that found expression in the writing of biographies, some of which were hagiographic but had the potential to humanize a story of growth and innovation. The present work values the importance of narrativizing such individual stories while situating them within a larger context of political change and economic processes. However, in its essentials, the work draws on the scholarship produced by economic historians on trading and business communities and their networks in the pre-modern and early colonial period, as well as the substantial work on Indian industrialization, and recently on business families and their relations with the post-colonial Indian state. None of these histories necessarily define themselves as business histories; they are concerned with issues of development and manufacture in the subcontinent, of entrepreneurship and the challenges it faced under conditions of colonialism and thereafter, and it is only retrospectively that we count them as our pathfinders in creating a subfield such as business history. It is also worth remembering that writing conventional business history for India, i.e., the history of a specific firm, is challenging given that archives are scarce and not accessible. It is only recently that archives of top business houses (Tata, Godrej) have been opened to the public, making it possible to study their organization and their business decisions creatively and comprehensively. Under the circumstances, business history in India, for the most part, tends to focus on specific communities and their regimes of circulation, their ability to negotiate with political regimes to carve a niche for their activities within the colonial economy, and more recently on big companies like the Tatas or the Birlas, where the individual story of a company is plotted within the larger context of colonialism and nation-building. The present work too focuses on the historical context in which business enterprises developed and flourished, but through the experiences of individual actors, whose lives and experiences offer a new lens on the complexity of the context in which enterprise had to be planned, executed and expanded. It does not claim to be a radical departure from conventional modes of history writing or of the conventional model of business history, but it attempts largely to tell a story of human agency and imagination and its legacy.

Business history as a field arrived late in India. There were reasons for this. For one, it featured very minimally in traditional economic histories of India in the nineteenth century, where there was predictably greater emphasis on agrarian experience and on the peasant misery and poverty as a consequence of colonialism. Imperial exploitation of the Indian economy was the dominant theme of histories undertaken by nationalist thinkers such as Dadabhai Naoroji, R.C. Dutt and M.G. Ranade. Some thinkers attributed India's slow and even arrested development to caste and the existing social structure that was seen to inhibit enterprise.

However, in the decades after Independence, there was a concerted effort to question these assumptions, including the Eurocentric bias in downgrading pre-modern and early modern India's commercial potential, and to argue against the assertion that Indian commercial enterprise went under without a whimper and that it was not organizationally resilient to confront the superiority of European capital or naval power. Indian trade was generally seen as a peddling trade, i.e., retail transactions undertaken by itinerant traders with small turnover in opaque markets, where demand could not be forecast. According to this description, wholesale trading was the exception rather than the norm, and furthermore, merchants were generally subservient to the political clout of an arbitrary pre-modern state. These characterizations were seriously contested by a generation of historians in the 1960s and 1970s who studied Indian trade in the Indian Ocean with a critical perspective and generated an impressive corpus of work. Their intervention effectively rehabilitated pre-modern and early modern Indian trading activity and demonstrated the resilience of the Indian commercial structure that dominated the trading world of the Indian Ocean. It had, in fact, several features of a quasi-capitalist initiative, structured around rational calculation of forecasting markets, made possible by wholesale trade and storage facilities, and a robust banking system that facilitated remittances and the raising of credit for trade and investment. The work done by historians like Ashin Das Gupta, M.N. Pearson, S. Arasaratnam to name but a few, highlighted the range and ramifications of Indian trade, plumbed its depths and strength and foregrounded some of the basic traits that characterized pre-modern and early modern Indian commercial activity. Among these features were robust and resilient community networks that ensured efficient circulation of information and credit, the importance of the ruling state in guaranteeing infrastructure and demand and the availability of export staples at competitive prices. However, it was also agreed that unlike in Europe, joint stock companies did not characterize the commercial operations of merchants who managed family firms and, by and large, used the 'commenda' mode of trading.

The field of Indian maritime history expanded substantially in the last five decades, focusing on the sixteenth century to the nineteenth century, when the rise of world Islamic empires provided the context for marked market growth and manufacture. This was also a period when India dominated the trade in the Indian Ocean. Indian merchants, along with other mercantile networks such as the Armenians and Geniza merchants of an earlier period, negotiated the market and cultivated relations with the ruling dispensation to drive an enormous set of operations. Predictably, scholars drew from these advances to engage with the debate on the capitalist potentialities of the Indian economy to reflect on the possibilities merchant capital had for making the transition to full-scale industrial manufacture. This provided a basis for subsequent experiments with business history that took as its starting point the operations of specific communities, such as Gujarati Banias (a specific caste cum occupational category engaged in trade, brokerage and banking), Marwaris and Parsis, and networks, the protocols they adopted for conducting overseas trade, predicated on correct market forecasts and calculations. However, the consensus was that merchant capital in India remained commercial and that the transition of merchant capital to industrial capitalism was undermined partly by the colonial intervention and partly by structural constraints associated with scarcity of capital and the cheapness of labour that undermined the drive to innovate.[9] Consequently, when business history emerged as an identifiable sub-field that looked at industrial corporations and business houses, it looked back to reference those moments, when Indian capital and enterprise experimented with forms of trading and organization to scale up operations, optimize profits and effectively procure and channelize supplies. Also, it drew attention to the fact that modern industrial enterprise was driven largely by traditional business communities, who made use of certain institutional devices such as the managing agency system (a form of business organization that undertook the management of joint stock companies) to run their business. For most of the period that we look at, the communities associated with business were Gujarati Hindu/Jain groups, Marwaris and Parsis, Bohras and Khojas, but not exclusively so; in fact, there are individual protagonists who came from non-trading backgrounds to enter the field of modern enterprise.

Conventional histories of modern business and enterprise in India predictably started their narratives with the European model of the joint stock detailing the history of the English East India company, a joint stock enterprise along with other European trading companies of the seventeenth and eighteenth centuries in India. S.P. Rungta's book *The Rise of Business Corporations in India 1851–1900* is the best example of such an approach. Rungta detailed the formation of modern European business, banking and insurance, as well as agency houses and managing agencies started by European traders and free merchants. Rungta also made an important point that in this enterprise, Indian contribution, albeit modest, was not insignificant, especially in banking. Pointing to the enterprise of liberal minded Indians, such as Dwarkanath Tagore, he referred to the Union Bank of

Calcutta, to a slew of steamship and insurance companies that he sponsored, and to the cotton textile mills in western India that Gujarati and Parsi capital invested in and oversaw. What was especially noteworthy, according to Rungta, was the rapidity with which the idea of joint stock and managing agency took hold of the Indian imagination. Rungta's work, however, did not focus on the rise and fall of specific houses but simply reviewed an account of business operations undertaken by a range of players in British India from the late eighteenth to the mid-twentieth century. In his review, the emphasis was on some select communities, on overall trends towards new forms of entrepreneurship and the impact of the first and second world wars on Indian and European enterprise. Rungta was primarily interested in the rise of the formal corporate sector and plotted the story of Indian initiative within it. What is absent in his account is the politics of business, the political constraints that stood in the way of a breakthrough and the distinctiveness of the colonial milieu in shaping Indian business.

Rungta's work, in many ways, provided a useful and workable template for attempting a history of Indian business—modern business, that is, for subsequent enthusiasts to follow. While there was nothing in terms of methodology to make Rungta's work a specimen of business history as we understand it now, its narrative framework and timeline have endured in the scholarship that addresses issues of modern business formation, the centrality of specific communities and their organizational networks in India. Additionally, we have inputs from political historians of the national movement who looked at the interests of business communities and groups and their vacillating relations with the imperial government as well as the nationalist organization, namely the Indian National Congress. A.D.D. Gordon's study of

businessmen in Bombay (1978) studied their political calculations
and their faltering attempts to balance their interests between
the call of nationalist politics and imperial collaboration.[10] The
case of Jamnalal Bajaj, as we shall see, embodied this tension and
contradiction, although Jamnalal himself was far too committed
a Gandhian to ignore the call of conscience when pursuing his
business interests. Claude Markovits followed in the same vein in
his 1985 monograph on business and politics,[11] and argued that
businessmen were not a homogenous bloc and that their political
choices were determined by their location and self-interest and
that it was far-fetched to identify a distinct capitalist identity. On
the other hand, economic historians Rajat Ray and Amiya Bagchi
looked more closely at processes of Indian industrial development,
particularly in the interwar years when exceptional circumstances
related to the war effort and government policies gave a fillip
to Indian industrial expansion. One of Ray's arguments was
especially significant as it referred to the risk-taking abilities
and proclivities of businessmen, who succeeded in taking over
the businesses of many Europeans. However, his work was not
strictly speaking business history, as it did not document the
rise and fall of firms but instead looked at the complexities of a
changing political situation that enabled nascent industrial groups
to scale their ventures and emerge as a full-fledged capitalist class.
Amiya Bagchi's monograph on private investment in India tried
to examine its genesis, arguing that tariff policies of the British
had restricted private enterprise. In his words, 'before World War
I, it was the governmental policy of free trade and after the war,
it was general depression in the capitalist system combined with
the halting and piecemeal policy of tariff protection adopted by
the government of India that limited the rate of investment in

modern industry'.[12] Bagchi was critical of colonial policies that inhibited industrial investment and did not see even the revised tariff policies as particularly conducive. What was important about these writings was, one, the perspective they offered on the consequences of imperial policies on indigenous enterprises and two, the wealth of information on the actual progress several industries such as textiles, cement, iron, steel and sugar achieved in the period.

These contributions enriched the economic history of late colonial India and contributed meaningfully to macro-economic debates on the impact of colonialism on the Indian economy and on the structural constraints that Indian businessmen confronted, especially the scarcity of capital that Tirthankar Roy's work highlighted.[13] However, it was with Dwijendra Tripathi that business history as a specific field of inquiry took shape, with the emphasis being on entrepreneurship and the behaviour of businessmen, trading communities and their complex relations with the market and the state. It did not follow the American model in that it documented the rise and fall of business firms and companies but instead preferred to identify and explain the phenomenon of entrepreneurship, on the processes that enabled groups and individuals to take certain steps in this direction, and go beyond their traditional calling. Admittedly, at this time, company archives were not as well developed as they are now; very few companies had their archives open and ready. Nonetheless, he saw the value of individual entrepreneurship as a key element in business history and consequently foregrounded the lives of entrepreneurs like Kasturbhai Laldas (1894–1980) to provide a more comprehensive appreciation of the context in which capital had to be invested and profits to be anticipated. He thus set up a template where individual entrepreneurs were the principal protagonists of business history; their background was crucial in explaining their temperament and ability to take risks and to negotiate with the political masters. In a series of workshops and publications that he oversaw, Tripathi brought to the table an impressive range of issues that looked at communities, networks, institutions and individuals. His *Oxford History of Indian Business* elegantly integrated elements of biographical sketches into a macro-analysis of the economic and political processes to understand the evolution of modern Indian business from a historical perspective and to suggest that the colonial interlude simultaneously distorted and fostered indigenous enterprise.[14] Needless to say, the work focused almost exclusively on the formal sector and did not address issues of small town or vernacular capitalism that Douglas Haynes identified in western India, where artisanal activity became entrepreneurial in the course of the latter decades of the nineteenth century.[15] Tripathi's biographical approach was followed by that of Medha Kudaisya, whose biography of G.D. Birla (2003) and the *Oxford India Anthology of Business History* (2012) reveal the important linkages between economic history and business history and business biographies.[16] Kudaisya's work elaborated on the role businessmen played after Independence and how, in fact, they came forward to partner the state in the development of the country after 1947. Their calculations went awry, especially during the period of the Licence Raj, when the regulatory apparatus of the state and the restrictions on foreign exchange and steel quotas made it difficult for business to expand. The conundrum of industrial expansion operating within the framework of a planned economy was explored by many historians, notably Stanley Kochanek and more recently by a volume on business and politics edited by Jaffrelot, Kohli and Kanta Murali.[17] Kudaisya's edited volume refers to a variety of writings that are rightly included in her anthology of essays on business history, even if these did not strictly conform to the more classical model of business history. What is striking about histories that write about business after liberalization tends to be biographical with detailed sketches of pioneering entrepreneurs. We have work on the 'Polyester Prince' Dhirubhai Ambani by Hamish McDonald, the biography of Rahul Bajaj by Gita Piramal, to name but a few, in addition to detailed studies of business houses like the Tatas and Birlas.[18]

Business biographies as a genre have proliferated in the last decade. These are either full-length biographies or are biographical sketches of businessmen mostly of the twentieth century. In terms of style as well as of orientation, these tend to be written for a larger public and celebratory in tone. Titles such as 'Business Maharajas' or 'Business Icons' play up either the rags-to-riches story or the continuation of a rich legacy narrative. It is important to note that while biography has generally been undervalued and seen as a stepchild of history, its value in documenting business history, especially in India, where archives are notoriously difficult to access, is significant. It is through semi-formal interviews that make up part of the biography and through private information that we are in a position to grapple with the messiness of business operations and the everyday challenges the men faced at different points in history.

The present work draws from this rich corpus of economic and business history while acknowledging the challenges in writing about individuals and their firms in view of the relative scarcity of data. It attempts to bridge the ground between macro history and individual lives, arguing that individual experiences often provide greater nuance and insight into the large economic and political processes and humanize the phenomenon of enterprise and entrepreneurship. Here it is useful to recall Gylfi Magnusson who said that a biographical approach 'is an important analytical tool for historians' and that it helps 'put history figuratively in the body'.[19] Lives are messy and inconsistent, but it is precisely in the ambiguity of human experience that we get access to the larger context, which is not reducible to either official statistics or conventional interpretation. Questions that dog us about the qualities some individuals possessed to be able to ride the challenges of a political dispensation while others could not are best addressed through micro-historical approaches. These give us some clues to the reasons for failure and success, whether these were structural or just a combination of good fortune and timing. Biographical details take us closer to the ability of protagonists to take calculated risks and adopt a pragmatic stand in relation to authority, to the reasons why and what it was about business that captured the imagination of someone like Dwarkanath Tagore in Bengal or Jamnalal Bajaj. Did the conceptualization and execution of enterprise stand for an intangible expression of modernity? Did it offer a conduit to a larger process for community improvement and public welfare? Was business seen as a trusteeship in the broad sense of the word? How did the businessmen of yesteryears provide a basis for subsequent generations to follow? These questions are addressed through the lives of individual men, their dreams and decisions that are revealing about the context in which they operated and, by extension, about the challenges that were peculiar to the subcontinent. Evidently, given the phenomenal success of some of these men, there was no question of cultural roadblocks; they were capable of thinking through innovative projects and striking big, both under conditions of colonial subjugation and under conditions of liberalization. In adopting what I call the 'snapshots' perspective, the book makes use of the voices of the protagonists and the firms they owned and managed. Thus, for example, in the case of Godrej, company archives are central to the story to document the processes by which the company was able to manufacture its products, distribute the same through a network of dealers and advertise aggressively to create a mass consumer base. In the case of an individual Parsi merchant, Jamsetjee Jeejeebhoy, we have recourse to his correspondence that gives us glimpses into how he envisaged the business of opium procurement and shipping and how he stabilized it, the protocols he adopted that included regular correspondence. We are not as fortunate as the other protagonists who have not left the same kind of documentary footprint. Consequently, the work also draws substantially from newspaper articles, secondary writings and references in order to broaden the very notion of the archive on which a historian is dependent. We are fortunate in the material that we have for founders and successors of Bajaj and Kirloskar, where we have personal reminiscences and reflections, several short biographical accounts that help us decode the factors in their success.[20] The interviews accompanying the Harvard Business School project on creative emerging markets are another excellent repository. These interviews reveal the circumstances in which crucial decisions were taken by leading businessmen and also present a vision of what they considered as good practice. It offers a useful contrast to the older histories undertaken by businessmen who wrote them in the first half of the twentieth century as an exercise in scripting their identity. We will have occasion to refer to some of the older vernacular histories written by business communities that were like a directory of eminent traders and what their activities consisted of.

In its temporal frame, the book covers the period between the eighteenth century and the decades leading to the opening and restructuring of the Indian economy. The choice of the period helps us contrast two kinds of imperial projects, the Mughal and the British, which fostered and inhibited (as the case may be) indigenous business enterprises. It also helps us reflect on the decades after Independence, reassess the salience of business to economic growth and evaluate the impact of a changing political context on business culture. The intricacies and challenges of the time period are traced through the actual experience of businessmen, whose operations help us reconstruct what the ground reality must have been. More than humanizing business history, it repositions the importance of actual experience that accumulated over time to generate an understanding of business-related ethics that provided the necessary ammunition to deal with government. This is not to assume or argue that businessmen were always informed by ethical considerations but simply to suggest that the idea of business itself underwent a transformation from merely a profit pursuing activity to that of a larger enterprise that had larger social potential. This is evident when we look at the vision of people like Ardeshir Godrej, T.V.S Iyengar or Jamnalal Bajaj, and the steps they took to realize it amid great odds. I hope the book is able to reflect some of the ineffable and intangible excitement that distinguishes many of these individual efforts, which I enjoyed discovering during the process of researching and writing, and I hope that readers too will share my excitement and enthusiasm.

1

Pre-Modern Business in the Age of Empire: Trade, Capital and Markets in Late Mughal India

The magnificence of the Mughal empire, a world empire comparable to its counterparts in Ching China or Ottoman Turkey, was evident in the splendour of the imperial court, the extravagance of its ruling class and the affluence of its merchant elites. As a world empire spanning over extensive territories and overseeing a dense web of cultural and economic transactions, its arteries were fuelled by flows of bullion that entered the royal mints to be converted into regnal coins—the silver sicca, the copper dam and the gold mohur—which were crucial to the business of gifting, revenue collection, trade financing and craft and commodity production.[1] Contemporaries were struck by the seamless absorption of metal and bullion into the subcontinent and echoed the sentiments that had been expressed centuries ago by Pliny the Elder, who referred to India as the sink of the world's gold. Europeans were less enthusiastic in their reactions and stridently vilified the trading classes in charge of the money trade. Writing in 1674, surgeon and travel writer John Fryer noted how Bania brokers were experts in the acts of thieving, dissembling and cheating and that their whole desire was to have money pass through their fingers![2] Without going into the admissibility of Fryer's observations, what is fairly clear is the fact that money was available in plenty in Mughal India and that men knew how to make it, accumulate it and redeploy it for social and commercial gain. Millionaires, particularly merchant millionaires, were, therefore, not an uncommon entity in several of the Mughal cities and emporia—Virji Vora, Shantidas Jhaveri, Mulla Abdul Ghafur and the Jagat Seths were embodiments of the prosperity that Mughal India enjoyed for at least two centuries, right until the middle of the eighteenth century. Their extraordinary success stands in stark contrast to the instances of bankruptcy and ruin in the aftermath of Mughal decline in the eighteenth century. The damage to commercial enterprise was, however, not irreversible. Pockets of stability and islands of enterprise emerged, enabling indigenous capital to survive regime changes and assume the mantle for capital accumulation and industrial development. Historians have tried to analyse the complexities and conundrum of Indian enterprise and their pragmatic approach to politics and the ruling state, whether it was the imperial house of the Mughals or the rule of the English East India company and subsequently the British Crown. We will have occasion to explore the strategies adopted by merchants and capitalists in the century of transition, thereby providing the crucial backstory for Indian entrepreneurship in the mid-nineteenth and twentieth centuries.

Money in Mughal India: Markets and Merchants in the Era of World Empires

'So turning to a description of the wonders of the Mughal court', the Portuguese traveller Fray Sebastien Manrique got it right when he wrote,

> I should say what most surprised me was the enormous quantity of riches, mostly consisting of that in the great Nacassaries, or treasuries which the Emperor possesses in various parts, great incomes enjoyed by princes and nobles of the Empire, and thirdly and lastly, the wealth or fortunes of the merchants, especially of those known by the generic title Sadagar and by the local appellation of katari.[3]

Unerringly, Manrique had located the linkages between the imperial treasury, the aristocratic establishments and the mercantile firms who combined to form the central axis through which money flowed and circulated. Each of the three entities worked in close unison, the Mughal state collected revenue in cash, thus fostering monetization and enabling commercial groups to position themselves within the apparatus of revenue collection and markets; the Mughal nobility spent their incomes to maintain a lavish lifestyle thereby encouraging specialized crafts manufacture and providing the demand for a range of export goods; and the merchants of Mughal India capitalized on the unprecedented commercial growth of the economy in the seventeenth and early eighteenth centuries. The consolidation of Mughal power backed by systematization of revenue flows into the treasury to stabilize the workings of the bureaucracy, the maintenance of infrastructure to ensure smooth supply flows of commodities and thereby, allowing a rudimentary national market to function efficiently, was directly instrumental in fostering high and regular levels of consumption and demand for goods from within as well as from overseas markets. Indian goods, especially textiles along with spices, sugar and a range of other items, were in demand across regions, satisfying the members of the provincial elites and aristocracies as well as in the larger world of the Indian Ocean. Indian cloth was especially valued among the rich and poor alike. The simultaneous rise of the Safavids in Persia and the Ottomans in Turkey helped configure a dynamic Indian Ocean economy, wherein the location of India as the dominant player and supplier of calico became critically significant. It was thus no coincidence that seventeenth-century India saw a massive expansion in the volume of international trade and shipping with ports like Surat, Hugli and Masulipatam enjoying unprecedented levels of prosperity. The Mughal state valued bullion and by default invested in the maintenance of trading channels and infrastructure, the benefits of which merchants made full use of. The French traveller Jean Baptiste Tavernier was full of praise for Indian roads and conveyances, 'and of the manner of travelling in India, which in my opinion, is not less convenient than all the arrangements for marching in comfort either in France or in Italy'.[4]

Money and its ever-growing influence and the need to guarantee its availability lay at the heart of official policy directives. The silver imports that flowed directly from trade were absorbed by the imperial monetary system, which turned out a prodigious quantity of pure coins and which subsequently entered the grid of revenue payments and commercial transactions. For the greater part of the seventeenth century, money was in abundance and credit easily available for trade that worked through a system of bills of exchange, or *hundis*. Mughal India had at its disposal standardized rates for remittances via bills of exchange that were extensively bought and discounted by traders. As Tavernier commented, 'On arrival for embarkation at Surat, you find there plenty of money. For it is the principal trade of the nobles of India to place their money on vessels in speculations for Hormuz, Bussora and Mocha and even for Bantam, Achim and the Phillipines'.[5] However, more than nobles who occasionally invested in trade as part of their portfolio, it was merchants who conducted trade on a massive scale, adding to the volume of trade transactions in the Indian Ocean. Merchants held a variety of portfolios—shippers who commanded medium-sized shipping made profits from both the freight business as well as from trade carried on mostly under the commenda system, which involved an agreement between an investing partner and a travelling partner who undertook responsibility for the actual transactions.

Shipping was a business that demanded large capital investment. The business of shipping was, for the most part, dominated by Muslim merchants of varying denominations—Arabs, Turks, Bohras and Khojas—who emerged as business magnates commanding exponential profits. Tavernier had occasion to speak of the palatial houses that belonged to Muslim merchants.[6] The great shipping magnates of the eighteenth century, Mulla Abul Ghafur and Ahmed Chellaby, were influential men who dominated the Indian Ocean trade and leveraged their connections within their community and with the Mughal court, or *darbar*, to accumulate huge assets that were ploughed back into business. While it is difficult to determine the extent to which political connections informed their commercial success, it is clear that they did not entertain political ambitions or carve out a space in the cities they lived in and worked from. As a result, we do not find merchants forming a lobby transcending caste, community and religion to bid for autonomous self-government like their Italian counterparts of medieval Europe. They did not at any time assume political agency or develop an explicit agenda to undercut the authority of the state. On the other hand, they were not impervious to the advantages of forging political connections and taking advantage of the patronage and clientism afforded by the state in early modern India. For the state, merchants were useful subjects; not only did they ensure the vitality of commercial transactions that played a key role in the state's revenue requirements and in sustaining bullion flows, they were closely embedded in state structures at multiple levels, as mint officers, as guarantors for revenue payments and occasionally as merchant–scribes.[7] The tendency to forge close relations with merchants intensified in the eighteenth century, under the regimes that supplanted the Mughal state as well as under the English East India company, whose growing political influence in the period generated unexpected opportunities for merchant capital.

The seventeenth century saw the advent of European trading companies and the establishment of their factories in several ports and urban centres in India. In theory, the companies were in charge of conducting the official trade between India and Europe, for which they sought preferential treatment and concessions. In fact, European companies also conducted a substantial volume of private trade within Asia, referred to as country trade, and in the conduct of which they were compelled to work with local merchants. Relations between Europeans, the Mughal state and local commercial society were not always smooth; the company officials deployed their superior naval power to blockade ports if they could not wrest the necessary concessions; on its part, the Mughal state with its superior land power, was able to thwart their procurement operations inland. Merchants were pragmatic in their dealings and utilized the convoy arrangements of the European companies in the high seas, and many of them, especially brokers and supply merchants, worked closely with companies and their servants. Until the middle of the eighteenth century, the influence of European trading companies was not apparent or uncontested. Merchants with clout, capital and influence never failed to approach the Mughal state to intercede on their behalf when goods were lost at sea, especially if they were under the convoy and protection of European trading companies. For Muslim merchants in particular, the creeping ambitions of the Europeans to control shipping and freight trade were ominous, and right from the start, the stage was set for a violent confrontation. Until the first quarter of the eighteenth century, Muslim shipowners were able to compete with European private traders and companies and even take them to court when the latter did not abide by the terms of their agreement with the Mughal state under which European convoy arrangements were obliged to provide protection to the local merchant fleet at sea against piratical attacks. In fact, the convoy was orchestrated in a way to delay the departure of ships from Surat so as to pre-empt the city's shippers from reaching markets on time and outprice their competitors. The 1740s saw several instances of altercation between Muslim shippers and the English East India company.[8]

With shore-based business mainly comprising brokerage and banking, the situation in relation to European trading companies was different. However, at no stage in the seventeenth century was the trade of the Europeans more significant than that of Asian trade in the Indian Ocean. Even if complete market integration was not achieved under the Mughal state, there is no doubt that political stability under the Mughals and the robust transport network provided by them via road and river gave a fillip to inland trade in a dazzling variety of goods—essential items as well as luxuries and high-value products. The marketing and financing of inland trade as well as of the export trade in the western Indian Ocean targeting markets in West Asia and East Africa was undertaken by Bania brokers and bankers who, through a system of advances, controlled the supply chain of essential and staple commodities. The bigger wholesale merchants were also bankers, drawing from their traditional expertise and occupational experience in minting and currency matters. Bankers enjoyed a very special status largely on account of the emphasis the Mughal state placed on the regnal coin, i.e., the coin issued by the reigning sovereign. All bullion had to be converted into the ruling sicca rupee (the only legal tender), and although technically minting was accessible to all, the crowds and queues before state mints at the height of a trading season made the intercession of private bankers essential. The latter enjoyed customary rights to convert and assay silver and foreign coins and thereby, in that capacity, determined the exchange business and currency market. Not surprisingly, bankers and brokers were men of affluence in Mughal India and more so in Gujarat, the premier maritime suba of the empire. These men accepted deposits, remitted money through hundis, or bills of exchange, and came forward with short-term loans to princes, pedlers and businessmen.

The success of merchants and the eminence of bankers was evident in virtually every major maritime region of India, whether Gujarat, Bengal or the Coromandel Coast. Each of these maritime regions drove a vigorous export trade to markets in West Asia and Southeast Asia, as well as in Europe. Bengal textiles were especially coveted in European markets, with the result that the trade of the European East India companies became significant for the local economy. It is in Bengal that we find the official and subsequently private trade of the English East India company assume disproportionate influence. In any case, Mughal rule integrated regions and regional economies via the mechanisms of revenue collection and aristocratic consumption. Revenue collection in cash meant that produce had to be marketed, while the growing demand for goods by the aristocracy resulted in accelerating flows of domestic and international trade. These connections between the producing hinterland and consuming, usually urban centres, were sustained and supported by an impressive credit and banking network that ensured flows of money from outside into official mints and of credit to fund and finance trade within the subcontinent. The hundi network of Mughal India was truly impressive, commanding the attention of traders and overseas travellers alike.

To put in perspective the strength and depth of Indian enterprise and wealth in the eighteenth century, we will track the lives and labours of some of these merchants and bankers from Surat to Bengal on the western and eastern seaboards of the subcontinent that Mughal conquests had helped integrate by the seventeenth century. In every way, from infrastructure to market integration, from monetization to sustaining elite demand and consumption, the Mughal state played a vital role in supporting commercial enterprise. Merchant subjects, by and large, were left alone by the state officials and notwithstanding occasional instances of venality, they were able to conduct their ventures to satisfaction. Occasionally, nobles participated in trade and presumably capitalized on the benefits of their office and privileges but did not always engross the market. Merchants and bankers held diverse portfolios, but the most important advantage that bankers enjoyed in Mughal India was their access to the minting rights. It was their expertise in assaying and minting coins that gave them the ability to manipulate exchange rates and combine trade, banking, remittance services and speculation. The state gave bankers a free hand, for their ability to mint coins and keep them in circulation depended on the financial health of the empire. Equally important was the demand for a range of elite goods on the part of the consuming nobility, not to speak of the turnover for medium- and low-range goods that moved inside the subcontinent and overseas.

Indian capital responded to the opportunities that the imperial Mughal experiment provided. For one, the monetization of land revenue that the state depended upon meant that merchants and commercial intermediaries were embedded in the inland trade of the subcontinent. The fillip to overseas trade, thanks to a larger political and market integration in the western Indian Ocean, encouraged Indian businesses to invest substantially in shipping, although this seems to have been restricted largely to Muslim businessmen. However, the shipping sector and the freight trade that shippers combined enjoyed extraordinary success even though it sustained most of the damage after the decline of the imperial system in the eighteenth century. While we do not have quantitative evidence on the value and volume of Asian trade in the seventeenth and early eighteenth centuries, there is no doubt that trade expanded exponentially and that the scale of profits was sustained through generations even if this did not translate into innovative practices of entrepreneurship.

A Shipping Prince, a Financial Magnate and a Merchant–broker in Mughal India: Select Case Studies

Our first protagonist is Mulla Abdul Ghafur, a merchant prince and influential shipper who commanded an impressive fleet of ships and whose operations dominated the markets of west Asia (Mocha, Aden, Basra) by cornering trade in spices and textiles, maintaining warehouses in India and overseas, and leveraging political support for his commercial ventures. Hailing from Patan in Gujarat, Ghafur was a Sunni Bohra who rose to fame rapidly.[9] We have very little evidence on antecedents or his back story; he emerges in European documentation around the end of the seventeenth century as a premier merchant, shipowner and freighter with considerable capital assets and influence within his *jamat*, or caste, as well as with the ruling Mughal dispensation in Surat city. Jawaid Akhtar refers to a Dutch comment on the Mulla's influence.

> This Abdul Ghafour is very wealthy and disposes of all the funds of the king's Gasie. Which is why this Gafour is more feared than anybody else is, even by the governor and the grandees and surely he could get such writs from the ecclesiastical judge of his majesty he might require.[10]

Ghafur's rise was indisputably part of the larger story of Muslim commercial enterprise in the Indian Ocean, where, thanks to the simultaneous rise of three major Islamic world empires, there was a steady demand for Indian products, which merchants were able to exploit. As old-time participants in the carrying trade of the Indian Ocean, Arabs, Turks and Gujaratis eyed opportunities for profit and expanded their investment in the traffic. Virtually all trading enterprises were family firms and made use of the commenda form of organization, which was seen as appropriate given the risks that Indian Ocean trade faced. It needs to be kept in mind that pre-modern enterprise operated under several risks, the most important of which was an uncertain and opaque market that was not easy to read. In an age of sail, when the monsoon determined sailing schedules, the interval between preparing goods for export and judging the actual demand for them was long and introduced an element of high risk standing in the way of high investment. Thus, as Ron Harris put it, there was a shortage of reliable collateral, asymmetric information between travelling merchants and passive investors and concerns over state interference over their property rights, all of which were real risks.[11] Under the circumstances, what the Muslim shippers and freighters were able to achieve was spectacular. They worked through close family connections and assigned responsibility to agents and commanders (*nakhuda* or travel partners) via the commenda system, who were made responsible for the business of their shore-based investors and for small travelling merchants and individual peddlers carrying small consignments of goods. According to Harris, 'the commenda was an equity investment contract, specifying investments and payoffs',[12] with the investment party providing capital to the travelling party.

What was the commenda system, and why was it ubiquitous in the Indian Ocean? In its simplest form, a commenda was a commercial contract involving two parties: a merchant with ready capital, credit or merchandize and an agent or factor with business acumen, reputation and a willingness to travel great distances to deploy his master's capital and sell the merchandize entrusted to him. Profits were arranged in accordance with the terms of the contract. The Surat shippers relied on this system; for example, we know how Mulla Abdul Ghafur used this arrangement working through his nakhudas or commander–agents, all of whom were family members. Ghafur maintained very close contacts with his nakhudas and relied on them to guarantee sales. Ghafur himself is reputed to have had the ability to read and forecast markets. Thus, he took calculated risks when he invested in a sizeable fleet of ships and aggressively dominated the freight business of Surat city. The confidence that small traders and freighters reposed in Ghafur's ships is testimony to the reputation that he enjoyed. He did not kowtow to Europeans or concede to their bullying tactics and openly countered the European convoy system deployed by European companies as a means of undercutting his business.

Political connections were important in Ghafur's business calculations. He appears to have had impressive political connections with the ruling Mughal administration, which may have constituted a major factor in the success and survival of his family firm. He commanded a fleet of twenty medium-sized ships that he fitted and freighted for the trade with West Asia. Gains in commerce were followed up with real investment in property; in West Asia, which was an important headquarter, we hear of his mansions and warehouses in Mocha, which illustrates the transnational nature of his business.[13]

The challenges that Ghafur as an Indian Ocean trader faced in the late seventeenth and eighteenth centuries were twofold: one was the growing interest of European traders (both company and private) to enter the western Indian Ocean trade, where through the convoy system that they instituted, they were able to manipulate shipping schedules and persuade smaller Asian merchants to use their shipping. On the other hand, there was also the very real problem of piracy, which the European convoys were meant to contain but which was often used as a fait accompli to delay the dispatch of the annual shipping. In the confrontations that followed on both these counts, we find Ghafur maintaining his own. As early as the 1690s, Ghafur had figured out the real intentions of the Europeans and came forward to flout their claims and speak against the apparent benefits of the convoy. While the establishment and continuance of the European convoy was structured around the idea of protection (a responsibility assumed by the Europeans thanks to their naval power), in fact, it operated in ways that were stacked against the Asian trader. According to Ghafur, the convoy officials deliberately delayed the departure timings, claiming that the ships of Surat city merchants had not all assembled on time. In reality, however, this was intended to benefit European traders and undermine competition from Asian traders. In retaliation, Ghafur ignored the instructions of convoy officers, slipped out of the safety net and then demanded compensation when attacked by pirates. John Ovington, the English traveller, had occasion to mention these acts of defiance and to demonstrate how Ghafur wilfully ignored the instructions of convoy officers, and demanded compensation for losses suffered at sea, many of which were fictive. In 1691, Ghafur even spread the news that the English had been negligent in their duties, which had caused him a major loss and for which he needed to be immediately compensated. Ghafur was able to get the city administration to speak on his behalf so much so that the English factory in Surat was besieged.[14]

Ghafur's investment in shipping speaks of both the size of his capital assets as well as of his risk-taking abilities. Locking capital in a fleet of seventeen ships was not to be lightly taken. The fact that he was able to do so demonstrated the profit turnover that he enjoyed. The fact that it was a family business where capital and information were tightly controlled was an additional advantage. His personal fortunes were estimated to be around Rs 85 lakh, which gave him enormous influence within his own community as well as with the Mughal court in the city.[15] Admittedly, in an unpredictable trading world as yet unmediated by technology, markets were not always easy to read, and we hear of occasions when conditions of glut upset Ghafur's plans. Yet, the fact that his business thrived for more than three decades and survived his death and family tensions indicates his business skills and organizational acumen. Contemporaries, especially European traders, were hugely impressed by his marketing skills and his capacity to leverage, as they found themselves outwitted on most occasions, whether it was in the West Asian markets or in the manipulation of the convoy system. For Asian merchants like Ghafur, the convoy system instituted by Europeans was not an unmixed blessing. While its underlying rationale was to insure Asian trade against piracy in the high seas, it also added to trading costs not to speak of the fact that private European interests in the convoy system used deliberate delaying tactics to pre-empt Ghafur's plans in the markets. Ghafur, on his part, like many of his Armenian counterparts such as Hasan Amadanai, did not hesitate to short circuit convoy arrangements by leaving earlier than was decided, in order to get a quicker start to their ventures and then demand compensation if ships were attacked by pirates and privateers. Whether these were acts of wilful arrogance or an expression of growing resentment against the expansionist aspirations of the Europeans is hard to say, but there is no doubt that Asian merchants, especially Muslim shippers, were suspicious of long-term European ambitions.

The size of Ghafur's firm and the organizational strategies adopted are difficult to gauge from the kind of limited evidence we have. We draw most of our understanding from European company records that mention his assets and capabilities only tangentially. There is, however, no doubt that he was involved in a measure of forwards trading: using his warehouses to accumulate stock and release it when prices were favourable.[16] The competition was fierce with both Turkish merchants (the Chellabies in particular) as well as with smaller players or peddlers who often glutted markets with their goods and thwarted Ghafur's plans. This, in a sense, was the essence and nature of pre-modern business in the Indian Ocean, whose markets were opaque and could not always be read, where small merchants, the classic peddler or itinerant trader, who combined trade and pilgrimage were content with small turnovers, which, in turn, could upset the apple cart of big merchants. Where the efficacy of Ghafur's business is apparent is its tenacity and ability to survive problems of succession. We find that after Ghafur's demise, the business was taken over and run fairly successfully by his grandson Mulla Muhammad Ali, notwithstanding the altered political conditions in Surat by the 1720s. By this time, the city administration in Surat was battling the aggression and monetary demands of rival contenders, especially the Marathas, whose attacks against the imperial Mughal centres threatened to destabilize the existing infrastructure and disrupt the smooth flow of goods and treasure. Even worse was the steady bankruptcy of the city administration, which, in order to buy peace with the Marathas, took recourse to a policy of taxing its merchant subjects. Mulla Muhammad Ali was among the first to bear the brunt of the state's new policies when the governor Haidar Quli Khan (1716–19) confiscated estates and ships worth Rs 85 lakh from the Mulla on grounds of disputed succession. While Mulla Muhammad Ali, through the good grace of highly placed nobles, was able to recover his losses, the situation did not improve substantively as the state let loose a reign of extortion, leading merchants to contemplate a coalition to affect a political rebellion. However, the rebellion that Mulla Muhammad Ali staged against the Mughal administration did not achieve the desired results, and what followed was a long-term decline in Muslim shipping and his family fortunes. What seems to have worked against the family firm was the rapidly changing situation in western India and the western Indian Ocean, where the declining demand for Indian products and falling consumption led to a glut in the market compounded by the aggressive expansion of European private traders who captured what remained of the falling trade. Backed by a strong navy and by support from the trading company that they worked for, European shipping absorbed much of the freight traffic and undercut Gujarati shipping. However, even the capital accumulated by Muslim shippers seems to have been substantial, exceeding what brokers and supply merchants commanded. Dutch scribe Jan Schreuder noted this in his memoirs when he recorded that the Mulna enjoyed more reserves than his Armenian and Bania counterparts. However, the latter, as we shall see, had more staying power and, notwithstanding altered conditions in the eighteenth century, were able to survive and carve a distinct niche in the trading world of late Mughal Hindustan.[17]

If shipping constituted the spine of India's overseas trade, then shore-based businesses of banking and brokerage gave it shape and flesh. Trade required commodities, and commodities needed to be bought and manufactured. Money and monetary advances were the essential fuel that drove the system of supplies and manufacture, which was the near monopoly of Hindu and Jain trading groups followed by Parsis. Building on centuries of commercial experience and financial expertise, commercial groups responded to market integration and expansion by expanding their trade operations. The business of brokerage witnessed an exponential increase as the demand for export goods went up. Markets were key to the Mughal revenue structure, which meant that commercial notables who were embedded in market operations emerged as major players of inland and export trade. Some became really influential, especially if they were close to the political establishment. Examples of these instances were men like Virji Vora and Shantidas Jhaveri, who made their mark as premier merchants and jewellers and who were able to hold their own as the leading subjects and notables of the Mughal state. Below them were middling brokers and intermediary merchants, who too commanded substantial assets and invested in the business of procuring goods for export and marketing imports—the Parekhs (Bania) and Maneks (Parsis) being instances in point. The success and consolidations of these families, however, was a later mid-eighteenth century phenomenon, by which time the trading world of India had subtly changed with European trading companies emerging as major political players in the regional state systems.

For the greater part of the seventeenth and eighteenth centuries, the European trading companies represented a very small segment of the business world. Not only did their business represent a very small proportion of the total trade of the Indian Ocean, but their political influence was also marginal. Barring their naval power, which the Mughal state was happy to press into the service of safeguarding the coast and providing protection to traders in the high seas, European companies were dependent on local brokers and interlocuters and on key intermediaries to secure limited trade privileges. Thus, for the greater part of the seventeenth century, the trade of Asian merchants in the Indian Ocean far exceeded that of the Eurasian trade, generating impressive inflows of bullion into the subcontinent and opportunities for increasing investment in textile manufacture. Merchant princes like Shantidas Jhaveri and Virji Vora who dominated the business world, did so quite independently of the European connection and were in many ways products of the Mughal system. Sudev Seth mentions the praise merchants like Shantidas showered on the Mughal state. Quoting the Chintamani Prashasti that went thus: 'who would not praise the virtues of Asaf Khan about whose radiance, intelligence and purity there are poems'.[18]

The career of Shantidas Jhaveri (1580–1659) is especially interesting as he was the acknowledged notable (the *nagarshet*) of Ahmedabad city. His was a rags-to-riches story, as his family migrated from Rajasthan to Ahmedabad sometime at the very end of the sixteenth century and his forefathers secured employment in a jeweller's shop. The family appears to have prospered under the successors of Akbar in the seventeenth century, gaining proficiency in the jewel trade as well as in the money business. *Sarrafi*, or banking involving minting foreign coins, exchanging old coins and dominating the market in bullion, and the jewellery business seem to have been closely integrated; for one, access to silver and gold or the bullion market was an essential precondition for the jewellery business, while intimate understanding of the court's appetite for precious ornaments helped jewellers enjoy access to the mint and minting rights. Shantidas Jhaveri's rise was meteoric as he made a mark as a great tycoon and businessman.

He did not invest very substantially in shipping, partly owing to his location in Ahmedabad, but was dominant in the freight business as well as the traffic in bullion imports to build up his own sarrafi business. Combining sarrafi with the jewellery business, he provided funds to the state and jewels to the Mughal court, whose appetite for luxury items was insatiable. The basis of Shantidas's wealth and proximity to the court was trade and banking; he transported goods on freight to West Asia and participated in sarrafi. He advanced loans to the Mughal rulers during critical times of war and succession disputes, as well as to European trading companies. The latter were forced on several occasions to defer to his control over the money market that he was able to manipulate. His understanding of the intrinsic value of coins and his ability to move them quickly to buy commodities gave him a huge advantage. The European factors observed how smaller men in the bazaar tended to follow him and other leaders of the pack; in their words, 'These people follow the greater ones, as the heard theire leader, for is Santidas or Miah Saw, or any of the great sawes (sahukars) keepe up their monies, all the rest must imitate them, though they knowe not theire owne reason'.[19]

Shantidas Jhaveri was based primarily in Ahmedabad, although he had his agents stationed all across Gujarat. As a Jain, he enjoyed substantial prestige within his community and, as a favoured Mughal merchant, enjoyed unprecedented powers of arbitration over other merchant groups. The influence that he exerted over the administration is indicated by the fact that in 1636, he was even appointed as the governor of Gujarat by Shah Jahan. It was very rare for merchants to be allowed to exercise political rights and functions, and it only speaks of his extraordinary influence and wealth. The Mughal rulers were well aware of his influence and sought to capitalize this to put forward their own agenda of providing a just and equitable administration to all. This was important when disputes among business groups threatened to disrupt the social milieu or when bankers hedged their bets on rival contenders to the throne. For the most part, merchants were closely aligned with the state, and not until the middle of the eighteenth century did their loyalties gravitate towards European trading companies, who were seen as more reliable political actors.

As a wealthy merchant banker with obvious political connections, Shantidas was fully capable of disarming competition from rivals. Admittedly, the English trading company was not as yet a real contender either commercially or politically, but their command over the fleet that protected shipping and their naval power gave them some leverage against the indigenous merchants. One of the ways this was expressed, as mentioned earlier, was in delaying the convoy that accompanied Indian shipping or to resist payments of compensation when goods were lost at sea due to piratical attacks. In 1636, we come across a major skirmish when the English factors reported how Shantidas held the city to ransom following losses at sea. It is worth quoting this:

> All this city is full of tumult, curses, and exclamations against us befor this governor (Saif Khan) about the junk of Dio by diverse banian merchants, the proprietors of her lading where of Shantidas here is a cheife one and hath earnestly requested us to acquaint you with his losse of 10,000 rupees, and do wonder wee are not shut by this tyme. The governor sent and threatened us the other day, and after much pretended kindness towards us for our liberty, hee charged us to send expresses with advise

into you of these people demand which is 20,000 rupees and must presently be satisfied.[20]

A close reading of these observations tells us a lot, about the trading milieu, about Shantidas' political clout, about the value of his investments and finally about the overall fragility of European presence in the city and also about the vitality of the state–business connection. Shantidas' influence in the court was a decided advantage, especially when it came to pressing negotiations with outsiders, in this case the English East India company, whose claims and demands were out of all proportion. The advantages of working with a diverse portfolio were also apparent: freight, money-changing, jewellery business and political entrepreneurship. Thus, Shantidas had substantial moneys locked in Surat's freight trade with West Asia; he retained his political connections as well as caste connections that enabled him to work closely with the mahajan, or the city's merchant assembly. He had full measure of the limits of the English East India company's strength and, on virtually all occasions, was able to wrest concessions and monetary compensation from them. According to Sheth, the banker benefited enormously from the patronage of the Mughal state, 'including receiving lofty titles that enhanced his social standing'.[21] Also, Shantidas, like other major merchant financiers of the period, had full confidence in the Mughal state system, identified themselves as Mughal subjects and remained anchored within the system. Not until the decline of imperial authority and the assertion of regional power in the middle of the eighteenth century do we find a shift in the political orientation of the merchants, who began to slowly gravitate towards other political claimants, including the European East India companies.

What profit possibilities did the brokerage business hold in the period under review? Expanding trade in the Indian Ocean involved an incrementally growing demand for Indian textiles, the manufacture and procurement of which exponentially went up in terms of scale. The cities of western India—Surat, Broach and Ahmedabad—were known for their premier businessmen and brokers, who worked through a chain of subcontractors and brokers to access piece-goods of various descriptions from the immediate as well as the remote hinterland. Many of them worked for individual shippers, while some worked for the European trading companies as well. A second responsibility of the broker merchant was to market imports that trading cities drew into their roadsteads and assume responsibility for their timely sales. The broker was a key player in the trading world of the Indian Ocean, and in the latter decades of the seventeenth century, he became a sought-after ally of the European trading companies, which appreciated the value of his services in facilitating the smooth conduct of overseas trade in textiles from loom to factory. For Europeans, brokers were invaluable intermediaries as they commanded intimate knowledge of the supply chain. Their understanding was crucial for European companies and merchants whose understanding of the playing field was hardly satisfactory, if not nonexistent. Having to negotiate suspicious government officials at every step of the transaction, to penetrate the supply chain, to beat down prices and to make sense of codes that brokers employed, it became increasingly necessary to employ a special broker and give him the responsibility for procuring goods and eventually for enforcing contracts for supply of textiles. The post of chief broker of the European companies became a lucrative post for merchants to compete.

Until the 1740s, notwithstanding the long-term decline that set in the trade of the Indian Ocean and the rapid strides of European private trade, supply merchants and brokers, primarily in charge of shore-based businesses, retained their connections with production centres in the hinterland and kept up their business with Asian merchants as well as with private traders and European companies. Many of them were increasingly aware of the fragility of the political situation in the aftermath of Mughal decline and of the growing aspirations of the English East India company. By this time, the potential of holding the position of chief broker to European trading companies had gained more traction, with the result that several leading merchants of trade cities—Hugli, Surat and Masulipatam—competed for it. In western India, especially Surat, the Parekhs (Bania) and Maneks (Parsis) fought for the post. As early as the seventeenth century, we hear of Tulsidas Parekh as an important contact for the English East India company between 1636 and 1667, undertaking to market the goods brought by the company, as well as providing short-term credit to procure purchases from the hinterland.

Brokerage was thus a lucrative line of business, especially during a period of rapid commercial growth that stimulated production and manufacture. Brokers typically were rooted in local and regional networks of kin and occupation that controlled information and came forward with credit and financial support whenever the need arose. Brokers in cities relied on sub-brokers or under-contractors, who in turn were very closely integrated with the world of manufacture and production through a system of advances and social assistance. Brokers—general and commodity-specific brokers—expanded their operations within the ambit of the family firm. We have the case of Tulsidas Parikh, who, like his counterparts, relied on a community and kinship-based network and specialized in the brokerage of specialized commodities like coral and silk. His brother Tapidas was also an important player and served to strengthen what was a family business. In fact, the family's fortunes took an impressive turn when Tulsidas' son Bhimji Parekh and his three brothers entered the business and assumed full responsibility as the English East India company's broker, managing its imports and exports.[22] Like all family businesses, however, this too suffered from dissensions and rivalries, but the greater challenge came from other competitors who competed for the post of the company's principal broker. The post evidently carried with it some benefits like that of an assured income as well as some political advantages of protection and immunity from interference by ex-Mughal officials and Maratha contenders. While competition for this position could become intense and disrupt everyday business, the fact is that the European connection for the greater part of the seventeenth and eighteenth centuries was an asset that merchants capitalized on. With the advent of European trading companies, the merchants were able to diversify their portfolio and use some of the new opportunities as a buffer against uncertainty and risk; however, it would not be correct to assume that by the turn of the eighteenth century, the European factor was in any way the decisive determinant of the city's trading scene. Trade with the ports of West Asia, sending goods on freight, handling massive bullion consignments, servicing long-distance trade with credit and providing services of brokerage to traders of all sizes, was undertaken by the community of Banias, many of whom dominated the trading scene in western India. Whether they would retain the dominance at a time when the existing political system showed signs of erosion was another story altogether.

Let us pause here to reflect on the options that Indian capital enjoyed in the period of high Mughal rule and the context in which capital operated and expanded. The Mughal state ensured peace and law and order through a carefully managed infrastructure that facilitated commodity trade and credit flows. The emphasis on revenue collection in cash fostered monetization, forcing the producers to go in for cash crops, which had demand among consuming elites and markets in India and overseas. The investment in luxury goods by the Mughal nobility helped in the manufacture of cloth and other items of very high standard, ensuring thereby strong niche markets for Indian goods. The simultaneous rise of other world empires in the Indian Ocean, such as the Ottoman and Safavid empires, was a major fillip to the world of Indian trade and exchange—shippers and traders scaled up their operations and investment to reap major dividends. They were helped considerably by the competitive prices of Indian goods in the market as they were by facilities offered by the Mughal state in terms of infrastructure and the relative neutrality espoused by the state towards merchants. This meant that capital was able to find lucrative avenues of employment, diversify portfolio and even engage in a degree of forwards trading. Mulla Ghafur, for instance, enjoyed warehousing facilities in Yemen, while merchants like Virji Vora were able to corner the market, build up reserves of commodities and release them when markets were favourable. Throughout this period, the benefits of political peace and administrative stability were major assets, especially when European trading companies entered the fray, demanded customs privileges from the state, tried to enforce contractual agreements for supply of goods, and used their naval power as a trump card against the state and local merchants. Admittedly, the Mughal rulers did not invest in a naval protection force of their own to maintain the rights of local traders on the high seas or negotiate with pirates and privateers and chose instead to turn over the convoy system of the Indian Ocean to the Europeans. This gave Europeans an important foothold in the overall political system, whether in Bengal or Surat, with long-term implications for the future. Also, the regional variations in India produced very different consequences for local merchant capital—Bengal, for instance, in the first half of the eighteenth century, threw up a robust state system that benefited above all premier merchants and traders whose wealth was truly spectacular, while Surat suffered a degree of dislocation in the first half of the century.

The Fluid World of Transition: Merchants and Money in the Eighteenth Century

Between 1707, when Alamgir, the last of the Great Mughals, breathed his last, and 1818, when Lord Wellesley had successfully dismantled the Maratha Confederacy, the Indian subcontinent had undergone a fundamental transformation. The process was slow but dramatic, with the great empire of the Mughals initially giving way to regional dynasts and military adventurers, including European trading companies, and subsequently to the establishment of the English East India company as the paramount power of Hindustan. The political transition was accompanied by a slow transformation of the trading economy that dislocated some groups and empowered others, especially those who retained the power to control and manipulate the money market to advance loans and extract interest. Transition politics relied crucially on merchant and banking intermediaries to move funds across borders and provide for armies on the move, with the result that monied men became the vital link in the chain that held intact the logistics of revenue and commercial transfers. At a time when money was in great demand and exposed to uncertainty, thanks to political instability and administrative confusion, bankers emerged for a brief while as kingmakers and political arbiters. Their access to money and to credit made them indispensable allies in the struggle for supremacy. We will focus on the period between 1700 and 1757, when some states, such as Bengal, grew and prospered and others, such as Gujarat, faced challenges and obstacles, leading to massive bankruptcies and crises. While the broad patterns in the political economy of the eighteenth century in its first as well as later phases remained the same, the decisive intervention of the English company in the affairs of Bengal after 1757 massively reduced the space for indigenous capital, quite unlike the situation in the western parts of the subcontinent, where indigenous capital was able to leverage the fragmented political situation and hedge their bets more effectively with potential and actual patrons.

What underpinned the new political economy in the period of transition, and how did this catapult the merchant to a premier position? Merchants had not been insignificant before, nor were they overlooked as important subjects, but there is no doubt that in the Mughal imagination, the pride of place went to the mounted knight, not to the calculating *baqqal*, or merchant. However, this changed overnight as successor regimes organized their revenue arrangements in a manner that made merchant intermediation crucial. The successor states that emerged in Bengal, Awadh and Hyderabad were structured around advances of bankers and their sureties, as well as around credit transfers within the region and outside it across borders during wartime. Thus, everywhere—from

Bengal to Hyderabad, Poona to Delhi and Surat to Benaras—bankers became central to the smooth functioning of the political–military system and thus became real power brokers. Thus, what characterized the eighteenth-century political economy was the rapid movement of money across borders and boundaries and the dominance of bankers in the business. Ironically, this occurred at a time when traditional trade and commercial connections were disrupted by war, invasions, political competition and the onset of a new colonial regime spearheaded by the English East India company. To explain the paradox, we will briefly look at the nature of transitional politics and how this indirectly benefited the banker, who, thanks to his social capital and accumulated reserves, was able to capitalize on the situation. We will focus mostly on western India but will have occasion to relate the region's historical experience to the larger subcontinental story.

The steady dismantling of the Mughal imperial system manifested in the inability of the central administration to collect revenues, thwart the aspirations of local bosses and their own subordinates and deflect the ambitions of provincial aspirants like the Marathas, Sikhs and Jats. What followed was a fragmentation of political authority and the articulation of regional polities that attempted to increase vertical control in their regions and to integrate local bosses and power holders into the administrative set-up that followed. In order to maintain a steady flow of revenues into the exchequer and to avail of liquidity during times of constant and endemic war, states turned to merchants for support. This could assume several forms. In Gujarat (Surat, Ahmedabad and Broach) in the first half of the eighteenth century, we hear of local Mughal governors extracting forced levies from the merchants. Equally we see merchants assuming a political role by coming to the support of one aspirant over another, although in the long run, merchants as a rule gravitated towards the protection of the English East India company, whose increasing influence was seen as a valuable counterpoint. Much of eighteenth-century politics, therefore, was mediated through bankers and merchants, whose funds became crucial fodder for war and military conflict.[23]

The Bankers of the World: The Jagat Seths in Bengal

In the reorganization and regionalization of political power in India in the first half of the eighteenth century, bankers and banking firms occupied a crucial role as revenue intermediaries, state bankers and war financiers. These firms were not just small individual bankers engaged in myriad lending transactions but were large, impressive family firms that were able to accumulate enough capital to function as state financiers, providing cash and credit for payment of salaries to civil and military departments. The Jagat Seths (bankers of the world) were among the most eminent of these firms as they stepped forward as sureties for the payment of the province's land revenue, working closely with revenue farmers and local landholders in charge of revenue collection, and controlling the state mint, ensuring the purity and currency of the circulating specie and earning huge discounts on exchange of old and foreign coins into new ones. The Jagat Seths extended financial support to traders as well as the European companies and as the contemporary historian Ghulam Hussain observed, 'Their wealth was such that there is no mentioning it, without seeming to exaggerate and deal in extravagant fables'.[24] At the height of their prowess, the house seems to have commanded a capital of more than Rs 700 lakh with an impressive annual turnover. The

English factor, Luke Scrafton, had much the same impression when he remarked how the Seth was the government's principal banker and how about 'two-thirds of the revenues are paid into his house and the government give their draughts (drafts) on him in the same manner as merchants on the bank'.[25]

What lay behind this extraordinary concentration of wealth in the hands of a single house? Did this formation hold lessons for the future? Can we see this as the early prehistory of Marwari capital and enterprise in modern India, especially in Eastern India? What was it about the community that migrated from Rajasthan to settle down in Bihar and Bengal, find its niche in the Bengal–Surat traffic, accumulate capital and invest in sarrafi, and subsequently take up the business of financing the crown? Was it the community's familiarity with trade and handling money? As migrants from Rajasthan, the community of Oswal Jains would appear to have sensed the benefits of commerce under conditions of Mughal stability and migrated to Bengal, where Mughal presence was light on the ground, local landed elements were powerful and commercial interests were oriented towards the traffic of the European trading companies. The firm seems to have extended financial assistance to traders and invested in the lucrative Bengal–Surat traffic in raw silks and cotton that supported a sophisticated credit structure and remittances through hundis. These were important advantages, especially after the displacement of Mughal authority by independent governors who focused on setting up a centralized bureaucratic state undergirded by an efficient revenue-extraction apparatus. This required the cooperation of local landed interests and bankers who stood as guarantors for anticipated revenues. The Seths fulfilled this requirement as they steadily gained influence within the Murshidabad darbar (that emerged as the major power centre in the eighteenth century) and over the minting establishment. By the 1720s, the Seths had established an absolute monopoly of the mint with the support of the ruling Nawab Murshid Quli Khan, and with this exercised complete influence over the money market. In fact, the control of the bullion market was so complete that the European trading companies were compelled to play second fiddle to the Jagat Seths until the English company succeeded in cutting them to size and exercising their growing political influence after 1757. The Battle of Plassey and the takeover of the Bengal administration through puppet regimes spelt the end of the pre-eminence of the bankers, at least in Bengal, whose economy suffered major dislocations under the English East India company's emerging economic dispensation under the aegis of English private trade and agency houses. While these provided fresh opportunities for new men to make money, the older commercial groups suffered an eclipse and retreated to other levels and layers in the commercial system.

The situation in western India stood in marked contrast to that of Bengal in terms of economic growth. Unlike Bengal, which enjoyed unprecedented prosperity in the first fifty years of the eighteenth century under the successor state of Murshidabad, western India, especially Gujarat, suffered the consequences of imperial Mughal decline and political fragmentation, which impacted trade and commercial activity. The decline of great arterial trade routes between Surat and Bengal and Surat and Agra impacted the availability of goods from the hinterland for export markets in West Asia, where political decline and market contraction combined to make things even worse for the shipper and export trader. Not surprisingly, shipping merchants and freighters suffered even if the regrouping of trade within the subcontinent and resumption of lower levels of trade with Muscat and West Asia staved off a complete calamity. Merchants and bankers, whose operations were primarily shore-based and were anchored in the inland trade and banking sector, retained their foothold and, over time, built up substantial assets that could be deployed in new investment opportunities generated by the requirements and organization of post-Mughal successor regimes. Thus, merchants and bankers in western India did not entirely lose their centrality, even if the prospects of working amid conditions of political decline and weak states were grim and challenging.

Every eighteenth-century regime in western India, including and notably the Marathas, made use of bankers' sureties and advances to keep intact their revenue machinery that involved the transfer and flow of funds and remittances through the regions they controlled. Backing these flows were the actual operations of trade that continued to function, connecting large regional units. For instance, the demand for cotton was conspicuous in western India, connecting smaller Gujarati urban centres and trade marts with Bombay; the traffic in opium connected Bombay with Malwa and Ujjain in central India; whereas the demand for cloth and other necessities in Maratha-controlled areas in the Deccan revived trade to a large extent. All these commercial operations set up networks of credit and remittances that came in handy for the transfer of revenues for political regimes. At the same time, there was the growing pull of Calcutta and the trade it commanded, namely that of raw cotton and opium with China, which impacted markets and networks all the way to Awadh and Benaras and to the Deccan and parts of central India. Dense and vibrant urban clusters proliferated in parts of central and western India as well as in eastern Uttar Pradesh (UP), helping bankers and merchants expand their investments in inland trade and remittances. Remittance networks doubled up as conduits for transferring revenues to the state treasury from various points, and it was no coincidence that active credit transfers undertaken by bankers in Benaras and Surat dovetailed with the trade routes that criss-crossed the subcontinent. In every political regime that came up in the course of the eighteenth century, bankers emerged as political entrepreneurs, providing loans and remittance facilities that gave them the much-needed leverage for continued stability. The commercialization of state structures in the eighteenth century was part of the larger context in which capital operated, encouraging financiers to maintain close relations with rulers.[26]

Thus, the trade supported by hundis and the use of the bills as a financing medium for political transactions provided the springboard for several successful merchants of the late eighteenth century. Within Gujarat itself, the merchant model encouraged upwardly mobile peasant groups to commercialize revenue farming and emerge as major political brokers embodied by men like Lallubhai, who hailed from a family of revenue officials.[27] What is striking about the eighteenth century is the massive commercialization of operations—the ubiquity of revenue farming, customs farming, trade in *mokats*, or the city's custom duties, as well as the massive transfers of funds that accompanied inland commercial transactions, which gave enterprising men of capital a huge leg up in establishing their pre-eminence and in developing valuable stock for the future. Samira Sheikh, in her elegant study of Lallubhai, argues that the dynamics of cotton trade were determined by the agrarian economy in the hinterland and that ministers like Lallubhai were agrarian entrepreneurs whose intimate knowledge of production and revenue assessment enabled them to acquire productive estates and thereby control transregional trade in Gujarat. Bankers and merchants were part of this circle and participated in inland trade vigorously. Among the most pre-eminent of these merchant-actors was the Gujarati banker, Tarwady Arjunji Nathji, followed closely by others such as Atmaram Bhucan in Surat, Lala Kashmiri Mal and Lala Bachhraj in Awadh and Gopaldas Maohardas and Manohardas Dwarkadas in Benaras. For all these men, the ability to command reputation in the money market as reliable financiers was crucial; more than their low overhead costs and sparse lifestyle, it was credit and the ability to raise it in the market that were their prized possessions. The fear of loss of credit was acute; honour and reputation had to be maintained at all costs. From childhood, children of bankers were taught through jingle and rhyme to be mindful of capital and use every conceivable means to double it, look after it and spend it wisely. The unprecedented success enjoyed by the eighteenth-century Surat and Benaras bankers suggests the dynamics of transition politics, to which we will now turn through the life story of Shri Arjunji Nathji Tarwady.

The Honourable Company's Shroff in Western India: Tarwady Arjunji Nathji

At the end of his professional life, around the end of the eighteenth century, Tarwady Arjunji was recognized as one of the richest bankers of Gujarat, whose advances and hundis had enabled the English East India company to overcome Maratha resistance and establish their paramount control over much of western and central India. Myths abounded about his wealth, such as how money-laden oxen carts traversed through several localities of Surat city. His reputation and credit-worthiness extended far and wide with the Mughal administration and the English East India company abiding by his counsel. To explain his extraordinary success, we need to carefully examine the context in which he found himself operating, the strategies he deployed in consolidating his capital reserves and investing them carefully, as well as the bargaining position he enjoyed with his sponsors, the English East India company.

Tarwady Arjunji was born to a Gujarati Nagar family that traditionally followed occupations of trade and banking, combining it with scribal employment. One fed into the other, for what is immediately striking about Tarwady's career was the proximate links he was able to develop with the administration and to the astuteness in forecasting political change. His family had connections with Benaras and, by default, with the Marathas, who by the middle of the eighteenth century had carved out an important sphere of influence in the city and emerged as patrons of the Hindu faith. Pilgrimage sponsored by the Marathas and trade in cloth, textiles and other goods that connected Benaras with parts of eastern UP and Bengal as well as with the Maratha provinces in central India enabled prominent banking families like those of Tarwady to consolidate their gains as bankers and remitters. These services came in handy and were useful in the long run for gaining leverage with European trading companies, especially the English East India company, which was making its presence felt in Surat in no uncertain terms. Nurturing political connections and backing these up with financial and logistical support was an important strategy adopted by businessmen, and Tarwady Arjunji was no exception. Given that there was no direct conflict of interests between him and the English company, unlike in the case of the shipper Mulla Muhammad Ali or his successors, it was relatively easy for the banker to profess his loyalty to the new aspirant and extend wholehearted support. As early as 1743, we find reference to the banker in English records as a major merchant and as an arbiter in commercial disputes.[28] By 1759, when the English company authorities were poised to take over Surat castle and assume responsibilities as qiladar, the banker was able to broker a deal with higher Mughal authorities in Delhi and secure the necessary permission, thus testifying to his diplomatic skills and soft power. Thereafter, he was ensconced as the company's shroff and persuaded to open a shop in Bombay and help with the company's business. In 1787, he was appointed treasurer of the English company in Surat. There was no looking back hereafter; the banker used the patronage of the English East India company to carry on his extensive dealings in cotton and raw silk with Bengal and invest in a variety of goods that fed the new cross-country trade routes, integrating regional economies of the period with the trading pole of Calcutta. With trade came banking and remittance operations that responded to political changes. Overseeing a massive credit network, Tarwady became the principal banker of the English company, providing it with massive loans, advances and money transfers.

What lay behind the success of the banker? What were the elements in the political set-up of late Mughal India that enabled some groups, especially in western India, to seize the opportunity and emerge as political brokers? For, at this time, there was no question of bankers and merchants transitioning to manufacturing and industry. What was feasible was sustaining existing levels of inland trade and commerce, which guaranteed bullion flows and remittances, which held out prospects of gain given the multiplicity of currencies in circulation. Traditional expertise in exchange manipulation and careful investment in inland trade combined with political choices of backing the right aspirant came in handy for the banker. The English company was obliged to support his cause; in 1759, the authorities invited him to diversify and expand his operations by setting up a shop in Bombay, providing the relevant commercial information for their concerns and even acting as arbitrator in disputes that were settled at the Mayor's Court in Bombay. The diversity of his portfolio was impressive; within the city of Surat, he offered loans to merchants, accepted deposits from residents, including widows, and thereby played his traditional social roles and took up the farming of the mokats on silk, a commodity that he extensively traded in. His working methods, like other bankers of his times, were scrupulously meticulous; he worked with a network of loyal and well-trained agents, such as Mulchand Dube and Arat Ram Tiwari, kept his ear to the ground on matters of bullion flows and the money market and came forward on several occasions to discuss matters of debased coinage and practices of credit transfers. He worked with low social and institutional costs; his agencies were staffed by men who were known to him or belonged to his family, and he maintained very close relations with the local governments, whose intercession he could then expect during times of stress and strain. The choice of political patron was guided by rational considerations: at a time of transition politics when bankers were accustomed to hedging bets and to supporting a variety of aspirants, there was the growing realization that English power was superior and, more importantly, commanded impressive financial resources that guaranteed the repayment of loans and advances. The ability to forecast future opportunities and side with the potential winners of the political contest marked Tarwady's career from the very start.

By the 1760s, when the English East India company became the real masters of Bengal and secured the prized possession of the Diwani (right to revenues from Bengal, Bihar and Orissa), the majority of merchants and bankers were disposed to an alliance with them, an arrangement that held concrete advantages in terms of legal safeguards for private property and of credit repayment. By the 1770s, it was evident that the English East India company was the most solvent of eighteenth-century political aspirants and that their march to paramountcy over the subcontinent was inevitable and a matter of time. They hedged their bets wisely, sided with the company and their rivals, but in the end stood firm with the English company. Not surprisingly, Tarwady came forward along with others to advance massive funds to help the company in its protracted struggle against the Marathas, Mysore and even the Nawab of Awadh, in whose service bankers like Lala Kashmiri Mal and Lala Bachhraj were employed. The existing remittance network was galvanized, annual transfers to the tune of Rs 15 lakh were made to defray military expenses in return for which the banker secured protection and privileges. These privileges were largely to do with the control of the exchange rate and creating monopoly conditions for his business. Tarwady's business firm would appear to have absorbed virtually all the capital in Surat, while his controlled network of agents enabled him to operate the credit lines and to invest in the growing trade of raw cotton in which Indians and European private traders participated. Thus, between 1782, when the first treaty of agreement (Salbai) was signed with the Marathas, and 1803, when the Second Maratha War began, the banker had built up huge assets and proximity to the company, enjoyed substantial dividends from the cross-country trades in cotton and opium and got ready to finance the Anglo–Maratha wars, which he did with alacrity and finesse, making huge profits by insisting on massive exchange discounts. During the wars, the contract with the banker to provide funds at the local currency to armies on the move, was the lifeline for the company, which, on every occasion, had to give in to the demands of Tarwady as far as the exchange ratio between currencies was concerned. It was the senior banker alone who had real power over the money market, which was expressed in his ability to command huge funds at any given time and determine the rates at which his Surat–Bombay–Bengal rupees or the Surat–Malwa rupee would be exchanged for local money.[29]

The end of the war and the formalization of British paramountcy put an end to the influence of sarrafs and money changers, especially as the British introduced a uniform silver rupee and made use of their own treasury transfers. Presumably, this would have cut into the influence and profits of the bankers, although we do not have evidence about the lives of his successors. Reading back from late nineteenth-century evidence, however, it would seem that Tarwady's wealth could not be sustained intergenerationally. On the other hand, there were others who had practised the same profession who were successful and went on to build massive fortunes while realigning their operations to the colonial economy that was articulated over time. Here, the operative factor was the rise of Bombay, which provided a new context for the realization of capital gains even during a century of war, conflict and transformation. Men like Rupji Dhanji, who migrated to Bombay, and Parsi shipbuilder Lowji Wadia came to the fore, representing a new capital firmly aligned to the English power and anchored in a new urban space that the early colonial city represented. The network of early colonial cities—Calcutta, Bombay and Madras—was in sharp contrast to the older Mughal system that oversaw a complex and differentially integrated set of regions. The colonial cities until the late 1760s did not have a hinterland to speak of, even if they established strong legal and military safeguards within their immediate settlements and peripheries. On the flip side, the settlements required markets and provisions, credit and commercial support to participate in the larger trading system and local ship repair and building facilities in order to keep naval and shipping fleets in good repair. The company authorities, in order to enlist these services, offered protection on the seas and military support against arbitrary exactions and demands from local powers, as well as legal safeguards for the protection of commercial property and claims.

By the end of the century, the older trading and commercial centres (Surat, Agra, Lahore and Murshidabad) had definitely given way to the influential colonial cities of Calcutta, Bombay and Madras that had consolidated their status as major entrepots in the export trades of the Indian Ocean and as major political nodes from which the English East India exercised its authority. Local merchants, for the most part, were unable to compete with the English as far as the external trade in the Indian Ocean was concerned. English interference and penetration into inland trade networks was especially pernicious in Eastern India, where they had staged very early victories, but not so in western India, where local capital was strong enough to work as more equal partners in trade and enterprise. Bombay provides a good example of Indo–British merchant collaboration.

Bombay and its Merchant Princes

It was not until the end of the eighteenth century that the island city of Bombay began to show signs of emerging as a major port city of the western littoral, commanding an impressive export trade in the Indian Ocean. For the greater part of the eighteenth century, Bombay played second fiddle to Surat even as the latter city languished. What gave Bombay an edge at the turn of the nineteenth century was the rise of the cotton trade and, subsequently, the opium trade with China. The consolidation of European private trade and its connections with Indian capital working out of Bombay, Gujarat and central India, the principal catchment areas for the export staples, gave the English city a much-needed boost. The company authorities invited other service groups to come and settle down in Bombay to strengthen the commercial infrastructure, with the result that merchants, artisans and men of capital migrated in substantial numbers, setting up small businesses and responding to unusual opportunities. The combination of political protection and the dynamics of a racially mixed society provided the basis for a robust mercantile culture that has continued to give the city its profile. As Govind Narayan Tembe put it in his description of Bombay, a miscellany of castes and religions was to be found in the city where 'one's eyes are dazzled by the heaps of freshly minted coins from the Mint'.[30] Tembe was eloquent in his description of the city's affluent classes, 'if one enters a merchant's house, one cannot help getting the feeling that one has entered the abode of Lord Kubera himself after looking at the opulent furniture, the grand vehicles, the demeanor of his servants and the obvious wealth throughout'.[31] All communities were found here; the city guaranteed an income even to the most ordinary migrant. Arabs, Parsis and Gujaratis migrated to the city in search of wealth and business, taking up the business of overseas trade and provisioning. Some, like Rupji Dhanji, a Kapol Bania, came to the city and took up the business of provisioning the residents by dominating the city's grain trade. His sons appeared to have accumulated sufficient wealth to take up the business of banking and remittance, eventually setting up a substantial partnership firm under the aegis of Seth Varjivandas. Through the greater part of the eighteenth century, banking establishments in Surat maintained branches in Bombay and came forward as major collaborators of the English company. Closely following on their heels were Parsis, who were particularly prominent in two major businesses, namely, shipbuilding and export trade in partnership with the European private merchants.

We will take up, in brief, the tale of Parsi enterprise in Bombay primarily to assess the scope for Indian capital expansion and commercial growth at the end of the eighteenth century and thereby to look more carefully at the opportunities transition politics afforded local groups. We do this also to contrast Parsi enterprise with that of Bania capital and to determine the extent to which a new spatial location like Bombay impacted Indian enterprise and produced long-term consequences. It is important to remember that both these groups—Gujarati Bania and Parsis— were sponsors of industry in the larger region of western India and drew from an earlier history of cooperation and collaboration with Europeans. While the colonial cities (Calcutta, Bombay and Madras) in their original moment of formation were not set up to foster Asian trade, they certainly required local collaboration for the ease of European business. Thus, grain merchants for city markets, shipwrights for repair work on European ships at the Bombay docks and men of capital to prosecute trade and business under the protection of the company and within the jurisdiction of the company's custom house were invited to set up residence. Over time, these men became part of the city's indigenous business class, expressing their commitment and political submission to the system that the ascendancy of the English company embodied. The Parsi community was especially attracted to the city of Bombay, as they sensed opportunities for their artisanal activity as well as their commercial appetite. The community had forged close links with the Europeans in Surat by the end of the seventeenth century, gained familiarity with their ways of working and entered into collaborative projects of trade and respondentia. Their skills in carpentry and ship repairs were acknowledged, and it was therefore not entirely coincidental that the Wadia shipbuilders moved to Bombay and carved a very distinct niche and reputation. Lowji Wadia was among the first to move to the island city of Bombay and display his extraordinary artisanal skills and consolidate his reputation as the shipbuilder for the English East India company.

Lowji Wasserwanji Wadia arrived in Bombay from Surat in 1736 accompanied by ten other carpenters to fill an essential requirement of shipbuilding and repairs that English ships needed. Impressed by the community's carpentry and building skills, the English East India company authorities held out important concessions for it to settle down in the city and work for them on a contractual basis. In 1740, Lowji Wadia was designated master builder, given a big salary and orders to build ships for a variety of operations, from fitting frigates to combat piracy and privateering on the high seas and littoral as well as repairing ships for the India trade. Construction of ships meant using wood and timber resources, with the result that the Parsis entered the timber trade in large numbers in collaboration with Europeans.[32] By the end of the eighteenth century, shipbuilding in Bombay entered its golden era as a number of ships were built and launched. The most important ship to showcase the achievements of the family was the frigate 'Cornwallis' built in 1800, so superbly executed that it was bought by the Admiralty. It may be mentioned here that the business of shipbuilding was not easy; there was the problem of access to good teak (from Malabar) and of racial prejudice against use of Indian crew and Indian-built ships. In fact, from the late 1780s, the builders faced resistance from English shipbuilders who raised an alarm that they would face ruin if the use of India-built ships for the England–India trade was encouraged. Notwithstanding these challenges, the family retained its hold over the business, accumulated substantial assets and maintained very close relations with the local authorities, which helped by ensuring almost monopoly control over all offices connected with the docks. That the community retained great integrity in their mercantile transactions was significant and undoubtedly helped in both consolidating their linkages with the state and in enabling the transition from commercial success to industrial ambition. Here, it is worth quoting from a contemporary periodical that referred to the scions of the Wadia family in glowing terms:

> Remarkable as is the fact (of Parsis holding a monopoly of all departments in the Dockyard) being contrary of other departments of the State, we are not aware of any instance in which they have abused the almost unlimited confidence reposed in them. The opportunities to do so have been ample; for in an extensive dockyard, where large sums of money, from

the mercantile nature of its multifarious duties are in a continual
state of transition, numerous avenues must lie open for the
surreptitious accumulation of wealth. But the integrity of the
Parsi has remained unsullied. This feature, so characteristic of
high moral principle, no less than the peculiar one.[33]

Other Parsi families followed suit and worked in collaboration with
European private traders and the East India company to establish
their foothold in Bombay city. The timing proved perfect—from
the 1780s the city began to come on its own and took part in the
burgeoning cotton trade of the region. By this time, some political
gains at the expense of the Marathas and Mysore had been secured,
and the company and its servants were impatient for more territories
and commercial gain. Local merchants sensed opportunities in
the changing milieu and used their traditional strengths to gain a
foothold in the new city and the new dispensation that came with
the political paramountcy of the English East India company. A
number of commercial groups and communities began to settle
down in Bombay without necessarily disrupting their connections
with their naval bases, and Bombay began to assume the features
of a major port city capable of drawing capital and investing it
in profitable channels. What made the Bombay and western
India story particularly compelling was the strength and depth of
indigenous capital that could work within the emerging colonial
dispensation without necessarily being subjugated by it. Indian
capital was not subservient to colonial forces, even if it was not
fully capable of subverting the latter or altering the terms of
reference for trade and financial dealings. This was not the case
in Calcutta, where colonial penetration came early, was backed by
territorial gains and was predicated on a ruthless extermination of
indigenous trade and manufacture. Admittedly, even in Calcutta,

there was a regrouping of local commercial interests and their successful adaptation to the new system, but not with the same level of financial solidity and capacity.

Concluding Impressions

We began with the Mughal state and indicated its role in promoting market integration and setting the stage for India's unprecedented commercial prosperity and expanding trade in the Indian Ocean. The golden years of trade threw up a range of enterprising merchants and bankers, who made full use of the situation and amassed extensive fortunes besides building up family firms. These did not always help in countering the challenges of Mughal decline and transition politics that set in after 1707. For a merchant who lived through the century of transition, the world of trade and exchange at the end of the eighteenth century was not the same. There were admittedly some continuities and familiar coordinates in place: Indian staples—cotton, textiles, sugar and spices—were found in all Indian Ocean markets, while imports of coffee, pearls and even bullion made their way into India albeit at a reduced level. The basic pattern of trade too had not fully altered; India sold manufactured goods and received, or at least preferred to receive, silver and copper for the most part. The state, in whatever avatar—post-Mughal, Maratha, local dynasties, etc.—pursued a policy of military fiscalism and was keen on commercialization of the economy in order to extract as much ready cash as possible. These compulsions helped the state–merchant nexus remain more or less intact. But on the flip side, the overseas markets had contracted—West Asian markets particularly suffered from political instability and, thanks to the entrance of private European competition, went through seasons of glut with goods remaining unsold. At the same time, there was a noticeable shift of Indian Ocean trade from the west to the east—from the markets in the Arabian Sea to those in the Bay of Bengal, which would gain further ground in the succeeding decades. These were no mean challenges that merchants had to counter, especially as the political context in the subcontinent had changed radically. By the middle of the eighteenth century, the political configurations of late Mughal India were no longer the same. The changing situation was apparent to the merchants, some of whom had the resources to adjust to the new conditions. Regionalization of state power, closer vertical links with local power holders (bankers, landed groups), the entrance of the English East India company as a dominant player and the restoration of inland trading routes and credit lines provided a new set of options for trading society, some sections of which benefited while others went under. There were regional variations as well; western India fared better, by and large; here, bankers and capitalists played a key role in accelerating the process of colonial expansion and thereby accumulating both capital reserves as well as political resources and strategies. In other parts of the subcontinent, substantial segments of merchant society, especially in older Mughal towns, suffered dislocations, while those who migrated to the new colonial centres were able to make a deal with the new power and calibrate their ventures. Merchants followed the money in whatever way they could, learning to scale up and outward whenever possible. It is to these enterprising merchant–capitalists that we will turn our attention, identifying their success stories and speculating on the reasons behind their fortunes.

2

New Merchants, New Cities and New Imaginings: Jamsetjee Jeejeebhoy and Dwarkanath Tagore

'While there are many large cities in India, it is widely accepted that Mumbai, though small in size, is the grandest of them all and home to the most outstanding things . . .' wrote Govind Narayan Apte in 1863 as he proceeded to elaborate on the magnificence of the city, the density of its settlements, the cosmopolitan character of its population and the splendour of its stunning buildings. What stood out in Apte's account was the spectacular display of wealth, embodied in the city's built spaces and in the standard of living of even ordinary folk and the diversity of the city's population. Apte went to the lengths of asserting that 'the ordinary people of Mumbai are more fashionable than the richest of the Calcutta babus', a sentiment that clearly reflected the urban transformation in India and the rising eminence of Bombay in the race to parity with Calcutta.[1] Apte was neither the first nor the last to comment on Bombay or on Calcutta, which dominated the export trade of India till the middle of the nineteenth century and was referred to as the London of the east. Before Apte wrote his account of Mumbai, we have the Iranian Abdul Latif Shustari, who worked

in Calcutta and lived in Bombay to oversee the affairs of Arab
merchants in the city and negotiate with the English officials.
His recently found and translated diary (1801–04) extols the
dynamism of Bombay, the kindness of its British rulers and the
immense wealth of the city's inhabitants, especially the Parsis.[2]
The diary also refers to the perception of residents in Pune about
the safety of Bombay as a settlement and where they preferred to
transfer some of their assets.

Shustari and Apte, writing from different professional
and temporal locations, had one thing in common. They both
appreciated the absolute centrality of the British presence in
determining the economic life and social contours of the cities
of Calcutta and Bombay and in persuading important segments
of the population to work as partners, albeit on an unequal basis.
This was especially true in Calcutta, which, by the end of the
eighteenth century, was a British–Indian city with substantial
investments by European capital and by Indian partners. The city
was often referred to as a city of palaces, of impressive buildings
built by rich Indians and Englishmen alike, although the racialized
distinctions between white- and brown-skinned towns remained
intact. Bombay, on the other hand, was more cosmopolitan,
with a diverse mix of demographic groups and a multi-racial and
multi-ethnic society. However, in the case of both cities, the late
eighteenth century, associated with the ascendancy of the British
in both political and economic spheres, marked a major shift in
the working of the commercial system and ways of doing business.
These caught the imagination of several men, merchants with a
hunger for profit and eager to embark on new ventures and take
risks. Many of them embarked on adventurous voyages, made
new friendships with Europeans and carved for themselves a

permanent place in the business annals of the cities they belonged to. Business success led to new modes of consumption and even charity, philanthropy and piety. If there were two figures who embodied this shift, the changing temper and commercial orientation, two uber-rich tycoons who left an indelible impact, they were our protagonists, Jamsetjee Jeejeebhoy (1783–1859) and Dwarkanath Tagore (1794–1846).

What accounted for their success? What lay at the core of successful Indian enterprise at a time when the ascendancy of the new power, the English East India company, and of British capital swept all competition away? How did Indians learn to work with new masters? How did they strike on their own? Was it to do with their personal temperament and risk-taking acumen, was it contingent upon local circumstances or did they draw from a legacy of stewarding trade and landing business? To answer these questions, we will need to go back to the actual material context in which Indians, especially men of capital, operated in the two cities of Calcutta and Bombay, both of which emerged as crucial nodes in a newly emerging global economy, to the specific advantages our protagonists enjoyed, not to speak of their individual attributes and appetite for success.

Early Colonial Indian Cities: The Age of Partnership

The second half of the eighteenth century saw the expansion of the colonial cities of Calcutta, Bombay and Madras. Calcutta enjoyed a head start largely on account of the political gains the English East India company made after the Battle of Plassey (1757) and the rapid expansion of British private trade in the inland as well as export trade of the region. Broadly speaking, there were two

sets of changes, both of which impacted Calcutta's built space
and social composition. Between 1757 and 1793, Asian shipping
from Hugli disappeared and was replaced by the Calcutta fleet of
British private traders who dominated the trade in the western
Indian Ocean and then drove it eastward towards China and
Southeast Asia. Peter Marshall points out how in 1777, the far
eastern region absorbed nearly 25 per cent of Calcutta's exports
and it became even more pronounced after the 1780s, when the
Calcutta–Canton trade dominated shipping and investment.[3] In
the years immediately following Plassey, the official trade of the
company registered a massive expansion without benefit to the
local economy as the company no longer brought bullion to fund
its investment. The expansion of private trade and the rampant
abuse of conventions and protocols by private interests had
deleterious consequences on the weaver, the primary producer
and even the intermediary trader, forcing the higher authorities
in the company and the board of directors in London to consider
regulations for English private trade. By the 1780s, the servants of
the company were barred from private trading, but by this time,
the old trading system had collapsed and most Indian merchants
were reduced to the status of working as *banians*, or junior
partners, providing access to supply chains and raising credit at
the local level as and when necessary. They were no longer in the
driver's seat of the economy.[4]

The rise of the banians in and after the 1780s signalled
the changes in the region's trading system, where the advent of
private British capital in aligning parts of the Indian economy
to the emerging global one became a major factor. The takeover
of the Bengal region coincided with major changes in the
British economy, where the success of the Industrial Revolution

necessitated the making of a colonial economy. India as a subjugated colony provided a huge market for distribution of British manufactured textiles while enjoying the wherewithal to produce a range of commodities that could be exported worldwide under British dominance. Thus, English capital flowed into India and was invested in commodities such as raw cotton, opium and indigo intended for export markets, thereby integrating India with a larger global economy presided over by Britain. Initially, the lead was taken by English agency houses that invested the savings and deposits of retired company personnel in export goods and took charge of remitting the profits to England by issuing bills of exchange on their principals in London. In 1790, there were fifteen agency houses in Calcutta controlling the trade in silk, indigo, opium, etc., within Asia. Agency houses depended on local intermediary merchants, banians in this case, who also capitalized on their knowledge of the local market and their accounting skills. Calcutta became home to several important banian families, who also responded to the opening of the trade and to the opportunities provided by the arrival of American clippers. Banians were employed by agency houses and held down important roles especially in overseeing cash accounts and monitoring finances.[5] Among these banians, mention must be made of Ramdulal De, Gauri Shankar Sen and Kaliprasad Datta, who worked closely with their European masters and even undertook scribal and clerical work for the company's revenue office. They lent their name to *benami* (anonymous) transactions, and as one of them mentioned in a judicial deposition, 'Master was to manage in Calcutta and I was to manage at the aurang'. It was from within this banian class, which enjoyed proximity to the British and even learnt new ways of doing business, that men like Dwarkanath Tagore learnt to model their business enterprise. Taking up residence in the glittering city and watching men make money out of trade and investment, banians emerged as a major social group in the city, extended their commercial networks and flaunted their wealth in conspicuous displays of piety and consumption. For these men, the idea of trade and commercial activity held the keys to wealth and status, and they were prepared to take risks and embark upon new avenues of wealth generation.[6]

The growth of agency houses began to assume considerable proportions after 1813, when the trade in indigo attracted huge speculation and investments. The boom in indigo exports was followed by a slump, and the result was the ruin of several agency houses and their constituents in the first commercial crisis of early nineteenth-century Calcutta.[7] The scale of Indian investment in indigo at this time was small so the effects of the crisis did not create the loss of confidence among Indian commercial men, quite in contrast to what happened in Calcutta, three decades later. Indian merchants watched the developments unfold between 1834 and 1847, when export trade revived leading to new forms of managing agencies that controlled major export–import trades and even floated sizeable enterprises and joint stock companies. This period corresponded to a more mature phase of the colonial economy as British manufacturers pushed their marketing and distribution quite aggressively through agency houses. It was in this scenario that Dwarkanath Tagore made his debut and emerged to become one of the greatest merchant magnates of the century. We will see how he adapted to the idea of the joint stock company and invested in modern commercial enterprise.

Bombay underwent a similar trajectory, although the timing of its take-off was delayed. Besides, the city's merchant princes' investments in export–import trade were more conspicuous than in the business of managing agencies. For the greater part of the eighteenth century, the English settlement of Bombay played second fiddle to Surat and was unable to register its presence in the region's trading structure. Chronically short of funds and dependent on the supplies from Bengal, channelled through the hundi networks of local bankers, it remained a sluggish trade city with minimal investments in infrastructure. However, the guarantees of peace and political stability and the imposition of naval control over the littoral helped persuade local capital and artisanal communities to come and settle down in Bombay, participate in the city's coastal trade as well as with the trade to West Asia. We hear of Indo–European partnerships in the respondentia (marine insurance) and the export–import business and of Asian merchants continuing with their ventures, albeit on a reduced scale. Bombay worked in tandem with Surat to prop up the existing trading structure that showed signs of revival after the 1770s, when demand for raw cotton had an impact on the subcontinent. British trading interests in cotton were realized through the political agenda of the English company whose successive campaigns against their main rivals, the Marathas resulted in the annexation of the cotton-rich districts of Broach in Gujarat. The rise of the cotton traffic from Bombay helped local merchants (Parsis and Gujarati Banias) who supplied the staple, deploy their credit bills to fund the trade and emerge as important partners of the British.[8]

By the end of the eighteenth century, Bombay too saw the rise of British agency houses[9] that worked with their Indian partners to invest in the cotton traffic, encourage the use of Indian shipping and emerge as partners and financiers for the

Bombay government of the East India company. The Bombay agency houses were formed by free British traders, independent of the English East India company, undertaking to invest on behalf of the company servants and retired personnel in the rising cotton trade of the region and to secure safe channels of remittance to England. Agency houses acted as agents normally for a firm in London and for their depositors in India. A good example of this in Bombay was that of Forbes and Company set up by John Forbes (1743–1821), whose interests covered brokerage, shipbuilding and banking. Agency houses in Bombay worked closely with one another as well as with some of the leading local merchants of the city. Shipping happened to be one of their principal lines of business interest, and this helped both local shipping interests (builders such as the Wadia family) as well as enterprising local merchants who invested in shipping and sent these to China and Britain. The timing also proved fortuitous, for with the outbreak of the Napoleonic wars in Europe, Britain was dependent on Indian-built ships to guarantee cotton supplies for their mills in Lancashire.

In terms of operations, however, the early agency houses, such as those of Forbes and Company and Fawcett & Company, were not as substantial as their Calcutta counterparts. But their presence in the city and their investment in cotton purchases, in encouraging and patronising India-built ships, ensured an important working relationship with Indian capital which became even more important in the succeeding decades. With the rise of the opium trade, agency houses and their Indian constituents found enormous opportunities for investment and capital accumulation even though the nature of capital investment remained mercantile. The meteoric rise and success of Jamsetjee

Jeejeebhoy was part of this larger commercial milieu in western India, rife with commercial opportunities, providing a readymade field for Indo–British partnerships, which, in turn, enabled men like young Jeejeebhoy to risk a foray and eventually emerge as one of the most successful businessmen of colonial Bombay. Contemporaries and later commentators never failed to extol his intrepidity and risk-taking temperament, which emboldened him to embark on five major voyages from Bombay to China and England. In fact, it was on one of these voyages that he made the acquaintance of William Jardine, who remained a lifelong friend and business associate.

China bound: Early life, Early gains

Jamsetjee Jeejeebhoy belonged to a Parsi family that was well acquainted with Bombay and the fact that its Parsi population had substantially benefited from the British connection as early as the late seventeenth century. For Jeejeebhoy's family, the decision to move to Bombay was therefore not surprising. By the 1780s, substantial sections of the community had already settled down in the city and made their mark as shipbuilders, providers of various provisions and services. Jeejeebhoy's uncle (who later became his father-in-law) traded in bottles—presumably wines and perfumes—and encouraged young Jeejeebhoy to pick up basic language skills and even undertake a trip to China in 1799. Both uncle and nephew were not unaware of the growing European investment in the China trade that depended on regular cotton supplies in the subcontinent. Jeejeebhoy's cousin, Merwanjee Manekjee, was a small merchant and seems to have entrusted some funds with him to try his luck. Jeejeebhoy seems to have

invested wisely and is said to have brought back, even after his
very first voyage, a small fortune. Even more significant than the
returns on trade was his exposure to a global trading economy that
was integrating markets in China with those of India and Britain.
He saw first-hand Chinese ports flooded with enterprising and
audacious private traders trying their luck in the tea trade, for
which cotton and subsequently opium were the most sought-after
currencies. He saw how Indian goods were crucial in this trade
and how he could intervene as a supplier, agent and even shipper.
Fortune beckoned him, and it was a matter of time and luck that
he would cultivate a reliable network of supply and information
and make his mark as one of Bombay's greatest merchants.[10]

For the greater part of the late 1780s and 1790s, Bombay
remained a quiet settlement with none of the advantages that
Calcutta enjoyed thanks to its control over the rich agrarian
resources of the hinterland. On the other hand, Bombay had
some advantages in that it retained its connections with the
markets in West Asia, thereby supporting indigenous capital,
and with production centres in Gujarat and central India, whose
goods (cotton and opium) became global commodities and
critical for the emerging colonial trade of the late eighteenth and
early nineteenth centuries. Thus, the rise of the cotton trade saw
European private capital channelled through agency houses and
indigenous collaborators, commanding a presence in the city,
placing orders for cotton, and also for locally built ships that could
transport the commodity to China and even to Britain. The rise of
Indian-built ships coincided with the outbreak of the Napoleonic
wars (1803–1815) in Europe, when Britain was not in a position
to use her own shipping to carry out the trade with China or with
India. Jeejeebhoy anchored his ambitions firmly with those of the

British free merchants and private traders, impressed with the tenacity of their commercial ambitions as well as with their access to superior shipping and naval prowess. On his second voyage, in 1804, for instance, he encountered stormy conditions during the height of the Anglo–French rivalries and was impressed with the naval expertise of the English. He came back from this voyage a richer man, convinced of the possibilities of trading with China and of collaboration with the British agency houses. His landing at the Apollo Pier after the second voyage was hailed by his family as a signal of great joy and good fortune and sealed his reputation as a successful merchant who had in no time established important connections in the coasting and China trade circuits that the European free merchants and agency houses had mapped out. It is likely that like other merchants of the city, he extended guarantee brokerage for European merchants, undertook commission and even invested in shipping both in Bombay as well as in Calcutta. It was often pointed out that, as Asiya Siddiqi mentions, almost all the country ships of Calcutta were owned by the natives of Bombay.[11] But how Jeejeebhoy was able to penetrate into the business in a very short span of time remains an enigma. This is especially so when we track his early years before he had stabilized his business. It could have been ties of kinship and community as well as personal connections, all of which enabled the four major voyages he undertook. It is likely that the network facilitated access to information and credit, which he used carefully and thereby built up a reputation of trust and integrity among his associates. There was also the luck factor; Jeejeebhoy's ventures coincided with the Napoleonic wars, which left Britain vulnerable and forced it to concede space to Indian-built ships for use in the China–Europe trade. Thus, by the time of his fourth voyage, which ended around 1805, he had accumulated a fortune of Rs 2 crore by exporting cotton to England.[12]

Jeejeebhoy's fifth and last voyage in 1806 came as the decisive turning point in his trading career. During this voyage, the ship *Brunswick* was captured by the French, who took off with his cargo and left him at Cape Town. Here, he made the acquaintance of the ship's assistant surgeon, William Jardine, which blossomed into a deep friendship and a lasting business partnership. By this time, the trading connections between India and China had expanded to fit into the emerging tea trade between England and China. The main players in the system were the English trading company with its treasuries in Canton and India, British private merchants, Parsi collaborators and subsequently agency houses, all of whom played a part in supplying the export staples (cotton and opium) to fund tea purchases and in enabling remittances to go through to England. Thus, private merchants were expected to hand over to the company's treasury at Canton the proceeds of their purchases in exchange for company bills of exchange on either Calcutta or London. By these multilateral arrangements, the company used the sale proceeds of private traders to buy tea for London while private traders secured the benefits of remittance to the U.K.

Parsis had a long experience of working with private European merchants in the China trade.[13] For Jeejeebhoy, the personal association with Jardine was timely, for agency houses had, by this time, emerged as major players in the China–India trade and in the interlocking financial arrangements with the company. What marked out Jeejeebhoy's initiatives was his ability to sense opportunities and to scale up operations and substantially modernise the undertaking. There is no doubt that his friendship with William Jardine and their decision to form a partnership yielded dividends. He altered the structure of his business in a number of ways. From selling a variety of goods on a commission basis and securing goods for the Canton market, he went in for specialization and increasingly focused on opium purchases and sales organized around the consignment trade.

The Opium Connection: The Making of a Business Magnate

The shift to opium as the principal export staple was a major development in the 1820s, the ramifications of which were not lost on Jeejeebhoy. He was aware of the profit margins in the traffic, of the locational advantages that he enjoyed given his access to important supply networks and of the relations that he had cultivated with both European agency houses (for instance, Jardine, Matheson & Co. and Remington Crawford & Co.), as well as with local capital and Hindu and Muslim businessmen. The ability to network and create a solid base of support and supply channels was key to Jeejeebhoy's success. The opium trade of western and central India was complex with several stakeholders, and it required great planning, foresight and trust to be able to command the distribution and supply of opium from the hinterland to Bombay and then from Bombay to China.

Opium was an important cash crop in India and extensively grown in eastern India (Bihar) as well as western and central India (Rajasthan and Malwa). It was an extensively traded commodity that enjoyed a sizeable demand in both overseas markets as well as in the subcontinent. As a group, the Bohras were particularly active in the distribution of the commodity and stationed their agents in Burhanpur that was from the late seventeenth century an important node in the network of opium distribution inland. There were other overland trading communities as well, who worked in close conjunction with local rulers in central and western India as well as with Portuguese officials stationed along the western littoral, especially at Daman, which became an important entrepôt for smuggling opium thanks to the lower rate of duties it imposed. Thus the map of opium distribution encompassed a complex political geography—it had to negotiate the jurisdiction of princely states in central and western India that stood to benefit by transit duties and customs and of the Portuguese in the western littoral that was the gateway to export.[14]

The demand for opium grew exponentially in the nineteenth century, when the commodity became the most desired one for goods exchange, especially of tea from China. The demand for opium as a recreational drug was seized upon by British merchants as well as by the English East India company, which sought to control the trade from India. In Eastern India, the company was able to exercise a monopoly over the production and distribution of the produce, but not so in western India, where a powerful conglomerate of merchants, intermediary distributors and local bosses controlled the trade in opium from the hinterland to the ports and also from the ports to China. In terms of volume, the traffic in opium by the early nineteenth century registered appreciable increases, outstripping cotton consignments from western India. Private traders, including Bombay's local Gujarati and Parsi merchants, bought huge quantities and exported the same on behalf of other merchants. Jeejeebhoy was very quick to jump in and establish his pre-eminence in the trade, thanks largely to his connections with agency houses as well as with local capitalists. The triumvirate of Jamsetjee Jeejeebhoy, Roger Faria and Motichand Amichand emerged as a major player in the opium trade that set the stage for the unprecedented influence of Jeejeebhoy as a merchant of eminence who set about organizing a diverse portfolio going far beyond his original business of guarantee brokerage.

By 1820, Jeejeebhoy was ready to restructure his business in a number of ways. By this time, it was apparent that the English company was not in a position to bring British private traders or their local collaborators under any control. Jeejeebhoy gave up his commission business and declared that he was no longer interested in this line and that he would never advance money to any private individual. He also disinvested from guarantee brokerage, which had been the lifeline of many Parsis. Instead, he chose to emerge as an independent player, a shipper, banker and a consignment trader for specific agency houses with whom he enjoyed an equal partnership. From his early apprenticeship with Parsi merchants, who traded with China (cotton), and his innate ability to build valuable personal connections with the Hong traders in Canton, with British merchants and agency houses in country trade (Calcutta–Madras–Bombay–Canton) circuit, he decided to first of all invest in shipping. In 1804, he bought his first ship, the *Good Success*, which he fitted with goods for the China market. Between 1818 and 1832, he bought four more ships, his most-prized possession being the 1000-ton *Fort William* built in Calcutta. With this fleet, he embarked on the consignment trade in a big way, working closely with big agency firms like Jardine that depended on supplies from the Parsi magnate.[15]

In September 1818, Jeejeebhoy proceeded to give his business a formal structure by developing a partnership firm with Roger

Faria, an Anglo–Portuguese merchant, Motichand Amichand, a Hindu Bania who had extensive contacts with opium suppliers in the hinterland and Muhammad Ali Rogay, a Konkani Muslim merchant. Together, this firm epitomized the early cosmopolitanism of Bombay and dominated the scene, especially in the export trade with China. The choice of partners—close friends as well—was judicious, as each of them brought very specific skills and expertise to the business. Through Roger Faria, he could work with the Portuguese networks off Daman; through Motichand Amichand, he had access to the Marwari syndicates that controlled the shipments of opium in the hinterland; and through Rogay, who was a shipowner, he could exploit information networks related to shipping and exports.[16] Between 1820 and 1840, the business grew exponentially with the firm consigning goods (cotton and opium) to agency houses in China. As consignor, Jeejeebhoy was responsible for financing the purchase of the export staples, and as shipper, he was responsible for the management of the voyage. His trusted partners—the agency houses—organized the sale at the other end and enjoyed the proportionate commission on sales. As shippers, his firm also claimed a share of the profits, and for a while it seemed like a win–win situation for all parties concerned. Admittedly, as consignor, he undertook risks and had to therefore ensure the quality of the product and its competitive pricing. He had to be equally confident about his China associates and their profit margins.

How did Jeejeebhoy manage the dense web of operations? Friendships and personal connections were key, but equally striking is the growing professionalization of the business. He personally attended to every detail and took exception to any carelessness that agents demonstrated when it came to market forecasting. His punctilious habits come to us through his letters and through the correspondence with Jardine, where the magnate is seen updating himself with market information and anticipating risks and market slumps. Operating the traffic was no easy task; in an age of sail, opium was transported by country boats and along muddy tracks, and markets were notoriously hard to read. There was also the political situation in China where the government was ambivalent about the traffic and often considered regulations and bans. Jeejeebhoy was a hard-nosed businessman who took risks and exhorted his partners to drive hard bargains. In one of his letters to Jardine, dated 12 February 1845, he instructed Jardine not to part with the drug without making the Chinese pay handsomely.[17] There was no question of Jeejeebhoy taking a moral position on the trafficking in drugs; indeed, for him, the commitment was to supply a pure product and to drive hard bargains. He was thus a modern professional who took pride in conducting the business on fair principles and expected others to do the same. Whether it was with his upcountry agents in India who provided him vast quantities of the drug or whether it was his associate Jardine, Jeejeebhoy was candid in his assessments and expectations. Writing to Magniac & Co. in 1831, he confessed that the stock of Malwa opium was less than anticipated and also how some of the material was inferior. He took responsibility for the same and assured his associates that he would guarantee better stocks. In another letter, he made the point that he was expecting better crops in the coming years and that, under the circumstances, they could hope for better market prices. This was clearly a hard-nosed businessman at work, who knew to forecast markets, take risks, and ensure supply chains. On the other hand, he did not spare his associates either—in his letter to Jardine (1849), he wrote how disappointed he was about the latter's opium transactions.

> I will candidly confess to you that my silence of late has been occasioned by a feeling of dissatisfaction at your transactions in opium on our account. Day after day I have felt a disinclination to enter upon a correspondence, the style of which is so different from what we have hitherto enjoyed and while I believe that it may prove disagreeable to you, I can assure you that it is not the less so to myself.[18]

The letter is telling; it gives the reader a sense of the quality of the partnership, one that was not unequal, and wherein Jeejeebhoy was not cowering before the Englishman and was in fact, hauling him to uphold better standards. Jeejeebhoy was not a dependent partner, and if he was excluded from certain sectors of business, it was only the dynamics of a colonial regime that forced him to hit the glass ceiling. His correspondence, especially in the late 1840s, in fact, holds a clue to the difficulties that he began to face in the export trade and the business of remittance around this time, when he was increasingly aware of his inability to send ships to England. While free British traders could do this easily, Jeejeebhoy could not, as it was more expensive to do so. In one of his letters, which Asiya Siddiqi uses as evidence of the asymmetry of the situation, he wrote, 'The result that always attends our country ships going to England would almost lead one to think that some evil destiny was attached to them, as we find the Free Traders can sail very cheap while our ships are burdened with immense expense'.[19] He elaborated this with some bitterness when he wrote how there was widespread prejudice about Indian country ships and that surveyors in England raised all kinds of objections and imposed penalties. The decade of the 1840s was a period of real challenge for the businessman, as it coincided with major changes in the financing and structure of the triangular trade, the decline of sail shipping and the rise of American competition. This impacted the remittance business as well in which he had important stakes.

From the very beginning, Jeejeebhoy was aware of the intersecting businesses of remittance payments and the opium and cotton trade with China. Remittances to British India and England were built into the structure of the trade, as all parties expected or were required to send proceeds from one company treasury (Calcutta–Bombay–Madras–Canton) to another not to speak of remittances back to England. The company absorbed funds for tea purchases in the form of bills that it issued on England, just as agency houses also stepped forward to do the same. Jeejeebhoy found bills on the company in London convenient as he could sell them to European traders. He had his agents stationed in London, who discounted bills and earned handsomely. Jeejeebhoy, under the circumstances, was forced to keep a watchful eye on remittance rates; his correspondence reflects his concerns on the fluctuating rates of exchange. By the 1840s, the bill business was not as easy as it had been in the previous decades; on 16 December1849, he wrote to Jardine mentioning how there were no buyers for bills and that there were large funds in London waiting to be withdrawn.

What Jeejeebhoy was giving expression to was part of a larger transformation that had occurred in the world of the Indian Ocean trade, where for a brief period, converging interests of the English East India company, British traders, agency houses and Indian capital came together to build a huge global enterprise. Once the status of the English East India company changed and it lost its charter of monopoly rights to the China trade, other foreign private traders, including the Americans, stepped in and competed with the Parsi businessmen like Jeejeebhoy in the bills business. As Jesse Palsetia points out in his biographical treatment of Jamsetjee Jeejeebhoy, American bills of exchange were now redeemable in London, and these, along with other western capital instruments, became a desirable medium of exchange for commodities among Europeans. This form of repayment disadvantaged Indian merchants, who found it difficult to sell bills in Bombay or secure quick repatriation of funds that were sent to London.

These difficulties were compounded by the advent of steam shipping in the ocean, which Jeejeebhoy's country fleet could not match. The new steam vessels were cheaper to run, while his own fleet was difficult to maintain. As he wrote in one of his letters to a friend,

> We have now in Bombay harbour an immense fleet of free traders who are willing to take on cotton to China for the very lowest freights, at which it is impossible to sail a country ship. Last year, many of our fine teak ships were laid up, and this season would have gone at miserably low freight.[20]

He complained about the lack of confidence people reposed in his fleet, forcing him to consider selling his ships. As it happened, there was around this time an unexplained fire in the harbour that destroyed his fleet. Whether this was a case of arson or was an accident is not clear, but the effects were disastrous. The apprehension about fire safety in ships spread among freighters and forced the Parsi businessman to give up on shipping and fall back on other forms of investment, in emerging insurance and railway companies.

Business After Opium

The difficulties faced by private traders during the Opium War and its aftermath and the delays in securing compensation after opium seizures did not entirely deter Jeejeebhoy from continuing with the traffic. Even as his shipping interests came to be scaled down, his firm continued to provide consignments to China and earn substantial profits that were wisely spent by his sons and successors. His faith in the British connection did not waver; he relied on their intercession in China and petitioned the higher authorities in London to press claims for indemnification. He trained his family in business and management methods, urging them to invest sensibly and read the market carefully, advice that stood them in good stead, especially during the fiasco of the 1860s when several families went to rack and ruin with senseless speculation in shares and cotton speculation. As a businessman, his commitment was to punctual performance and to maintaining standards. There were no moral qualms about trading in narcotics; for him, as for his European counterparts, the idea was to make huge profits by managing a business efficiently and fairly. He fully bought into the liberal narrative of private enterprise and profits, a part of which he turned over to philanthropy and investment in civic improvements.

How did Jeejeebhoy see himself? Thanks to his extraordinary success and his connections in high places, he became an influential subject who found it important to intervene in the public life of Bombay city, conduct philanthropic operations, especially for the less privileged members of his community, and earn official recognition from his patron-rulers. According to Palsetia, the activities of Jeejeebhoy were part of an older, pre-colonial mercantile culture that invested in charity as a resource to increase their social capital. However, there were new elements in the charity business as well. At one level, Jeejeebhoy's charitable intentions derived from the urge to promote himself within his community and within British colonial society, where he felt at home and wished to be first among equals (in this case the British). But at another level, there was a modern managerial aspect to the projects that were not simply extensions of personal vanity. This is clear when we look at the way charities were set up and managed. These spoke to both a larger public good as well as to a community network. Charity was both an important means of enhancing his public image and persona as it was of consolidating his position within the community organization or Parsi panchayat, as well as being a new modality of creating private–public partnerships in a rapidly developing commercial city with new infrastructural and civic requirements. Jeejeebhoy thought beyond his community; he was a full-time participant in the building of Bombay and its civic infrastructure. For Jeejeebhoy, wealth was to be ploughed back into civic facilities that were a form of investment for the future, not just in terms of building individual status but of collective well-being. In these efforts, he saw the government as a key partner and not as an adversary.

Among the philanthropic activities that Jeejeebhoy undertook, mention may be made of financial arrangements towards the redemption of loans by debtors languishing in jail for poor relief, as well as setting up medical relief in the form of a new hospital in collaboration with the government, the existing medical college board, the medical fraternity and local inhabitants. Towards this effort, Jeejeebhoy offered to pay into the treasury of the Bombay government an initial sum of Rs 50,000 to be held in trust at 6 per cent per annum, provided the government came up with a proportionate contribution. In terms of access and organization, the scheme ran into some trouble. According to scholars like Palsetia, Jeejeebhoy's intention was to capitalize on his unique position as intermediary and take greater control over social projects that included special and preferential treatment for his community. This was not compatible with the government's viewpoint that saw Jeejeebhoy's 'exclusive' philanthropy as antithetical to western ideas of public good. Eventually, a compromise was reached on 11 November 1840, and the Bombay government proceeded with the hospital, which they named after Jamsetjee Jeejeebhoy. It had a capacity of 300 beds with special wards for patients recommended by him.

The other charities that Jeejeebhoy undertook were related to the civic improvement projects in Bombay and schemes to help the poor and the destitute, especially within his community. What made his interventions (setting up of asylums, a fund for vagrants, etc.) stand out was the emphasis on good management. While he did not run these as businesses, he expected them to be soundly operated on sustainable principles. Like his commercial ventures, his partners, in this case the government, did not always extend unequivocal support. Jeejeebhoy expressed his disappointment on a number of occasions; he reacted bitterly to the court of directors' initial reluctance to his schemes and donations that he wanted treated as a public–private partnership. He wrote that he wished he could convey to the court of directors the seriousness of the indigent population in Bombay and how essential it was to provide institutional support. The disappointment did not result in a major shift in his attitude towards the British, whose support he relied upon and whose connection he believed was good for the country. As a loyalist, his work was appreciated by the government that bestowed on him the baronetcy in 1842. With this honour, he had made it to the list of the most important notables of the city, whose commercial genius and social vision were celebrated by one and all, associates in the city and overseas. The address that marked the occasion went thus:

> neither is it necessary to dwell upon the benefits which the trade of . . . this port (Bombay) has derived from the enterprise and magnitude of . . . your commercial operations, nor to point out the great extent to which . . . you have availed yourself of the means of doing good derived from your . . . mercantile knowledge and experience, joined to a conciliatory disposition and the probity of your character, as well as from your position in the native community, by arranging differences and settling disputes, so as to save the parties from the evils of a tedious and expensive litigation.[21]

The address thus acknowledged the enormous contributions that Jamsetjee Jeejeebhoy had made for the city's commerce, which was seen as a vehicle for public improvement. The governor Lord Elphinstone referred to his extraordinary contribution asking rhetorically, 'which other world city could boast of a citizen who had devoted a quarter of a million sterling to purposes of public charity and benevolence.'[22] Jeejeebhoy himself saw trade and commerce as essentially a productive social activity, and in this, he echoed the official rhetoric of the English free traders, who saw Laissez-faire and free trade as the most important conduits for change and progress. For this, business had to be conducted around principles of probity and intelligence—senseless speculation was not something that he ever espoused. Risk-taking was an essential ingredient of successful enterprise, but this had to be supported by fair and consensual practice, intelligent market forecasting and product control. As a successful merchant firm, his philosophy was transmitted to his sons, who, unlike their contemporaries, did not get sucked into the vortex of speculation and gambling in the share market of the late 1860s.

Jamsetjee Jeejeebhoy was indisputably one of Bombay's most important merchant–princes of the nineteenth century. This was not just a consequence of the colonial connection; it was the outcome of a conjunction of circumstances, personal temperament, locational advantages and robust information and business networks. Interestingly, in the case of Jeejeebhoy, networks transcended community and were multiracial and multiethnic. For the British administration in Bombay and its European merchant elites, Jeejeebhoy was an invaluable ally. It was not just the generosity of his donations and endowments; it was also his acquiescence with the emerging capitalist project under the direction of the colonial state that made him a valued subject. Jeejeebhoy was not just a lackey or a comprador but was in every sense a modern businessman who knew to strike a deal when he saw potential and invest in social projects that would transform the city that he had made his home as a young boy. He passed on his good business sense to his son and successor, Cursetjee Jeejeebhoy, who, unlike his contemporaries and even family members, did not succumb to the share mania of Bombay in the 1860s; instead, he carried on with the consignment trade in cotton to British firms and invested in banking and insurance, which were emerging as significant businesses. There was as yet no transition to modern industrial manufacture, but in terms of careful management of trade and enterprise, the house of Jeejeebhoy sustained and responsibly its fortunes and did not suffer from inter-generational convulsions.

If Jeejeebhoy set the tone for a new form of business and the basis for Anglo–Parsi collaboration in the fields of export trade and shipping, Dwarkanath Tagore (1794–1846) experimented with similar projects in Calcutta. The lives of these two businessmen present interesting contrasts and convergences. Both men lived through a period of colonial consolidation and saw unprecedented opportunities in the English connection, whether it was law, security of property or profits from commercial enterprise. Both valued their English friends and sponsors and reposed great confidence in the establishment, which they saw as crucial to the development of the country and to the liberation of its people from poverty. Like the Parsi magnate, Dwarkanath believed in the utility of free trade and industry and even went to the extent of professing the advantages of making India a settler colony. His hopes were shattered at the end of his life, when he faced huge losses in business, leading to a complete retreat from productive commercial activity that others of his class emulated. With this catastrophe, Bengal and its men, unlike Bombay and western Indian capitalists, turned their backs on business for almost half a century.

Dwarkanath Tagore: The Merchant Prince and Business Pioneer of Bengal

A German aristocrat visiting Calcutta in the 1840s who had the good fortune of enjoying the Tagore household's hospitality in Calcutta had this to say of Dwarkanath Tagore: 'Dwarkanath

Tagore, who by his ability and enterprising spirit, has become one of the wealthiest merchants of India, is also one of the most hospitable man in that hospitable country'.[23] He was not wrong in his impressions; by this time, Dwarkanath had tasted dizzying success in various enterprises, from land management and litigation consultancy to trade and managing agencies. Dominating the business world of early nineteenth-century Calcutta, he was a versatile personality—an entrepreneur with a diverse portfolio who dared to dream big and experiment with new forms of business organization, promoting a slew of joint stock companies dealing with coal, steam transportation, banking and silk filatures, sugar factories and land-related consultancy. He made a colossal fortune, hobnobbed with royalty and literati in Europe, and saw himself as a catalyst for modernization for change that would help catapult India into heights of development. Dwarkanath's meteoric rise, helped by an intrepid temperament and adventurous spirit, occurred in a very specific context of Calcutta's rise as a major city of European private trade and capital fuelled by agency houses that blazed a new trail of enterprise and organization.

Socially, the two men—Jamsetjee Jeejeebhoy and Dwarkanath Tagore—belonged to very different backgrounds but were products of a similar context and shared a common appetite for commercial profit and management experiments, thanks to an openness that characterized the community and sub-caste they each belonged to. As a Parsi, Jeejeebhoy was predisposed to trade and enjoyed the benefits of artisanal experience and of community networks that responded to the European/British private trade connection. Dwarkanath belonged to a sub-caste of Brahmins, known as the Piralis, celebrated for their enterprise, sense of adventure and openness. Dwarkanath's immediate ancestors moved to Calcutta in the eighteenth century, where they responded to opportunities generated by European trading companies in their settlements. Some opted for service with the English East India company; one of them even worked as *diwan* (manager/collector) for the French trading company at Chandernagore. The family supplied the commissariat at Fort William in Calcutta, accumulated land and real estate, and enjoyed holdings in both Calcutta (Jorasanko, the main estate) and in Bangladesh. Born in 1794 to Rammani Tagore and adopted by his uncle in 1799, Dwarkanath found himself in an environment when English education and the benefits of western learning were becoming obvious. He went to Sherbourne School, where he developed his English language skills in addition to his proficiency in Sanskrit and Persian. By the time he left school, his family had acquired estates in Orissa and Bangladesh, and through careful application of new revenue laws introduced by the English East India company, enjoyed the reputation of being responsible landlords familiar with the provisions of the Permanent Settlement of 1794. Apprenticeship in commercial management of land was an important asset, yielding both revenue as well as commercial contacts. Unlike his Parsi counterpart, Dwarkanath's mastery of zamindari accounting and of the new rules of revenue and judicial administration initiated by the English East India company gave him both an intimate understanding of the real estate business and revenue management and held out real prospects of income from a lucrative consultancy on litigation that he ran for a number of years. He charged handsomely for his service, earned Rs 1000 every month, and invested this in the acquisition of more land, capitalizing on the distress of defaulters under the Permanent Settlement of 1794, under which those landlords who failed to pay their revenue had their estates auctioned off. From here, Dwarkanath set out to understand the workings of English commercial enterprise by accepting an appointment in the salt department. Even before this, Dwarkanath had appointed English managers in his estates under consideration of efficiency; he had thus the opportunity of learning their methods of supervision firsthand as well as their understanding of commercial enterprise. It is very likely that this experience enabled him to add a number of new factories (silk, indigo and sugar) to his estates. The decision was also informed by the growing expansion of commercial agriculture in Bengal in this period, thanks to the rise of private trade and agency houses that broke the English East India company's monopoly of the India trade and resulted in a massive expansion of indigo production and export. Indian investment in this traffic or in the operations of agency houses was not substantial, but Dwarkanath was too astute to miss the signs of the commercial revolution in Bengal.[24]

Around this time, in 1822, Dwarkanath took service under the company's salt department, where he acted as *serishtadar* (officer in a district court) to the collector and salt agent, Trevor Plowden, with whom he also developed very close and intimate personal relations. Working for a meagre salary, Dwarkanath learnt a great deal about revenue administration, made useful contacts and accumulated capital and information that would serve as a useful launchpad for his own business operations. Just as his business flourished, his social life too thrived. He made influential connections, hosted impressive parties and soirées and built an impressive reputation. Professionally, he was known for his commitment to integrity and for a zero-tolerance attitude towards corruption. This meant that he was able to draw on capital deposits from subscribers who went along with his plans for expansion. The most significant of his projects was in the banking sector. Formal banking was underdeveloped in Bengal; the existing banks were hardly adequate, and so in 1828, Tagore made the decision to float the Union Bank, a bank independent of the government with a capital of 500 shares. The bank followed modern organizational principles and appointed directors. The bank did very well in the early years; its paid-up capital increased, and right through the first commercial crisis, when agency houses that had overinvested in indigo went bust, managed to remain strong and enhance Dwarkanath's reputation as 'the dominant figure in the Calcutta business world'.[25] Both the Union Bank and Tagore stood like a rock, helping select creditors like John Palmer and thereby consolidating the confidence of British associates. Tagore himself was not confident as yet of launching his own entrepreneurial career, but by October 1834, he was ready to take the plunge. By this time, he had sufficient capital stock accumulated from landed income, consultancy and commercial agriculture. The situation too seemed right—after the first commercial crisis that saw the fall of several agency houses, a new form of managing agency was finding traction among indigenous businessmen who discovered the transformative aspects of western education and the enormous social potential of trade as a vehicle of public improvement. Like Jeejeebhoy, Dwarkanath reposed complete, even naive faith in the British connection as an emancipator of poverty, superstition and everything that was wrong in Indian society.

The Managing Agency System and Indo–British Partnership

The aftermath of the first commercial crisis in Bengal, which saw the collapse of major agency houses in the wake of the indigo crash (1829–30), was marked by a new form of entrepreneurial activity in the form of managing agencies. These were partnership houses mainly interested in India's export trade of sugar, indigo and silk, but unlike their predecessors, the agency houses oversaw the formation of joint stock companies.[26] While it is not clear how many such partnerships emerged, we know for a fact that the more prominent of these firms—Carr, Tagore & Co., Oswald, Seal & Co. and Turner & Co.—were powerful and accommodated very substantial Indian capital. These houses directed a huge export trade with Britain and Europe as their principal destination and, following the example of agency houses, handled huge consignments of indigo, sugar, silk, saltpetre, etc. Dwarkanath's estates were an important catchment area for many of these goods—sugar, silk and indigo—in which he had already invested substantially.

What really marked Dwarkanath's enterprise at this time was not his ability to integrate his operations with the European firms but to experiment with a new form of business altogether, that is, the joint stock business, and secondly, the ability to effectively work out principles of backward integration. We see this in his early entrepreneurial management of landed estates and his ability to forecast the potential of commercial crops and in his decision to initiate banking operations. The founding of Union Bank and its ability to bail out agency houses in crisis helped gain the confidence of senior European businessmen like John Palmer and float his own independent business ventures with Europeans. Carr, Tagore & company was launched in 1834 with much fanfare as the first biracial enterprise. This was primarily an export firm that consigned cargoes to Europe. The company had its correspondents in London and Le Havre who handled the consignments and managed the business on that end. Very similar to the earlier agency houses, the company of Tagore invested substantially to control production and processing of the commodities it exported—indigo, sugar, saltpetre, hides, rum and timber. This was done by buying up existing silk filatures (owned by the East India company) and by experimenting with rum production in his estates. This failed, but it marked Tagore's never-say-die spirit and his vision that went far beyond the efficient management of the old consignment trade. One of the manifestations of his disposition to innovation was the organization of joint stock companies, something that Indians had not experimented with yet. There were risks in this, for the joint stock principle did not have legal backing in India.

Dwarkanath was more than aware of the challenges ahead. There was the question of capital and subscriptions and of shareholders willing to come forward to accept liability. Here, his personal credit rating and his track record proved major assets. The first venture was in connection with the acquisition of the Raniganj Colliery in Burdwan, which gave him virtual control of coal supplies under the management of the Bengal Coal company that was formed by merging it with a rival colliery. The move was actually audacious, as conditions were far from optimal for Tagore's managers. We have an evocative description of the problems that his manager faced—floods, fires, labour strikes.[27] This was followed by several other joint stock companies, all of which involved the use and exploitation of coal. The enterprises were the Calcutta Steam Tug Association, the Steam Bridge Ferry company to facilitate movement of passengers and cargo across the Hooghly and the Indian General Steam Navigation company (established in 1844). All these companies were dependent on coal for fuel and energy and thus were serviced by the Bengal Coal company. Much more than his Parsi counterpart, Tagore was dipping into the demand for transport infrastructure and making the move from trading and consignment management to joint stock companies that oversaw coal processing and organizing transport services. These companies were modern entities, run on professional lines, reliant on subscriptions and shares and functioning through a board of directors. For instance, with the Calcutta Steam Tug Association, there was a managing agency contract in place. The deed provided for the existence of the association for a term of five years with half-yearly meetings of shareholders to approve accounts and declare dividends. The initial call was for a capital of Rs 2 lakh, divided into shares of Rs 1000 each, to be invested in the purchase of two steamboats. No shareholder was to hold more than twenty shares, and individuals were to have one vote for one share, two votes for five shares, three votes for ten shares and four votes for twenty shares. The association was to be conducted by a committee of five annually elected directors under whose control the secretaries were to manage the details of the business. Carr, Tagore & Co. were appointed secretaries and paid 5 per cent on the net earnings of the steamers.

Why Dwarkanath opted for the joint stock model has remained a matter of speculation among historians. It is likely that with the Steam Tug Association, the intention was to attract capital, which was not always abundantly available. The joint stock enterprise helped distribute risk while assuring him control over the board of directors. There were social considerations as well; the idea of a steam tug association carried with it explicit connotations of public service attached to the enterprise, which Tagore hoped would attract more capital subscriptions. According to Kling, the venture was meant to instil a sense of public participation among men of capital. In terms of actual realization, this did not work and the investing public was quick to see through the benefits that the association gave agency houses. The Steam Tug Association, for instance, absorbed Tagore's coal and docking facilities, and the ease with which agency houses used control of public companies did not inspire investor confidence in the long run. However, there is no doubt that the Calcutta Steam Tug Association was the most successful of Tagore's undertakings. It never paid less than 10 per cent per annum in dividends. When it launched its second tug in 1836 and doubled the capital by issuing new shares, the company had clearly established a reputation for itself. As Krishna Kripalani, one of his biographers, observes, 'Dwarkanath had a hawk's unerring eye. When he espied game from a distance, he lost no time in swooping on it. He was imaginative and could see ahead. He knew that a tugging service from Calcutta to the mouth of the Hooghly River was an economic necessity. A sailing ship would ordinarily take a fortnight to negotiate the hundred miles of the dangerous waterway full of shallows and sandbars, while a tugboat could do it in two days'.[28] Transport and investment in transportation seem to have caught Tagore's fancy, and quite in contrast to his Parsi counterpart, who did not invest in steam shipping, Tagore went full steam ahead. He thought far ahead and fantasized about a speedy mode of transportation connecting Calcutta to England via the Isthmus of Suez. The possibilities of using such a route seem to have impressed him and in 1835, in partnership with his friends, he founded the Bengal Steam Fund to promote the opening of a steamship line. Unfortunately, for Tagore, rivalries between different merchant lobbies (Calcutta and London) thwarted his project. His Midas touch did not work so well with other ventures as well; there were notorious failures, albeit not his doing, but that brought discredit to his house.

None of these failures can undermine the importance of Tagore's initiatives. He was a great dreamer, an entrepreneur with a vision that envisaged trade and industry as a vehicle of social improvement that he had learnt while collaborating with the English, whose value system he fully endorsed. Not only did he learn from their commercial strategies and practices, he thought of himself as a member of an international community and genuinely wanted to secure for his country the benefits of modernity. Enterprise was one route to this achievement. It was not an easy decision to make, for it needed real vision and business acumen to step forward to invest substantial amounts of capital in enterprises, capitalize on the confidence of his well-wishers and promote joint stock companies. Floating joint stock companies was Tagore's second great achievement, as he grasped the essentials of managing these entities that absorbed public subscriptions and had to demonstrate commitment and profits to the shareholder. The willingness to shoulder responsibility by adopting a new experiment in management was what elevated Dwarkanath's status. Admittedly, there were gaps in management, and the tendency to retain control of the company by buying up as many shares as possible prevailed. This tendency, in fact, did not encourage good practice and became a typical feature of Indian business. On the other hand, given the fact that these were maiden ventures in the field of joint stock, the appetite of Tagore to take risks and make profits stands out, especially as he came from a landed family and not a commercial one. As it happened, this also proved to be a drawback, as he was a man of varied interests and compulsions and did not always devote single-minded attention to his operations. He delegated work and was not always prudent when it came to the selection of partners and managers.

The Rise and Fall of Union Bank: Reversals and Retreat

The establishment of Union Bank in 1829 was the first major entrepreneurial venture of Tagore, intended primarily to fill a gap in the banking sector that remained underdeveloped at this stage. Among the formal banks worth talking about from this period is the Bank of Bengal, which was established under a charter enjoying the protection of the English East India company and authorized to issue notes against a proportion of government securities lodged with the Accountant General. Initially the notes of the Union Bank were accepted by the Bank of Bengal, but in 1834, owing to pressure for money, the Union Bank withdrew the government paper it had deposited as collateral with the Bank of Bengal, and its bills were no longer accepted. Notwithstanding this constraint, the Union Bank thrived by lending money to European businessmen. Like all his other ventures, this foray into banking was a major victory as it discounted bills of exchange and short-term promissory notes and received deposits at 4 per cent, which were subsequently invested. Its status with the government remained ambivalent, for when the proprietors applied to them for a charter of limited liability, the government refused, insisting that this came under unregulated 'indigenous banking'.[29]

These reverses did not deter Dwarkanath Tagore, who hoped to expand the business and move into the higher echelons of the exchange business that was handled by the East India company and the European agency houses of Calcutta, houses that were less interested in indigo and more in the bills business and who were decidedly against the attempts of Dwarkanath to enter this sector. In fact, the obstacles that Dwarkanath faced at this time are strongly reminiscent of Jeejeebhoy's crisis relating to shipping and remittances around the same period. According to Kling, at this point, Dwarkanath made three unwise decisions: one was to increase the bank's capital, followed by a decision to enter the exchange business and finally to overinvest in the production of indigo. Thus the directors were persuaded to vote for a massive increase of the bank's capital base—Rs 15 lakh to Rs 21.6 lakh in 1836, to Rs 32 lakh in 1837, and to Rs 80 lakh in 1838. By 1839, the capital stood at a whopping Rs 1 *crore*. From here, the pressure to invest capital in the exchange business and in indigo exports followed. While earlier, Dwarkanath himself was impatient and keen to get into the exchange business, which he anticipated would give him enormous profits and the reputation of being a big player in a global business, he seems to have dragged his feet when the Union Bank began its policy of overinvestment in indigo. What followed was a massive investment in indigo advances and loans to indigo producers against the security of property and equipment. Ignoring warning signs of a possible crash, the investment went ahead even though Dwarkanath himself was distracted and preferred to leave actual operations to his managers. It is here that a basic flaw in the system came to the surface; clever and artful accounting manipulations kept shareholders in the dark, and the fact that dividends continued to be paid meant that the bank was overstretched and waiting for a calamity to strike. In reality, declining indigo prices created a downturn, leading the bank into a vortex of bad debts. Mercantile houses in London handling indigo with their agents in Calcutta fell like a pack of cards and Tagore's bank lost a huge amount—Rs 4 lakh, according to a conservative estimate. The bank declared itself insolvent as Calcutta geared up for its worst commercial calamity. Tagore's empire crumbled, although it must be mentioned that he was able to hold on to some of his joint stock concerns that were bequeathed to his unworldly son, Debendranath Tagore.[30]

Dwarkanath was not physically present when the crisis struck. He was in England recuperating from health issues and died in 1846 before the Union Bank closed its doors. By this time he seems to have disengaged from the active affairs of the bank and seemed to turn a blind eye to the unfolding situation. What explains Dwarkanath's blindness in this regard? What was he actually contemplating, and why did his attention and forecasting waver? For someone who had meticulously acquired skill sets, expertise and capital and for someone who knew the world of international business, why did he sell his shares and withdraw from active management of the bank at a time when it needed his wisdom and prudence? We have no clear answers; what we do know is that when the crisis hit the Calcutta money market, Dwarkanath was in England and that even before this he was making preparations for his voyage to England. It is likely that by this time, he was participating more expansively in the cultural project of British rule. He travelled extensively to Europe, imbibed the cultural tastes of the times and was in every sense a partner in the empire and its culture. Even as he was disappointed about the attitude of several European merchants and resented their lack of cooperation in some of his decisions, his faith in the British connection never wavered. For him as much as for Jeejeebhoy, the rule of the British provided opportunities for self-improvement and it remained for the commercial elites to take the reins and lead India into a century of improvement and material progress.

Dwarkanath Tagore invested considerably in charities and patronage of the arts. He engaged in traditional charities—

providing financial support to worship and festivals as well as in secular endowments. He donated to public subscriptions, to the blind and the destitute. He campaigned against public begging and worked to sponsor a poor relief scheme. Like his Parsi counterpart, he campaigned for medical services for the poor. In fact, the similarities between the two men who were millionaires of their times—Jeejeebhoy and Dwarkanath—hold a mirror to the dominant ethos of mercantile elites of the period. Both were European by cultivation; both recognized the virtues of English commercial and management practices and both crafted their persona as cosmopolitan subjects with a deep sense of identification with the country in which they were born. In every way, they embodied a very special moment in the history of British India when racial animosities had not hardened and when some Indians and Englishmen embarked upon a mutual project of profit, enterprise and management without the burden of moral and ethical confusion. Jeejeebhoy did not see anything fundamentally wrong in peddling opium; Dwarkanath did not see anything intrinsically wrong in taking tough decisions against his tenants or in stuffing boards with yes-men in order to get his orders passed and realize his goals. Both men were responsible for fostering cordial relations between the British and the Indians and saw the East India company as their chief adversary and British free merchants as their allies in the campaign against the company. However, there were occasions when racial sentiments surfaced but were not enough to persuade Dwarkanath to remain oblivious to some of the flaws in his own countrymen. As he put it in one of his letters, it had been 'painful' to 'point out the errors of my countrymen'.

But 'the regeneration of my countrymen', he asserted, could be accomplished only by 'candid and fearless exposure'. [31]

The Legacy

What lessons do the successes of our protagonists hold for the historian of Indian business? Regardless of retrospective wisdom, there is no doubt that both of them, in their individual capacities, were adventurous men who saw in commercial enterprise and management the potential for profits and a lifestyle accompanying it, as well as its potential as a conduit for social improvement and public welfare. It is the latter aspect that makes both these men truly modern—men who recognized British rule to be the purveyor of modernity in which they were not only eager to participate, but in which they reposed great confidence. In the case of Jeejeebhoy, the practices of modernity lay in documentation of business dealings, in an abiding commitment to commercial integrity and probity and in providing services to a larger public. There was an inherent bias towards the fostering of the spirit of modern urbanism, which the city of Bombay represented and which was assiduously cultivated. Jeejeebhoy was a notable of Bombay; it was a city that he identified with closely, and he was in turn recognized as a city notable who was invested in improving its public space and civic sphere. His associations with Englishmen proved to be momentous, enabling him to amass a fortune that was unprecedented, especially if one remembers that he began virtually penniless but was driven to find his destiny. He found this in Bombay, in the city's burgeoning global trade. He took risks, sought adventure and perfected the art of consolidating personal connections and setting up networks of information.

His ability to work with people seems to have been a huge asset, and it was no coincidence that his firm was multiracial and multiethnic and served to drive a lucrative business. He invested in shipping, something that Indian merchants after the mid-eighteenth century were loath to do, and it was with his fleet of ships that he managed a massive shipping and consignment trade. In the closing years of his life, he was aware of the limitations of his enterprise and the symmetries of the colonial situation, but this did not deter him from continuing with his ventures and bequeathing to his successors a viable business that survived intergenerational changes. Do we attribute this to a management philosophy that he spoke of in his letters? Did this resonate with his successor, who we know did not indulge in senseless speculation in the late 1860s, when all of Bombay virtually went insane with gambling in the share market? We do not have ready answers, but there is no doubt that the profits accumulated from opium provided the basis for future investment in banking and insurance.

With Dwarkanath Tagore, the legacy for business was more ambiguous. While Dwarkanath himself made a fabulous fortune and capitalized on his family's status anchored in land holdings, embarked on modern business enterprise with even greater intrepidity, and resolutely endorsed the British connection as the vehicle for India's transformation, he did not transmit the same enthusiasm or even business acumen to his son, who in any case was spiritually inclined. It is also likely that the non-commercial origins of his enterprise resulted in a paralysis of policymaking, deterring him from taking the same level of interest, especially in his later years, or diffusing his business ethic to family members. At times, Dwarkanath appeared distracted and moved from one enterprise to the other quite in contrast to the single-minded devotion he showed in his litigation consultancy business. What seems to have moved him was the company of free traders and merchants whose practices and entrepreneurial spirit rubbed off on him. His family fortunes and personality gave him an advantage in building a reputation as a genteel merchant prince in the social circles of Calcutta. The fascination for things European also meant that he left his business unattended during his visits to England. Whether or not his absence was instrumental in aggravating the crisis related to the Union Bank is not clear, but there is no doubt that the fall of the bank while he was away in England was key to the collapse of his commercial endeavours. As it so happened, Dwarkanath died in England, buried in foreign soil, his grave a testimony to a very important moment in Indo–British partnership.

The partnership was short-lived; after the crash of the Union Bank and the second commercial crisis in Bengal, business confidence disappeared even as the social divide between European business interests and Indians widened. Once Tagore's empire crumbled and collapsed, there was a general loss of confidence in doing business and the landed elites of Bengal retreated to land and colonial employment. On the other hand, the model of joint stock companies that Tagore promoted remained a model to be emulated; in fact, in western India, where investment in industrial manufacture took off in the latter decades of the nineteenth century, joint stock companies became the norm. With this, a new age of Indian capital expansion began in which Bombay assumed precedence over Calcutta. The elites in the two cities entertained distinctly different imaginings, one associated with commerce and business and the other with land, rentier incomes and colonial education and employment. These choices should not necessarily be seen as binaries and polar opposites; in both cases, the salience of European association was not questioned. In cities in western India, such as Ahmedabad, entrepreneurs sought the help and assistance of Europeans and Americans in a private capacity to float manufacturing units and companies. In Calcutta, the appeal of colonial modernity worked as a catalyst to the articulation of a powerful proto-nationalist imagination on the part of elites, manifest especially during the days of Swadeshi.

3

Powering Industrial Enterprise: Parsi Business Families in Late Colonial and Early Independent India

The latter decades of the nineteenth century saw the maturation of industrial enterprise in India, with several business families coming forward to experiment with new forms of organization and taking risks such as investing in modern industrial projects. The rise of families such as the Tatas and the Godrejs not to speak of others like the Birlas and the Bajajs through the latter decades of the nineteenth century and moving ahead in the twentieth century attests to a period of dynamism in the business history of India. It was during these years that Indian capital came of age and took the leap to enter new sectors and experiment with new models of entrepreneurship. These were informed by a new imagination that looked at steel manufacture as the medium of modernization and prioritized technical and scientific education as crucial inputs to sustain industrial development. It was during this time also that indigenous capital and business families demonstrated a willingness to take risks and to experiment with new strategies of expansion and diversification. For instance, in the case of the Tatas and Godrejs, professional management of companies was a conscious policy decision along with transparency in methods of financing. The house of Tata avoided the worst aspects of corporate governance and emerged as an ideal, rational managerial corporation embodying the best, even if not the most recognizable face of Indian capitalism. Mircea Raianu suggests that 'Tata was in a category of its own displaying "characteristics of both indigenous and expatriate" firms, in addition to some which appear largely unique'.[1] Our other protagonists were no less impressive: both Godrej and Bajaj were devout nationalists and responded to the call of 'swadeshi capitalism' to build a range of manufactures for India and to emerge as dedicated captains of industry in India. Far more impressive than their wealth was their commitment to the ideals of stewardship that were expected to steer an emerging republic to prosperity and growth. In this chapter, we will focus on the early years of the house of Tata—the circumstances in which the founder–owner and his immediate successor set about building a massive industrial empire—and follow it up by looking at another Parsi company, that of the house of Godrej, and the products it turned out in the two decades after Independence. We will, therefore, be focusing on specific members of the family whose lives corresponded with a particular stage of India's industrial development from the late nineteenth to the middle of the twentieth century.

It is not entirely coincidental that both our protagonists were based in Bombay and western India, which, by the second half of the nineteenth century, had already consolidated its pre-eminence as a commercial and industrial centre. It was here that investment in industry was contemplated, and capital moved from being commercial to industrial, especially after the brief interlude with share speculation in the aftermath of the cotton boom of

1865–66. By the late 1860s, Bombay had recovered from the share and cotton crisis in which leading business families had suffered. This was even more true of business groups in Ahmedabad, where capital had remained locked in safer ventures and where individuals experimented with the idea of moving into industrial manufactures. This was largely occasioned by their exposure to European activity, to personal associations and friendships and an informed appraisal of the milieu that culminated in early manufacturing ventures. Predictably the industry of choice was cotton with its principal components, weaving and spinning, but which were not differently organized, mechanized and located not in workshops but in factories. The early success of Tata in launching the Empress Mill had a backstory, which was about Indian capital in western India moving towards industrial investment, experimenting with joint stock and learning to adapt European technology to local conditions.

Cotton, Capital and Enterprise in Western India

By the 1850s, western India had undergone the first wave of post-pacification measures after the rounding off of British conquests. The establishment and consolidation of British rule, the exposure of Indians to British policies and practices and the informal associations Indians in the capacity of junior administrators cultivated with European superiors had important consequences. While large-scale export trade and institutional finance were dominated by classic colonial firms in eastern India, the situation was different in the western regions of Bombay and Gujarat, where Indian capital worked in tandem with European capital in the sectors of cotton speculation, trade and subsequently banking. In Gujarat, although the handloom industry suffered setbacks because of British textile imports, it continued to provide for a substantial section of the domestic demand. Bombay's trade in raw cotton and opium was an important source of capital accumulation for merchants and bankers in Gujarat and Bombay, the case of Premchand Roychand being but one instance in point. While, admittedly, the cotton crash in the 1860s left many commercial men in a state of bankruptcy, it is also worthwhile remembering that many recovered and were able to contemplate new ventures and experiment with new modes of wealth generation via industrial manufacture. This was evident with businesspeople in Ahmedabad who decided to go in for industrial ventures departing from conventional commercial enterprise. As a city with a long and deep commercial history, with a substantial indigenous financial sector (sarrafi), which invested in internal trade and distribution, it was not surprising to find men like Ranchhodlal Chhotalal, a Nagar Brahmin who worked with the government, seriously contemplate the revival of textile industry in the city. If, in fact, the exposure to modern ideas and institutions triggered a major social and intellectual awakening in Bengal, it may well be argued that western India saw in industrial enterprise an important conduit to modernity. Whether it was Ranchhodlal Chhotalal, Jamshedji Nusserwanji Tata (J.N. Tata) or Pirojsha Godrej, the desire to forge major industrial and commercial ventures represented a radical shift in temper and orientation, enabling them to emerge as genuine captains of industry.

Brief snapshots of some of the businessmen are in order here to give a sense of the context in which men like J.N. Tata began their journey and capitalized on expertise and experience to take risks and envisage a new form of organization. Ranchhodlal Chhotalal is a useful example to highlight the risks and opportunities that marked the changing circumstances in which individuals came forward to experiment with industry and manufacture. Chhotalal enjoyed the benefits of a decent education, acquired proficiency in Persian, English and Gujarati and started life in government service. He worked as a clerk to the assistant collector of customs in the government, as a result of which he developed a number of important contacts that persuaded him to think differently and to try his hand in setting up a spinning and weaving company. While his stint in administrative service was marred by controversy and allegations of corruption, he dared to dream and brave all odds to set up a mill with English machinery and go public for raising capital. He forecast quite correctly that the market was in a position to absorb both yarn and textiles and that there were gains in scaling up and mechanizing production. With the help of his friend George Fuljames, he obtained details of the textile industry in England and issued a notice for capital subscriptions, which were not easily forthcoming. Not a man to quit, Chhotalal persevered until he launched the Ahmedabad Spinning and Weaving Mill in 1859.[2] He had to overcome insurmountable difficulties; not only was capital in short supply, but even machinery that had to be imported from England came late and had to be transported in bullock carts! None of these factors deterred him as he went ahead, installing the machinery with the help of an astrologer friend. The latter appears to have had rudimentary knowledge of mechanics and ran it well enough to assure his investors, pay reasonable dividends and subsequently expand his operations. Several mills followed; his son took up the mantle of management even as others came forward to place Ahmedabad on the industrial map of India.

Bombay too witnessed a period of growth and industrialization around the same time, although the process was delayed because of a financial crisis in the 1860s. Bombay's surge of commercial prosperity was largely due to the opium trade, which saw increasing Parsi and Bania investments and, in the case of the former, a major share in the shipping and consignment business. Between 1830–31 and 1860–61, according to Claude Markovits, the value of merchandise exports from Bombay increased sixfold and the value of opium sales alone increased more than tenfold. In terms of imports, Bombay's imports increased only fourfold during the same interval, the major increases being in cotton goods and metals.[3] Bombay's trade balance was thus more favourable even if its export trade rested on fragile foundations given the speculative nature of both cotton and opium. Speculation in cotton in the end proved to be disastrous as the city was gripped by a share mania in the 1860s, leading to the utter collapse of the financial market and of several business houses. However, what was striking was the willingness to take risks on the part of some businessmen, and in the case of men like Premchand Roychand or J.N. Tata, the ability to ride the storm and look to the future and tap the existing potential for investment and manufacture.

While we do not have clear estimates about the proportion of capital derived from cotton and opium invested in industry, what we do know is that the floating of companies became pervasive among indigenous businessmen. Between July 1873 and December 1874, as many as twelve factories emerged in Bombay, with many more in the following decade.[4] The Oriental

Spinning and Weaving Mill was formally floated in 1855 by Dinshaw Maneckji Petit in February 1860, Mangaldas Nathubhai established the Bombay United Spinning and Weaving company, in March of the same year, Petit promoted his mill, while, in September, Mancherjee Merwanjee Bhavnagari and Pallonji Kapadia established the Eastern Spinning and Weaving Mill. The progress of the Bombay mills was such that by 1860, the city boasted of ten textile companies with 6000 employees. All of them were joint-stock companies. Given the constraints of capital and technical support, this was an impressive record attesting to the temper and orientation of business groups in the region, something that consolidated into greater optimism, leading to the expansion of mills in both Bombay and Ahmedabad and subsequently in other cities such as Surat, Nagpur, Sholapur, Madras and Delhi.

It is in this backdrop of a growing industrial temper that we need to examine the rise of the house of Tata and their expansion and diversification and to reflect on what it was about the house that did business differently. Like their counterparts, theirs was also a family business, and they too adopted the broad principles of the managing agency system. Yet they brought in new elements into the project—an open and catholic attitude to the use of technology, which they were prepared to learn, import and adapt; a familiarity with overseas markets; and putting together a global network of agents. These practices were, in part, a feature of the community; Parsis had always been adept at learning and imitating artisanal methods and practices and this predisposition, combined with modern education and exposure to western institutions, seems to have given them a head start in modern business. Whether it was J.N. Tata's enthusiasm for learning the nuts and bolts of the textile industry in England or Ardeshir Godrej dabbling with actual locks and lockmaking, the community's embrace of new methods and practices was always on full display.

The Tatas: Founding Moments

The family's manufacturing profile was crafted by Jamshedji Nusserwanji Tata (1839–1904), who belonged to an old and established trading family in Bombay, thoroughly familiar with the business of export trade and agency in the course of which the family had built up important government connections. His father worked closely with the British as a provider to the commissariat department and had a network of contacts extending up to China. J.N. Tata cut his teeth in extending his agencies in Hong Kong and Shanghai, developing real expertise in the process, after which he went to London to set up his agency for handling bills and the remittance business. The timing happened to be disastrous, for his arrival in London coincided with the cotton crash and the share mania of Bombay in 1865–66, and Tata realized that the bills he carried were worthless. But the calamity taught him valuable life lessons and strengthened his resolve to work with caution. As a result, Tata, who was in London when the crash happened, was able to persuade his creditors to grant him some laxity. His biographer F.R. Harris had this to say of the young adventurer:

> Few men of Mr Tata's age have ever found themselves in a more unenviable position. He was a stranger in a strange land, at a time when traffic between the businessmen of East and West was still somewhat rare. He had arrived in England bearing scrip, which he hoped would prove not only negotiable

but profitable security. He found his pockets stuffed with waste paper, his credit impaired, and the good name of his firm already at stake. It required a stout heart, a clear brain, and a steady character to meet such a situation. Fortunately for his firm, Jamshedji Tata possessed al these requirements. He put the position before his creditors, and before the banks, so ably and so frankly that they, impressed with the honesty of the man, appointed him his own liquidator. But the crisis through which he had passed left an indelible mark upon Mr Tata's character, and confirmed in him that need for caution which formed his guiding line in after life.[5]

The experience was transformational as he set up assembling his resources and building his reputation. The occasion also gave him the opportunity to study textile mills in England closely and to contemplate a new set of strategies to embark on a programme of industrialization for India. Tata's family location was a significant factor in his personal and professional development; the fact that the family was well-networked in Europe meant that he was exposed to new ideas and temperamentally was well-disposed to launching new schemes in India without ever becoming provincial or insular in his outlook. In 1948, Frederick James, an admirer of Tata, mentioned in his address to the Society of the Arts how Tata wished to make 'India a great industrial power and to this aim, he brought a restless and inventive energy, a prophetic insight and a high conception of science'.[6]

Fortune, they say, favours the brave, and in the case of the Tatas, this axiom worked quite literally. Even as the family was beginning to readjust to their finances, the contract for a British commissariat in Ethiopia in 1868 worked to their advantage so

much that they were able to restore the China branch of their
agency house and accumulate sufficient capital to think of
new investment outlets. J.N. Tata arrived in Bombay to see an
exciting and altered landscape dotted with chimneys in factories,
beckoning him to a new world. The time seemed just right and
ripe to take the leap. Persuading his father to allow him to buy
a crumbling oil pressing factory in 1869, he converted it into a
textile unit, christening it the Alexandria Mill. The name was
apt, as the young businessman scaled one height after the other.
Running the mill efficiently, he was able to sell it for a profit and
return to England to study the sector even more closely. In 1894,
he set up a new mill, this time not in Bombay but in Nagpur,
which was at the head of a rail line and was in close proximity to
the raw material, i.e., cotton-growing areas. This was the central
India Spinning Weaving and Manufacturing company, later
called the Empress Mills, which started operations on 1 January
1877 and generated impressive profits soon thereafter, thanks
to excellent management practices. In 1886, Tata registered his
second company—the Swadeshi Mill—for production of finer
varieties of yarn and cloth, and in 1903 he opened the third and
last company, the Advance Mills, in Ahmedabad. The mills ran
well and made impressive returns.

What accounted for the apparently seamless success of
J.N. Tata? Evidently, he had calculated the demand for cloth
effectively even though this was a segmented demand. But more
important was his investment in technology that he was prepared
to experiment with to scale up his operations. For instance, he
introduced the ring spindle, which he had come across in England
and despite the fact that it required intensive labour, he pressed
ahead while making sure that his workforce was looked after

with proper relief schemes. It was here that the innovative and humane aspect of the Tata enterprise stood out; from very early on, the men in charge were expected to and trained to engage with capital, labour and management creatively. The success of the enterprise spurred the founder to contemplate new schemes, and it seemed only appropriate that he would switch his interests and investment to steel, the material of twentieth-century modernity. However, this was not an easy decision, for unlike textiles, which were anchored within an older artisanal tradition and a network of access to the raw material, iron and steel production required unlimited power, capacity to mine and process, not to speak of huge capital outlay and a skilled labour force.

But J.N. Tata was not the person to back off or turn back on his dreams. It is said that he had attended a lecture in Manchester in 1867 about the greatness of iron and that the idea of iron and steel works had taken root from that point onwards.[7] He came across a report on the financial prospects of iron in the Chanda district by German expert Ritter Van Schwartz and decided to approach the authorities for permission to prospect for the same. Nothing came of it, and it took more years to secure a prospecting licence for the Lohara and Peepalgaon areas of Chanda district. Anxious to add to his understanding of a new industry, Tata left for England and the US to secure technical knowhow, which he then applied on his return. In 1903, the exploration of Chanda district went full steam ahead, but once again the deposits did not yield much. But by 1907, with the help of the renowned metallurgist Charles Perin, Sakchi was 'discovered' in present-day Jamshedpur. After months of toil and tedious travel, Perin and his men found about 3 billion tons of ore—that too near the railway station, which meant that the transportation issue was also sorted. Unfortunately, J.N. Tata did not live long enough to see his pet project through, and it was left to his successor to take the steel story to its logical conclusion.

However, by this time, the family had achieved a global reputation for prudent management, for withstanding reverses and for embracing professional methods. All this was based not on hearsay but on performance data and hard evidence. Not only had J.N. Tata recouped from the losses of the disastrous Bombay cotton speculation, not only had the family forged important contracts and connections with the British authorities, they had been able to retain global connections through their managing agency business to rebuild a branch of their agency in Hong Kong with the help of Ratanji Dadabhai Tata. In 1887, Tata Sons came into being as a private trading concern, with J.N. Tata, his two sons, Dorabji Tata and Ratanji Tata, and a cousin, Ratanji Dadabhoy Tata, with a modest capital of £1575. The formation of Tata Sons as a managing agency was intended to help with marketing and to find and penetrate new markets in India at a time when political conditions were not entirely conducive to indigenous business. Until the first great war, Indian industry enjoyed no protection, and it was not until 1905 that a department for commerce and industry was set up. Also, adverse tariff policies went against Indian textile interests in order to safeguard those of Manchester. This meant that Indian industry worked against all odds.[8] Indian businessmen like the Tatas were careful to hedge their bets, keep their relations intact with the government and simultaneously put pressure on the government to enable them to function more effectively.

As far as J.N. Tata was concerned, he was determined to see through certain projects, as he was convinced that no country that did not manufacture iron and steel could become industrially great. Additionally, he envisaged a power project that would support mills in Bombay and reduce its dependence on Bengal and Bihar coal. Thus, towards the end of his life, Tata laid down a blueprint for two of his most cherished projects that his son Dorabji would take forward, namely the building of an iron and steel factory and a power generation scheme for his mills in Bombay. Neither of these were easy ventures to put into operation; capital was perennially in short supply; the colonial state was whimsical and could not be relied upon to encourage domestic production; and, amid the prevailing policy paralysis, it required extraordinary entrepreneurial drive and wisdom to make these dreams real. The Tatas had all of this in plenty. With nerves of steel, Dorabji got into the fray to invest in steel production. The timing was perfect, with the country gripped with swadeshi fever, encouraging princes and people to come forward and invest in what was seen as a homegrown venture. Thus, the decision to float the Tata Iron and Steel company was enthusiastically received. The colonial government remained tepid in its response, while the London money market remained unimpressed and reluctant to come up with any capital for investment.

With the swadeshi winds behind them, the Tatas were eventually able to attract capital from Indian princes (13 per cent of the capital in 1911 was held by the rulers of fifteen princely states) and the rest in the hands of Bombay millmen. The government too eventually stepped forward, and the project went into action. As Dorabji recalled, many years after this momentous event, 'as for the first time in India's financial history I had succeeded in raising for industrial purposes such a vast sum from the hidden wealth of India for the development of our mineral resources'.[9] The company was formally registered in 1907; factories were erected in the sleepy hamlet of Sakchi and soon a bustling township emerged. Tata Iron and Steel company Limited (TISCO) went into operation with a plant capacity of 100,000 tons of ingots. This was definitely a spectacular achievement, speaking volumes for the vision of a man and his family. While the venture was wrapped in the rhetoric of swadeshi, it would be an exaggeration to see this as purely a swadeshi enterprise or as a fallout of delayed government support; rather, it has to be located within the imperatives of global commerce and the single-minded vision of India's premier business family that was truly global in its outlook. The company had some advantages on its side; by this time, Indian pig iron was competitive and was its cheapest producer, which gave the new company a great advantage. The Tatas realized this and soon pushed sales of the company's pig iron in China, Japan and Southeast Asia. The ability to leverage information and rely on long-term business connections without alienating the state was among the greatest assets the Tatas enjoyed and which saw them attain heights of prosperity.

With the second project, the hydroelectric one, too, the Tatas faced capital scarcity and once more depended on Indian princely states to step forward. The intention behind the project was to produce and capitalize on power and deploy it for his textile mills. Power generation was flagged off in 1915, and by the end of 1919, the Tatas were capable of satisfying the requirements of the Bombay region. From here, there was no looking back, and the company went from strength to strength, setting up cement manufacturing companies, electrical and chemical concerns and engineering companies. When the First World War broke out, the Tatas were already a mini industrial empire, even though its management and priorities were not clearly defined.

The two great wars and the years between them constituted a significant period for Indian business groups that found unexpected opportunities. The imperial government, having to run a mammoth war effort, was compelled to cut down on its exports and focus on war production, thus giving indigenous manufacturing in India a big boost. The demand for indigenous goods went up, enabling manufacturers to reap substantive gains even though productive capacity could not be stretched indefinitely. The government went all out to help businesses by relaxing certain provisions of the Factory Act (1892) relating to strikes and industrial action. The result was an all-round expansion of the Indian manufacturing sector (textiles noticeably) and the coming of age of Indian industry, with the Tatas commanding the heights of the new economy. TISCO survived the depression years and given the product mix of the Tata mills catered to every segment from cement to steel, from power to chemicals and salt. TISCO not only oversaw a huge expansion of production but also sponsored research and development, enabling the manufacture of high-tensile steel and Tata Steel's high-quality tensile steel (TIScrom) to be used for railway coaches. The entrepreneurial spirit seemed to burn consistently, as the Tata Locomotive and Engineering company was launched in 1945 to produce locomotives, wagons and boilers.[10] The lead role they played in the war effort made them a business entity to reckon with—equally and reciprocally, the house realized that the gains secured were temporary and that structural constraints had to be addressed if industry was to be secured and placed on a stable and sustainable footing. No businessman could ignore the fact that war-induced demand would not offset structural issues and that a clearer articulation of business interests had to be forthcoming—a resolve that eventually found fruition in the Bombay Plan of 1944. In all of these ventures, it was J.N. Tata's grandson and Ratanji Tata's son, Jehangir Ratanji Dadabhoy Tata, who was at the helm of affairs. J.R.D. Tata was appointed chairman of Tata Sons in 1938, and it was left to him, the dynamic 'Jeh', a cosmopolitan, ingenious entrepreneur, to manage one of the largest conglomerates of industries in India, to figure out how he would 'run an empire of steel, aviation, electrical power, insurance, cement, oil and soaps and textiles.'[11] It was under J.R.D. Tata that the capacity of TISCO was expanded, Tata Chemicals was launched, TELCO was formalized and Air India was envisioned.

But for the moment, let us focus on two other aspects of the Tata story in the period under review, namely the founding of the township of Jamshedpur and the setting up of philanthropy and educational activities that gave and have continued to give Indian industry an exemplary model of public–private partnership. As mentioned earlier, the objective of this chapter is to highlight those figures who forged a new conception of industry, manufacture and enterprise in a very specific moment of India's historical development, namely the late colonial era and the decades following Indian Independence. The building of the township of Tatanagar, or Jamshedpur, is an important even foundational moment in the making of the reputation of the Tatas, something that other families such as Godrej emulated in the form of a township in Vikhroli, a suburb in north-eastern Bombay. For modern historians of capitalist enterprise in India, the process of land acquisition by business has more critical and complex dimensions. As Mircea Raianu suggests, the investment in land acquisition by the Tatas was a complex process that exploited the ambiguities of law regarding land occupancy and acquisition, with the result that businessmen almost always acted as landowner, litigant and capitalist all rolled into one.

Planning an Industrial Empire: The Making of a Township

If the decision to scope mineral deposits had been a momentous one and set the house on a path of industrial experimentation, then the resolve to build a township was equally significant compared to what P.C. Tallents in the census report of 1921 described as 'the romance of the century'. Always ready to think out of the box, such as setting up a mill in Nagpur outside the safety zone of Bombay, the Tatas, under Dorabji and Ratanji, were determined to set up their concern in a site that was described as wild and inhospitable and to build a settlement that would help in the centralization of production functions. Whether this was a move to neutralize potential discontent and labour unrest over housing or whether it was a genuine move to build an idealized space is hard to say, but there is no doubt that there was something innovative about the way the house of Tata went about it and their principle of sharing welfare among a wider social constituency and of investing in urban development. As R.D. Tata said to his shareholders in 1928, 'we are not putting up a row of workmen's huts in Jamshedpur—we are building a city'.[12] This was a case of paternalism or welfare capitalism based not just on sentiment but on rational principles, which enabled the company to develop its reputation and retain its autonomy.

The process was not as easy as it sounded. It involved acquiring land, adhering to the prescription that insisted on use of this land for public good and then embarking on a massive building project. The latter was sustained by the steady advances the business house made in its steel production. Acquiring the land involved negotiating with existing laws about acquisition that insisted on the use of land for public benefits. The house of Tata thus had to exploit legal loopholes to acquire land, defend its acquisition, manage it for a factory and thus act as employer, landlord and sovereign. What is interesting about the venture in its early stages was how it demonstrated the workings of social and ideational networks that operated in smaller princely states. The choice of the site, for instance, was thanks to his relations with the geologist working for the state of Mayurbhanj, who brought the attention of R.D. Tata to the rich iron deposits in the Gorumahisani district. Protracted negotiations and finally the decision to build an industrial settlement in British territory and acquire lands belonging to tribal groups and intermediaries resulted in the foundation of the new township. The Pittsburgh firm of Julian Kennedy and Axel Sahlin was approached and given a contract for designing and engineering works. The nucleus of the town emerged between 1909 and 1912, initially to cater to about 10,000 residents. This expanded exponentially in the succeeding years when more aesthetic and design considerations came up in the expansion project. What is useful to emphasize is the pioneering nature of Tata's investment in land as a viable route to industrialization and turning out a successful experiment that successive post-colonial governments have had to reckon with.

The industry-cum-township model was undoubtedly an important one for a number of reasons. It was an illustration of optimizing economies of scale, of urban experimentation. It testified to the ability of the Tatas to work in sync with a rapidly changing environment. The decision to look into the interior and exploit the reserves of what were seen as wild and savage country and turning these over to the industrial project was undoubtedly an important step and inspired many others to follow suit. The same can be said for their range of philanthropic and educational activities, all of which carried a very distinct signature of vision and commitment, something that every member of the family seemed to carry. J.N. Tata's commitment to principles of basic honesty, integrity and business common sense was resolutely remembered—business was eventually about trusteeship with a real commitment to shareholders who trusted them with capital, to workers who provided their labour and to society, which stood to benefit from all-round economic wellbeing. In fact, as R.M. Lala points out in his biography, J.R.D. Tata never stopped recalling the wisdom of J.N. Tata, who abided not just by financial probity but by real integrity of thought and mind. Whether it was higher educational institutes, such as the Tata Institute of Social Sciences (TISS) and the Tata Institute of Fundamental Research (TIFR), or hospitals and cancer centres, the watchword was social responsibility and excellence.

To what extent was the success of the Tatas a consequence of individual talent, community support and linkages? Or was it facilitated by circumstances, a matter of contingency that could never be discounted in any risk-taking enterprise? That the house of Tata was well served by family members is undisputed, and that the mantle was handed down to first cousins and relatives without prejudice was undoubtedly a factor that went in favour of the family. In every sense, J.R.D. Tata was an appropriate successor to the legacy that the founder had painstakingly built and bequeathed. Talented and humane, he had the good sense to delegate and spot talent and subsequently nurture it. Men with vision were drawn to him, and it was not just coincidence that well-meaning public servants approached him with plans and schemes. We have, for instance, the example of the chemical engineer Kapiram Vakil, who drew his attention to the Okhamandal site in Gujarat, where he saw the potential of recovering slat and minerals from saline water, which would eventually constitute an inorganic chemical compound.[13] As in Jamshedpur, the Tatas lost no time in developing a township to serve as the nucleus for industrial growth. It is also remarkable that the family with its various branches was able to sustain their ventures and support them in whatever capacity and retain an openness of temperament to the fostering of scientific research and development. Like in the case of other business houses, the interwar years benefited the Tatas in getting them new spaces and the opportunity to leverage the imperial connection while developing new ties with Indian nationalist circles. There is no doubt that in the years after Independence, the family would face serious challenges and even disillusionment with some policies of the Nehruvian period, but that is not to suggest that the family had not developed adequate resilience to tide over the 1950s and 1960s and consolidate their premier position in the business landscape of modern India. What stands out about the Tatas is the international orientation and cosmopolitan outlook, which were deeply and securely grounded in the local with no apparent fault lines. It is difficult to analyse this or even suggest that it was a manifestation of a model minority conduct that does not bring out the richness and dynamism of the family and the corporation they built in the first half of the twentieth century and took it forward subsequently. They seem to have provided a blueprint for others to follow—we see this especially clearly with the case of the Godrej family, yet another Parsi family of Bombay who began as locksmiths and security architects, were infused by the swadeshi spirit and were experimenting with design to turn out a product that would challenge the finest of workmanship that the west had to offer.

The Godrej Saga

Like so many Parsis, the family of Ardeshir Burjorji Sorabji Godrej (1868–1936) came from Gujarat, settled down in Bombay and made use of western education and the spaces that empire provided to think imaginatively about the kind of future India deserved. Beginning his life as a principled lawyer in East Africa and refusing to compromise, Ardeshir returned to India in 1894, determined to do something innovative that would give the country a basis for future growth and prosperity. Ardeshir was deeply impressed by both the powerful nationalist rhetoric of self-reliance and of non-British rule that had enslaved and impoverished India, as well as by the craftsmanship and skill of Indian artisans whose work and worth had to be reclaimed and rehabilitated, albeit within a new mode of production and organization. His early flirtation with the making of fine surgical instruments ended in disappointment as he confronted the problems of marketing a product without the 'Made in England' label. This reverse did not deter Ardeshir, who, with funds provided by friends, turned to the manufacture of locks. Why the lowly lock has been a question that historians have tried in vain to answer. It is possible that lockmaking was primarily a localized and specialized business (Aligarh, Howrah and Dindigul) that was hand-made, making it expensive and cumbersome and almost impossible to upscale. Yet there must have been an indication of the potential for such an item to which was added the swadeshi zeal of doing something homespun but capable of deploying modern techniques. More than the Tatas, it was Godrej, especially its founding father, who was a committed and proud advocate of nationalist ideas and went ahead with what seemed to be a crazy operation. Here, it would be instructive to recall a charming report about him in the *Times of India* newspaper in 1927, by which time Ardeshir had moved to the manufacture of fire-resistant safes for India and which could compare with the very best the advanced west could offer. The piece, titled 'The Swadeshi Urge', went as follows:

It was past 6 and fagged out mill-men were winding their way when a representative of the Herald drove through the more or less dusty streets of Parel to see a venerable Parsi gentleman experimenting with scent bottles. 'Ye asses and donkeys, ye foolish children of India, what have you done for the motherland, what have you done for the Swadeshi enterprise? If you see your mother bleeding in so many parts of her body, will you leave her alone and continue enjoying your lives at your cost? Do you realize Mother India has been bled white by foreign exporters who have made us slaves of their tastes and goods.'[14]

The reporter went on to write that although the gentleman may have appeared cranky, he had earned the reputation of having experimented amid odds with homemade safes and lockers and looked around for investors until he had found a perfect solution to manufacture fire-resistant safes to be able to issue a challenge to the government of India to test them against fire and to demonstrate that his was by far the best product available in the market.

The report was clearly an allusion to Ardeshir, who was projected to be eccentric and talented but persevering. It was not easy to pursue the development of a product with little capital or to take the risk of putting it in the market and securing its use. Yet what strikes the reader of his life and labour is an extraordinary spirit of adventure and commitment to self-reliance and equally to modern, scientific methods of manufacture without compromising the skill and status of the artisan. This was by no means an easy balance to maintain. In 1897, with a small capital fund of a few thousand rupees, he purchased the necessary materials and implements and mobilized a few skilled artisans from Gujarat to establish a workshop in a small, rented shed. He turned out a range of fine locks and made it a large-scale industrial product in no time, an achievement that is both staggering but also representative of the swadeshi movement in the history of Indian enterprise, when sheer ideology helped overcome odds and produce an unusual and unshakeable faith in industry. Three years into the business, he entered the business of safes, which was almost entirely dominated by imports, but Godrej was not deterred. Care and attention to quality and design made these safes impregnable and won huge approval and market support. Spectacular displays of fire-resistant safes followed in the cities of Bombay and Calcutta, marking a proud moment for the maker and his product. By the time of Ardeshir's death, the company had been formally registered with a surprising range of goods, from locks and safes to soaps, announcing the advent of a new, young and vibrant manufacturing company. Sales estimates were impressive; sales of safes and cupboards went up substantially, just as the net profit of Godrej soaps showed encouraging trends.[15] On his death, the mantle passed on to his younger brother Pirojsha Burjorji Godrej (1882–1972), an able successor with vision, perseverance and a systematic approach to the consolidation of the new venture. He went several steps further and established a plant at Vikhroli, which included a space for research and design. Like his brother, he was moved and influenced by the humanitarian ideas of Gandhi, especially on trusteeship. Viewing business as a trusteeship that ought to guarantee the interests of all stakeholders was a key idea that he gave expression to; this included workers, shareholders and the larger public. This new ethical imperative found expression in labour welfare measures, in quality products for the middle class at affordable prices. The company under him ran a very successful advertising scheme, as a result of which Godrej products like the Storwel became objects of deep emotional attachment. Service after sales was another major concern, which testifies to the values of the business house and family. Like J.N. Tata, Pirojsha appreciated the strategic role that industry had in fostering development and, in the words of Karanjia, 'took upon himself the trusteeship of the country and the people's welfare'.[16]

Why was the family able to achieve such success in a relatively short spell of time? Was it only to do with the individual excellence of the leaders? Or did it have anything to do with the new values of professionalization adopted by the house? Or was it the political and social context of the times with the consumption of objects such as the Storwel and the office chair being intimately connected with the emergence of a new middle class? The answer lies in all of these, but what is of importance is the efficiency with which Godrej was able to leverage and secure a virtual dominance in the tubular steel furniture market by upholding the swadeshi principle and of marketing security and self-reliance. Much more than the house of the Tatas, the Godrej house kept in sync with the vision of India's leaders, especially Nehru post-Independence. Whether it was in the design or in the marketing of their goods— furniture for home and office—the idea was to experiment with and undertake a project on Indian modernism. Godrej seized the opportunity to adopt Nehru's aesthetic vision of modern India and commissioned the first modernist workspace, for example, the offices of the Madhya Pradesh State Electricity Board.[17] Amongst the chairs that made up the office space, the CH 4 became iconic, embodying the values of minimalism and modernism. This chair was seen as a catalyst in transforming old office spaces into modern ones. Made from electricity-resistant material, hundreds of thousands of chairs were turned out in the familiar olive–green colour and placed in every office space in the country. The fact that it was inspired by international design spoke volumes about the family's commitment to excellence and openness, and yet its value and utility were solidly grounded in the domestic context. Another impressive quality about the company and the family was the ability to operate amid extremely difficult conditions of steel shortages, thanks largely to its management protocols and the far-sightedness in working with government departments and obtaining the quotas for steel. The professionalization of the company and the care taken to gauge the consumer's wants and opt for creative advertising techniques made Godrej a household name, producing a real affinity among customers for the product and the family that it embodied. Godrej stood for trust, excellence, safety and security, and its products were seen as family members to be cherished and bequeathed.

The story of Godrej in the decades after Independence is a story of its objects, notably the Storwel, the office chair and the typewriter, each of which became a mass consumer item and an integral element of homes and offices. The story of Godrej and its manufacturing experience is also about shortages of steel and the challenges of working within the 'Licence Raj' or 'Permit Raj', a quota permit system for licences that prevailed at the time. While the company and its owners and managers chafed at the restrictions of the licence quota system, they abided by the regulations, something that is worth noting about the ethics they upheld. It testifies to the context in which Godrej operated and expanded, one in which business and politics worked for a while as partners in development.

The post-Independence period saw the articulation of an industrial licensing policy through the enactment of the Industries Development and Regulation Act of 1951. Under this act, any new industrial undertaking or expansion under the 'scheduled industries list' required licences. This was not intended to hamper private industries but largely to prevent undue concentration of wealth, protect small-scale industries and ensure a degree of regional distribution of industries. Where the regulations proved irksome were in relation to the provisioning of steel that was strictly managed. For a company that made steel furniture, this was not an easy condition to overcome. On the other hand, it recognized the potential that steel furniture had and took all possible steps to ensure the production of a fine product and its distribution through a network of dealers. The level of innovation that followed was truly striking right from the beginning and spoke volumes about the resolve that the Godrej family demonstrated without having to compromise either personal integrity or professional excellence.

Safes and Almirahs: Chairs and Typewriters

Aware of the potential that steel cupboards had in a market that valued security and was apprehensive of both vermin and theft, Godrej went ahead in refining steel storage spaces, taking the basic wooden almirah as its model and adapting it to new material, i.e., steel. Having cut his teeth in the manufacture of locks, the move to steel storage units was a matter of time and a logical progression. The decades of the 1920s, when this was contemplated by Ardeshir, were relevant in that the family was able to deploy the values of swadeshi and balance these with government connections to earn their laurels. This was the time when industrial development in India was tacitly encouraged by the government when the range of Godrej safes and locks found acceptability in a range of homes and government offices. This meant that contracts from government departments began to pour, which the company capitalized on. In fact, the advertisements of the period (a strategy that the family company began to use very early on) spoke of how the company guaranteed the safety of office papers from theft and vermin. In 1921, Godrej commenced operations to manufacture the steel almirah with sophisticated locking and bolting features while reiterating their commitment to the use of good steel, which they never compromised on. By 1944, the company went on to produce at least four ranges of cupboards, six models of fire-resistant safe cabinets and seven models of the Godrej six-patent almirah.[18] The same year also saw the introduction of the Storwel, which would eventually become synonymous with efficiency and storage. The company by this time had established its reputation as a supplier of safe storage, and by focusing on a specific product and branding it, it was planning to make the Storwel a mass product. By 1950, an aggressive campaign for advertising the product was underway, and it took no time for the Storwel to become a standard feature in every home and office. The ads also emphasized the business ethics of the company, one that played clean and safe. The '55 not out' advertisement, for example, is evocative; the ad observed how Godrej played with a straight bat and how the company was known for its adherence to norms and for being a 'safe and clean people who have made Godrej a household word'.

It was not as though the company did not have stiff competition in the steel furniture sector during this time. Allwyn, Steelage and Bungo were rivals, but Godrej scored better as it had the advantage of a buffer provided by the contracts of the government. The making and refining of the cupboard in many ways embodied the personality of its founders and makers, who had a curious enthusiasm for design and workmanship and who found, in the use of pickled steel, an expression of commitment to modern design. Thus, pickled steel was reiterated time and again as the unique feature of the product, not to speak of the locks, levers and the final coat of lustrous paint that helped the product stand out. To this was added the appreciation of an emerging economy in post-Independence India, where, along with all the regulations and restrictions of the Nehruvian planned economy, there was a clear set of trends expressing the wants and desires of customers who wanted convenient and durable storage that would last a lifetime! Whether it was the office, where seating (tubular chairs), filing cabinets and storage almirahs were required, or the home, with middle-class families beginning to think of storage space and furniture differently, the company seemed to read the pulse correctly and produce the appropriate product. The company designed its promotional material carefully and emphasized how steel furniture had begun to symbolize values of efficiency and productivity in offices and to embody values of cleanliness and space in homes. As one of its promotional materials pointed out:

> Steel furniture has a special appeal for the modern housewife. It can make a small room spacious, modern rooms gracious, old rooms new. It has the added advantage of reducing work in the home. Its flowing lines and even surfaces are easy to keep clean, neither harbour dust and vermin nor absorb moisture.[19]

Godrej factories soon began turning out Storwels literally by the hundreds despite the extreme constraints on steel supply. It was not as though Pirojsha did not have anxious moments about not being able to work to optimum capacity, but what was impressive was the tenacity the company showed in working the licence quota system by maintaining close contacts with the bureaucracy and to ensure government contracts for their products. It is worthwhile quoting one of the office circulars we come across in this connection: In 1952, an official circular urged the personnel to make an all-out effort to secure orders, particularly from such departments of government as are in a position to issue a sub-quota certificate in our favour.

> Whilst giving a written quotation, you should not ask for a specific quantity or category of steel, but you may certainly advise the department concerned that we could considerably expedite delivery in the event of the department giving us a sub-quota certificate or releasing to us steel, our own steel

allocation from the general SPI quota being so meagre that a long delay in delivery was inevitable.[20]

In fact, the letters and circulars of the company to which we have access thanks to the Godrej Archives amply demonstrate the company's ability to leverage its position as one of the prime suppliers of government equipment and work the quota system to its best but not unfair advantage. Often, other customers had to wait for orders to be fulfilled, but on balance, the situation did not diminish the capability of Godrej to produce and market its office equipment and in particular the Storwel.

The company even intervened in public debates about steel shortages and the best ways to deal with them, even as it exhorted its branch offices and stockists to explore any option that they found feasible. In 1955, the steel situation was particularly thorny; the *Times of India*, in its 16 November 1955 edition, reported how the government of India had re-imposed controls on the supply of structural steel products and to ask state governments to pay world prices if they wanted steel a year in advance. The newspaper took the government to task for its opacity, observing that 'though the decision was taken a week ago, New Delhi has not chosen to take the country into its confidence', and also highlighted the importance of looking at private enterprise and its requirements that were increasingly hard to fulfil as the 'import of structural steel was by no means easy now'. The government, as it happened, fell back upon imports—New Delhi had ordered steel to the tune of over 1,50,000 tons—an amount that was barely enough to meet two months needs of private enterprise. By 1958, when the country was battling a full-blown foreign exchange crisis, it seemed that the only way out for the government was to explore the prospects of importing special categories of steel in short supply on deferred payment terms and, if necessary, allow industrial associations to participate in the programme of such imports. As the *Times of India* put it, on 1 July 1958, 'the foreign exchange crisis has to be met by a vigorous wielding of the axe. But it will be a pity if, in wielding the axe, the government damages the very sinews of industrial production on which the success of the plan depends.'[21] Correspondence with their various customers indicated how the company was working amidst supply constraints; on 27 March 1958, writing to the director general of supplies and disposal, R.K. Sanjana, the sales manager, mentioned how they could not adhere to their delivery time and how their stock of steel was completely exhausted. In its letter dated 5 June 1958, the firm informed the garrison engineer of Amritsar division that they could not complete the order for supply of Storwel cupboards as their stock of steel was practically exhausted and the delivery from producers had been inordinately delayed. They also informed their customer that they had intimated the fact to the director general of supplies and disposals and begged consideration for deferred supplies.[22] In the same year, in the annual meeting of the All India Manufacturers Organization, N.D. Sahukar, the general manager of Godrej, referred to the problems of the steel industry and of those industries that depended on steel and how many of them were working under 50 per cent of their capacity.[23] The 1960s did not show a substantial improvement in steel supplies; the year 1964 seems to have been especially severe; many sheet processing industries were closed down for lack of steel sheets of suitable gauges; even the Godrej Plants output had been hit hard and the scarcity of steel had reduced the working capacity of the plant, throwing more than 400 workers out of employment.

These challenges notwithstanding, the company was able to continue with the production of Storwel, expand its range, go for new models and distribute them all over the country, truly making it a pan-Indian object. It was consistent with the company's desire to project itself as swadeshi with a difference. Thus, advertisements and catalogues emphasized the links between the nation and enterprise, the reputation of the company and the brand value of the product. Over time, the focus changed from being a reliable product to a good-looking one and even before the opening up of the economy, the company had opted for new sleek designs and colours; the Centurion and Classic models, for example, testified to this. These initiatives were critically dependent on professional management, distributorship and advertising that made up the anatomy of a modern manufacturing company, which is what Godrej aspired to be. The documentation that the company maintained was quite extraordinary—thanks to the archive it supports, we have very fine details about the way the company functioned, how designs were refined and patented, how these were operationalized in the plants and how the assembly line of products reached the market through a network of stockists and distributors. In every way, the business family demonstrated its ability to forecast the market, create a demand and participate in a new project of consumption. This included office furniture and the typewriter, making the family and company leading providers of office equipment. It was indeed hard to imagine an office in the 1960s, 1970s and 1980s that did not have the ubiquitous almirah and tubular chair, not to speak of the typewriter.

The making of the office chair was a natural progression in the chain of equipment manufactured by the company. For one, the company had already gained expertise in the use of tubular steel and the various processes that it had to be subject to. At the same time, it had a ready market—the office furniture segment was not unknown to the company—and it made business sense to improvise with the material to turn out all kinds of chairs and seating devices, from the average chair for the ordinary office goer to the executive revolving and tilting chair for the boss, from hospital equipment to public seating in cinemas. Designing the chair was not easy; although, as a standard chair, it was meant to fit all, the actual design of the object was not as easy as it seemed. But given the vision of the company and the readiness of the family to experiment with design and learn from expertise overseas, we come across several design and manufacturing initiatives: the manufacture of CH 6 without arms for the office personnel and CH & A (revolving chair) for the executives, being instances in point. With no help in terms of samples, the company sourced catalogues from Thailand with great difficulty to turn out a line of chairs. Particularly important was the Typist Chair (CH 2 and CH 3) that was continuously refined—a testimony to the dynamism of the family and the firm to experiment with the product. The absolute determination to improve products and satisfy the aspirations of customers was what marked the family, and its manufacture of objects of everyday use helped it acquire a kind of familiarity and affection that made the experiment truly unusual. This was well illustrated in the case of the manufacturing of the Godrej typewriter in 1955, which became ubiquitous in virtually every office and announced the ingenuity of indigenous manufacture. Spurred by the efforts of Naval Godrej, who was the son of Pirojsha Godrej and the nephew of Ardeshir Godrej, the manufacture of the typewriter became a reality. Technicians were given the necessary training; alloys of special ferrous and non-ferrous materials were used and very few of the components were imported, thus keeping in line with the mantra of self-sufficiency that the family had always espoused. An incredible amount of planning went behind the process for fixing types and keyboards. Notwithstanding the scepticism of many and the challenges of competitors, Godrej went ahead, and by 1959, an improved model M8 was introduced, which enhanced sales. The company never stopped improvisations and refinements; in 1967, Plant 3 at Vikhroli undertook the manufacture of VEB Optima Model M-12, which enjoyed a huge demand with production doubling between 1965 and 1970. In 1970, a new model named after Godrej founder Ardeshir—the AB—was launched, and it remained in the market for nine years. The company went from strength to strength; the 1983 Godrej Prima made a splash, and over 6,00,000 typewriters were manufactured in a span of thirteen years, from 1983 to 1996.[24]

The individual stories of each of the Godrej products, from the Storwel to the chair to the typewriter and then on to the PUF refrigerator, embodies the personalities of the family members who worked in their individual ways. Each of them brought to the table an uncanny understanding of the market, an implacable will to succeed and an openness to learn and achieve excellence. Thus the attention to detail, the need to enhance the product and the focus on product management and professionalization is evident in the way the family communicated the brand value of its products, which in turn helped make the family an eminent one in the business landscape of Bombay. The close association of the family with the city is also apparent in the way it chose to integrate its operations with the social, cultural and environmental concerns of the city, giving others a convenient blueprint to follow. It is here that we will turn to the building of a township in Vikhroli, which anchored the company to a space located in a suburb in the city.

Classified Ad 10 – No Title
The Times of India (1861-current); Mar 6, 1949; ProQuest Historical Newspapers: The Times of India
pg. 5

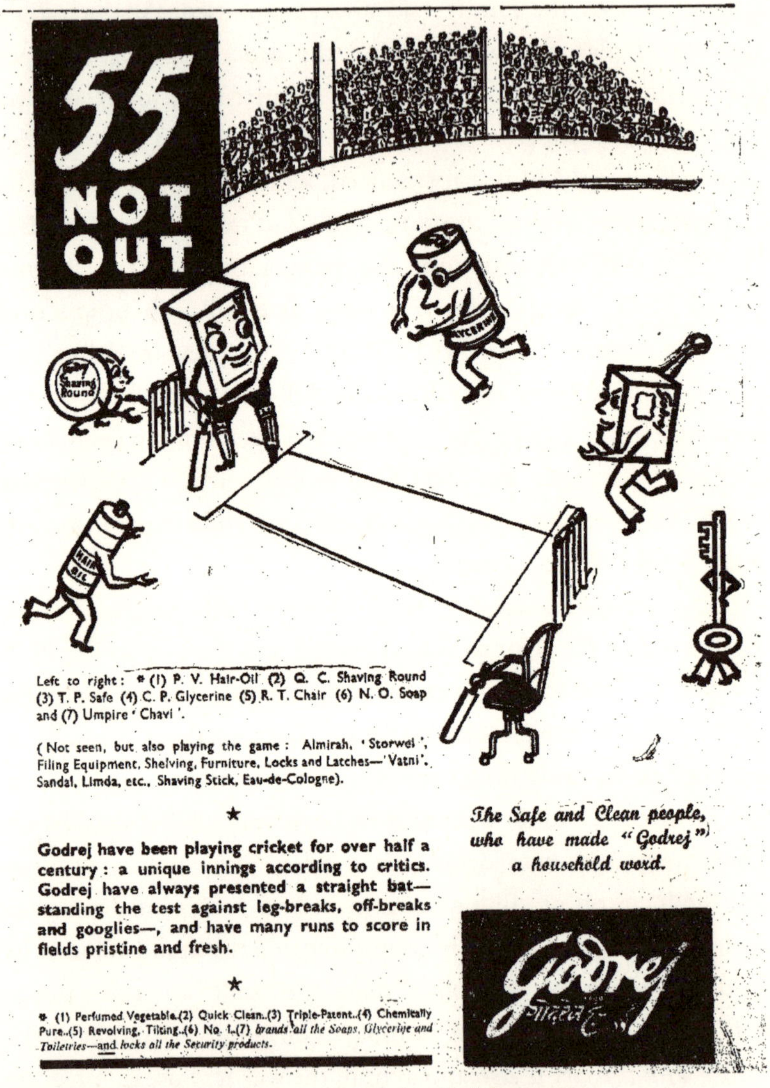

55 NOT OUT

Left to right : ✿ (1) P. V. Hair-Oil (2) Q. C. Shaving Round
(3) T. P. Safe (4) C. P. Glycerine (5) R. T. Chair (6) N. O. Soap
and (7) Umpire ' Chavi '.

(Not seen, but also playing the game : Almirah, ' Storwel ',
Filing Equipment, Shelving, Furniture, Locks and Latches—' Vatni ',
Sandal, Limda, etc., Shaving Stick, Eau-de-Cologne).

★

Godrej have been playing cricket for over half a
century : a unique innings according to critics.
Godrej have always presented a straight bat—
standing the test against leg-breaks, off-breaks
and googlies—, and have many runs to score in
fields pristine and fresh.

★

✿ (1) Perfumed Vegetable.(2) Quick Clean..(3) Triple-Patent..(4) Chemically
Pure..(5) Revolving, Tilting..(6) No. 1..(7) *brands all the Soaps, Glycerine and
Toiletries—and locks all the Security products.*

The Safe and Clean people,
who have made " Godrej "
a household word.

Godrej

Source: Godrej Archives

Vikhroli: The Planning of a Township

It was in 1943 that the sale of land measuring about 3000 acres was confirmed by the High Court of Bombay to Naval Pirojsha Godrej, fondly known as 'Naoroji'. The sale was confirmed by a letter dated 16 July from the Collector, Bombay, Bombay suburban district to Payne and Co. attorneys of Godrej, after which possession took place. Five years later, the same plot was transferred to Godrej and Boyce in order to create the nucleus of an industrial township.[25] The process of acquisition in this case was quite different from what we saw in the case of the Tatas; for one, this was smaller, and for another, the process was not as contentious and contested. The area itself was marshy and swampy and not easily amenable to settlement. And yet Naval Pirojsha persevered and worked in close concert with architects and engineers to transform the swamp into an industrial Eden. By 1960, four modern structures emerged to house industrial plants, not to speak of residential spaces for personnel.

Pirojsha like his father or his successors was more than just a profit-seeking industrialist. A deep and abiding commitment to serving humanity and to environmental concerns was evident, especially in the way he conceived of the township and the plants that it accommodated. These were airy and planned amid trees and foliage to relieve workers and personnel from the monotony of industrial labour. In a compilation of the notices on the Godrej family by Dr Viraf Minocher Dhalia, there is an entry on Pirojshanagar referring to the ways in which its founder planned schools and space: 'away from the hum of productivity of men and machines, you may on a weekday morning run into the joyous laughter of little children on the wide-open compound'.[26] In fact, this abiding commitment to standards and to service characterized the Godrej project and vision, which was a fundamental commitment to the basic human values and to the highest industrial standards. Notwithstanding steel shortages and constraints that followed from the quota policy of the government, the company maintained its performance standards, something that the government recognized and acknowledged. In the choice of its manufacture (steel furniture, safes, locks, typewriters and bathing soaps), the company and its directors seemed to have correctly judged the demand for them and developed strategies to make these everyday products. For this, credit surely went to the creative and enterprising dreams of the founder, Ardeshir, and his successors, who were committed to the swadeshi ideals without compromising standards or the openness to learn from existing technology overseas and adapt it appropriately. Not surprising then that the company made steel ballot boxes for India's first democratic election or took trail-blazing decisions to develop the typewriter and perfect the Indian soap. The story of the safe, Storwel, soap and typewriter speaks volumes of the ways in which the company built its enterprise step by step, developed modern ways of doing business, developed networks of distributors and stood for self-sufficiency that endeared them to the state. Standing proudly and even assertively for private enterprise, the company never forgot its commitment to consumer satisfaction and industrial excellence that made its goods much more than consumer items; they represented a bunch of social values eagerly adopted and espoused by a new and growing middle class. In a featured supplement to the *Times of India*,[27] it was pointed out how service to the consumer was the keynote of their policy, just as ethical concerns for the workers informed their labour welfare programmes.

The expanding strength of the company was built on three pillars: one was workmanship and standards of excellence in the range of products that were turned out; another was a loyal and effective network of distributors and stockists entrusted with selling the product and ensuring after-sales service; and finally, there was a concerted advertising and marketing strategy that the company adopted and refined. Just as the foundations of the company were built on principles of family solidarity, the emphasis on loyalty and reciprocity was cultivated quite self-consciously with distributors. The latter were carefully chosen, regularly monitored and asked to consciously improve their performance and fill in the gaps. It was the dealers who knew the market, so it was entirely appropriate that the company would work closely with them. Annual conferences of dealers were convened, and sub-dealers were appointed when the market got too big. This was a strategy that old-time employees such as Johnny Fernandes referred to.[28] Whether it was salesmen or authorized dealers, the company was able to communicate the value of familial loyalty; we have on record an interview of T.V.V.S. Chowdhary, a salesperson operating for Godrej, who mentioned how he and his concern felt proud to sell Godrej products.[29] Ananthswamy, a dealer working for Godrej in the southern region, also said how meticulous Godrej was in monitoring work orders and how he identified with Godrej and its style of functioning; in his words, 'at least until 1990, I soaked in Godrej, I thought Godrej, I breathe Godrej and I live Godrej'.[30] Godrej was especially meticulous in monitoring the work of stockists.

By the 1990s, the Godrej products were household and office names, and the family was recognized as one of Bombay city's premier business elites. While in terms of assets the family lagged behind the Tatas and the Ambanis, it managed to retain the imagination of its consumer base with the family itself standing for a brand. It is a family company, with the Godrej family holding 50 to 100 per cent of all companies it owns and holds. Family members work like trustees, and it is remarkable that in its long history, it has not experienced a split and that younger generation executives start like all others and work their way up. There have been moments when Godrej products were dismissed as fuddy duddy and seen as being out of sync with contemporary aspirations for fancy furniture, but this cannot take away from the dynamism that characterized their operations, especially in the four decades after Independence, when working conditions were not easy, especially in view of the government's steel quota policy, repressive tax regimes and labour unrest. The company survived all of these challenges, and it was largely due to the individual resolve of the family members. Each of them who took the baton distinguished themselves with their professional expertise, and this is what marked them off from many other business families. Naval Godrej, for example, was an expert on machine tools, a keen critic of government policies that, by the late 1970s, were crippling manufacture and took important steps in giving the machine tool industry the much-needed push and momentum. He worked alongside workers, scrutinizing every detail, and, according to the company's biographer, B. Karanjia, inspected every machine that came by. It was ironic that a man who was dedicated to the cause of both labour and enterprise should have been the victim of a stabbing incident and suffer from poor health until his death. The stabbing incident itself, occurring at the height of labour agitation in Bombay, attracted widespread outrage and anger among all sections, including trade unions, which gives us a measure of the presence that the family commanded in the city.

Bombay, or Mumbai as it is now known, has always been a businessman's city. With the Godrej family, the influence is also manifested by the sheer amount of landed property they own. As Bombay's biggest private landowner (3400 acres), they have protected about 1750 acres of mangrove swamps on the property and have consolidated their position as committed citizens and philanthropists. In the lives and labours of two of the most premier and pre-eminent Parsi business families, we find the story of a young nation finding its feet, of remaining local while experimenting with the global and of negotiating the complex tangles of a semi-planned economy and an autarchy. The two business houses were known for their ethical understanding of business and management, which they put into operation. In subtle but significant ways, they let successive governments know that they were in for the long haul and that they were not susceptible to threats. Their presence and success amid great odds set the stage for business to assume greater heights and independence even though their counterparts did not always follow their direction and opted for newer strategies to balance the relations between state and enterprise. In part, this was inevitable; business, in India, like anywhere else in the world, had to operate in a specific context and remain mindful of challenges and opportunities. Hedging bets was part of the game, and yet in the profiles of some of our protagonists, ethical considerations held precedence and marked them out as men for all seasons.

4

Money in the Bazaar: A Story of Indigenous Credit

Let's take a respite from individuals and move to an abstract entity—the bazaar. Generally associated with plenitude, the word 'bazaar' immediately evokes impressions of a physical space stacked with produce and transactions. The bazaars of the east are especially captivating, with the souks of Turkey and Egypt and the bazaars of Mughal India bringing to mind colours and excitement, an array of splendid commodities and fabled merchants dealing in exotic goods as well as objects of mundane necessity. Was the bazaar then just a built space stocked with goods, regularly featuring transactions and sales being negotiated between sellers and buyers? Or did the bazaar, over time and in specific contexts, encompass more complex layers, meanings and dimensions? We ask this question for two reasons: one, because the bazaar in India had a very specific connotation with a specific set of functions ascribed to it during the nineteenth century, when it functioned not merely as a built space for buying and selling but as a crucial intermediate space responsible for the funding and marketing of agricultural produce in the subcontinent and encompassing a complex range of functions through a set of financial instruments and practices. The second reason behind the question has to do with its representation in official colonial discourse, where it was contrasted to the formal sector of regulated business and described as informal, dismissed as unregulated, and by default evaluated as vernacular and not capitalist enough. How far are these assumptions valid, especially in view of the fact that the bazaar played a crucial role in sustaining commercial flows in the subcontinent, integrating different segments of the economy? We will have occasion to elaborate on these questions and to identify how the space that we define and acknowledge as the bazaar, threw up influential men of capital and commanded a web of complex transactions in the nineteenth century under conditions of colonialism. By the late nineteenth century, the bazaar had emerged as a very distinct tier in the colonial economy responsible for the provisioning of goods and commodities within the subcontinent, connecting the world of Indian rural produce to the consuming hinterland and for supply of goods to the export centres on the coast and interacting with the larger world economy. The expansion of the bazaar thus testified to the dynamism of urban–rural linkages and also to the power and flexibility of capital in integrating complex segments of the economy. As Anand Yang argues in his book, *Bazaar India*, rural markets and their workings have been neglected, and the focus on the bazaar is useful to reconfigure the agrarian geography of India and thereby interrogate the assumptions of existing historiography.[1] In course of this chapter, we will attempt to understand the bazaar and its changing contours that were reconfigured in a context of massive market integration under conditions of colonial rule to examine its mechanisms and its vitality that made it an influential sector in the economy and even provided men of means a way to transition from trade to manufacture. We will not focus on individual kingpins of the bazaar; rather, we will take up random examples of bazaar enterprise and, in the process, foreground the bazaar itself as our principal protagonist. This comes through in the histories that indigenous business and banking communities wrote in the twentieth century, wherein invariably it was the ubiquity of indigenous capital and business—in the forms of commission agency (*arhat*) and banking (hundi)—that was recorded in meticulous detail. For indigenous capital, the bazaar, in its varied segments, was the site of activity, reputation and accumulation.

A Matter of Definition

What is a bazaar? How do we define it? How do anthropologists and historians look at it? Under what conditions did the bazaar come to assume certain characteristics and meanings in the nineteenth century? As we have already indicated, at a very general level, bazaars were spaces where sellers and buyers met periodically to affect sales and purchases of either specific commodities or a range of goods. The dictionary definition of the bazaar supports this characterization, seeing it as a market held through the year consisting of shops and stalls. The term itself had Arabic–Persian associations before making its way into the Indian vocabulary. Culturally, the word bazaar was associated with a degree of coarseness removing it from and pitting it in contrast to the world of courtly consumption and taste. However, as an entity and actant, it was important enough for the state to engage with it and to intervene in its workings to its advantage. It was not entirely independent, for it had multiple stakeholders—heads of states, religious orders and merchants—all of whom were interested in its revenue capacity and would not allow for its uninterrupted abstract power. Control over the bazaar became in the Indian context especially pronounced during the eighteenth century, when British power, in its quest for dominance, forged connections with bazaars and their men whose purses were opened, sometimes prized open to fund and finance campaigns. C.A. Bayly's work brought this dimension out brilliantly as he saw rulers, townsmen and bazaars as critical players in the eighteenth century of transition, when conquest and consolidation of British rule witnessed the resurgence of bazaars and bazaarmen, who through their provisioning of supplies and credit, became king makers.[2]

The men of the bazaar, for early British observers, were primarily bankers who had accumulated capital through trade and brokerage and who subsequently deployed cash and credit to leverage political connections and assume a key position in the political economy of the period. It was their funds that fuelled the movement of soldiers and goods and services, as a result of which their intercession could not be discounted even after political success had been accomplished and a new colonial economy was set in motion. For nineteenth-century British officers and observers, the bazaar men were shroffs, or bankers, whose influence derived from the intimate understanding they had of money, exchange and the currency business, which was crucial for trade and politics during the transition. It may be useful to recall here that through the eighteenth century, bankers and their financial instruments had emerged as a critical conduit for the working of the revenue establishment and for remittances that states and armies required across borders.[3] The remittance network, in turn, was predicated on commercial flows that determined the exchange rates between one currency and the other. The bankers or shroffs who knew the business and dominated the exchange trade were key for any state establishment, not to speak of the aspiring English East India company that relied on Bengal funds routed through bankers of Benaras and Surat to sustain their wars in western India. During the course of the eighteenth century, we come across sporadic references to the 'bazaar shroffs' of Surat—those connected with the money and exchange market in the city of Surat and who dominated the Surat–Bengal trade in raw silk and cotton. Predictably, they handled credit transfers and remittances along this route, which became increasingly important for the English East India company as it relied on money transfers from Bengal to support its struggling settlement of Bombay. The officials of the English East India company had occasion to comment on this, especially after 1765, when the Surat–Bengal trade sustained a long-term decline, thereby raising the exchange rates between the two places. With the decline of this traffic, the bills of exchange business suffered disruption as the terms for exchange became distinctly unfavourable for the English company authorities.[4]

The remittance or hundi network dominated by shroffs became increasingly important during the course of the eighteenth and early nineteenth centuries, when Bania funds and credit and their hundi networks supported the processes of long-distance trade and of imperial conquest and consolidation. In fact, one fallout of the British conquest was the setting up of new credit agencies and branches through swathes of western and central India. Bankers everywhere, including in those states ruled by princes in Rajasthan, were key allies of the state if they saw it as a stable political player. Seth Piramal, for example, was potedar of the state of Bikaner and also enjoyed the confidence of Ranjit Singh (Shekhawati). It was only after the formal conquest of India by the English East India company and the introduction of important measures such as the abolition of multiple currencies and the company's takeover of treasury transfers that the disproportionate influence of bankers diminished. Some of them lost their traditional business in financing the needs of rulers, and some even suffered the consequences of commercial instability in the period of transition to a new and fully articulated colonial economy. There were, however, regional variations in this story; certain regions, such as Bengal faced severe depression, while other regions, like western India, where the process of subjugation was delayed and staggered, the indigenous trading groups were able to maintain their resilience and integrate their functions with the nascent colonial economy. As mentioned in the context of Parsi enterprise in the opium trade, inland trade networks in western and central India were activated by the colonial traffic in cotton and opium and helped indigenous financiers and merchants to consolidate their position. The latter were helped by the presence of princely states in Rajasthan and of the Marathas in parts of central India and by the Portuguese ports along the coast (Daman and Diu) that worked as efficient transit points in what was largely a clandestine trade. This worked against the English company authorities in enforcing a monopoly on production and distribution of opium and helped Indian merchants and financiers work with Parsi traders and European private merchants of Bombay. The business of provisioning opium and before that cotton was undertaken by bankers and brokers who established important agencies of commission and expanded them in the succeeding decades.

The Maturation of the Colonial Economy and Market Integration

The articulation of a colonial economy in India was a long-drawn process with several constituent elements: a dominant European sector that controlled the export–import trade of the subcontinent; a supporting structure of inland trade connections that channelled goods into the principal port centres and second-tier market towns; and an agricultural sector that accommodated a substantial subsistence economy and was taxed for revenue by the colonial authorities. Like any typical colonial economy, India became a captive market for massive quantities of manufactured goods—primarily textiles turned out by Lancashire and Manchester—and a principal supplier of raw material and cash crops, including cotton, food grains, opium, indigo, jute and leather. However, the profound transformation that India underwent in its export–import trade composition was only one aspect of the changing milieu. In the initial decades after colonial conquests, within the overall domination of the Indian economy by the English trading company, there were extensive trade dealings by British private traders and free merchants who depended for supplies of their export staple on Indian merchant networks, especially in western and central India, where we find the best evidence of the early bazaar economy in operation. The functioning of the opium business in the nineteenth century is a clear and concrete instance of the bazaar economy in operation, one that involved the financing and marketing of primary agricultural produce and transporting it to port cities and other important markets inland. The bazaar in this case was dominated by big bankers (sahukars), who entered into contracts with local petty traders. Amar Farooqui's work demonstrates how the wholesale opium trade was concentrated in the hands of the Malwa sahukars, who were engaged in large-scale speculation and gambling in stocks, an indication of futures trading.[5] These sahukars also traded extensively in cotton and grain and handled the network of remittances that constituted a key feature of nineteenth century markets. British expansion and the consolidation of princely states under British rule helped bankers set up kothis, undertake the business of lending, remittances (hundi) and the financing of agricultural produce. In his work on market towns in north India, C.A. Bayly mentions how bankers in Benaras financed the pilgrimage trade, the trade in silk sarees and silk goods. In Allahabad, on the other hand, bankers worked closely with traders engaged in the traffic of castor oil, indigo and mild drugs. The expanding networks of Agarwal and Oswal banking families in central and western India, investing in the production and trade of sugar, indigo, opium and drugs, as well as the movement of Marwaris into the Ganges Valley and Calcutta, constituted the early history of the modern bazaar that emerged as a prominent tier in the economy of colonial India.[6]

The workings of the early nineteenth century colonial economy were predicated on the connections between British free traders and agency houses and indigenous businessmen whose knowledge of local markets and access to credit resources came in handy. Indigenous brokers and bankers, termed as banian in Bengal and guarantee brokers in Bombay, were essentially compradors advancing money to the foreign agency houses that employed them, agreeing to sell goods imported and buy goods to be exported. They agreed to guarantee bills used for the purchase of commodities, which was the most critical function performed by them, especially in view of the lack of confidence that European merchants had of smaller merchants and dealers working in the interiors. These men had substantial means, enjoyed credit ratings in the market and had enough clout to attract capital and ensure the smooth flow of trade transactions.[7] With the expansion of the railways and the transport and information revolution (wire telegraph in particular, that made it easier to forecast markets), new arrangements and new players came to the fore. For one, the very infrastructure of the railways was designed to access export items more easily for British trade and reduce costs; as Thomas Williamson, the revenue commissioner of Bombay, wrote in 1846,

> the great trunk line running by the Malseje Ghaut in the direction of Nagpurr, would be most direct which could possibly be selected to connect Bombay to Calcutta. Commercially, it would be best for the cotton of Berar, while for the first 120 miles from Bombay we would proceed in the immediate direction of the military stations of Ahmednuggur, Jaulna and Aurangabad.[8]

The sentiments embodied a classical colonial mindset; the underlying rationale for the colonial state was to reduce costs of carriage so that imports could be pushed easily into the interior and agricultural goods like cotton could be exported to global markets more easily. While the distribution of goods across the subcontinent was definitely facilitated by the railway network, indigenous distributors were not entirely displaced; rather, they were integrated into the new system. In fact, their intercession and participation through financial instruments and commercial practices helped in reconfiguring a three-tiered colonial economy, wherein the bazaar occupied the intermediate but crucial space. Thus, Rajat Ray argues that with the development and expansion of the railway network, the export–import European firms, such as the Rallis and Volkarts, built their own upcountry network but could not entirely dispense with the indigenous commission agency houses (*arhatiyas*) who rapidly emerged as principal movers of the bazaar economy. These men, according to Ray, were different from older brokers, for they did not just guarantee the payment of the price of goods but guaranteed bills or hundis through which trade transactions were operated.[9] The arhatiya fulfilled a number of key functions—he gave a contract of guarantee undertaking delivery at the due date and at the price determined and a promise that any difference would be paid by him. The arhatiyas were truly the kings of the bazaar as they financed trade and marketing of agricultural produce—both staples for domestic consumption as well as export commodities.

Vernacular histories of indigenous capital undertaken by business communities in the early twentieth century are explicit in detailing the density of transactions undertaken by them in two major sectors of the economy, both of which were interrelated. One was the ubiquity of commission agencies and sarrafi businesses (hundi chitthi), which they ran in the hinterland centres, and the other was the connections they maintained with premier European business houses in the major port cities of Calcutta and Bombay. Both these activities were intimately connected with the larger segment of financing and marketing agricultural produce, the major portion of which was oriented to the domestic market. Thus, even a cursory glance at the history of Indian trade and businessmen by Mohan Badjatya indicates the extraordinary web of commercial transactions conducted by Bania groups (Oswals, Maheshwaris, Agrawals, etc.), whose presence was marked through the length and breadth of the subcontinent. It may help to list some of the entries in Badjatya's work that speak for the pervasiveness of the bazaar transactions and foreground the vitality of the bazaarmen. Below are some translated excerpts from the work that give concrete examples.[10]

One such example is provided in the case of Messrs Basantlal Gorakhram, an Agrawal firm that established itself in Bombay some years before, currently managed by Seth Basantlal, Seth Gorakhram, Seth Dwarkadas and Seth Barasilal. The headquarters of their business was in Bombay and ran a vibrant trade in cotton and grain, a commission agency in these staples, and had extensive *godaam*, or storage spaces. The firm owned a ginning and pressing factory in Datia and a sarrafi and an arhat each in Karachi and Badayu. A similar instance is provided by Messrs Samarthrai Khetidas, an old firm based in Ramgarh, established by Khetsiadas and currently run by his son Motilal with branches all over India. In Bombay, the house had an establishment in Marwari bazaar, where the business of hundi, sarrafi and arhat was undertaken. The house had a branch in Amristar that controlled imports of foreign cloth and also ran banking concerns. It maintained gin factories in Mansor, Nayanagar and Gulbargha, where they traded in cotton as well. There is also the case of Messrs Hiralal Ramgopal, an Agarwal family whose business was established by Keshavdas several decades ago and expanded by his son Ramgopal. It had an office in Bombay on Memon Street, where they ran banking and arhat. The house had an agency for foreign companies and owned ginning factories for cotton that they supplied to mills like the Nagpur mills.

These instances are just a few among many entries that dot the pages of Badjatya's directory. They illustrate and highlight the close links between inland trade and the provisioning of commodities for export trade, as well as that between banking and brokerage, which accompanied the maturation of the colonial economy that left spaces and opportunities open for indigenous capital. This was especially so after the expansion of the railways that accelerated trade flows and encouraged migrant business groups to move into nodal centres and port cities. Traditional business groups from Rajasthan migrated in large numbers to dominate the inland trade as commission agents for big traders and as bankers whose financial instruments were crucial in financing agricultural production and marketing. How did this happen? The answer to this question lies in both the communities' reserves built over time in the upcountry trade as well as in the obstacles faced by multi-nationals in penetrating the bazaar sector of the economy. Tom Timberg refers to Marwari migration to Bombay and Calcutta in the nineteenth century, which quickened after the railways. They served as agents to European firms (Rallis and Andrew Yule) and then entered the business of supplying jute to industries in Bengal.[11] Subsequently, they acquired jute presses to set up solid foundations for their control over the sector. The interwar years saw the community's rapid expansion leading to associations formed by Marwari traders and then directly entering the jute business by setting up their own jute mills or acquiring them from others. In Bombay and Ahmedabad, we find Gujarati and Marwari capitals experimenting with cotton futures, opium and bullion. Instances of Khetsidas Harmukh Rai and Cheniram Jesraj Nathuram, who started with opium trade and then moved into cotton, illustrate this trend. Another prominent firm associated with cotton was that of Bhagvandas Loyalka, who arrived in Bombay in 1866 and experimented with opium, cotton and commission agency. The Somanis were yet another prominent Marwari family dealing in

cotton and futures markets. The Ruias were guarantee brokers
to the Sasoons and were renowned as cotton kings.[12] Most
of the merchants mentioned by her were related to the cotton
export business.

These men who represented nascent indigenous capital in
metropolitan colonial cities did not embody the bazaar that is
the subject of our inquiry but were intimately connected with it.
For these men to get access to staples, whether grain or cotton,
to ensure the distribution of select imports, it was vital to forge
connections with a different strata of bazaarmen also drawn from
traditional business communities and who specialized in the
financing and marketing of agricultural produce. Their strength
lay in their experience of working with a quasi-monetized
economy where they dominated inland movements of credit
and produce distribution. Their financial instruments—the
hundis—sustained every commodity market or bazaar, and while
it appeared unregulated to European observers, it had its logic and
commanded a complex and sophisticated form of organization.
Following the pathways of colonial expansion—as the British
extended their commercial networks—they invested in cotton
and opium as export goods and capitalized their connections with
markets and rulers. The bazaar did not represent a monolith and
was characterized by several levels; some started as shopkeepers
and became money lenders, others dominated large-scale grain
markets and financed crop production. Thus, between 1780
and 1820, Marwari migrants, mostly belonging to the subsect of
Shekhawati Agarwals, established themselves in grain markets of
the Doab; by 1850, they had offices all over India. Inland exchanges
were accelerated by the railways and produced, according to
Rajat Kanta Ray, 'an integrated exchange system'. In Ray's words,

'the bazaar in its wider sense meant the system of banking and trade that ensured, through long tried-and-tested indigenous methods, the massive flows of money, credit, crops, manufactured goods and precious metals within the domestic commercial economy of India'.[13] What did this bazaar look like, and how did it work? What kind of capital did it command?

The Working of the Bazaar

Even today, a cursory stroll in a crowded *mandi*, or bazaar, in a three-tier town of India gives us rich images of huge volumes of goods waiting to be traded, processed and distributed. Rows of tractors with sugar cane, bustling crowds in grain markets and dark, dank godowns bursting to their seams with produce bring home the density of wholesale transactions in India. Observers in the early twentieth century pointed this out in great detail, their attention drawn to both the low profit margins as well as mass selling at low margins. The American trade consul at the turn of the twentieth century observed how, 'In doing business with the great masses of people (in India), the margin of profit must be extremely small; however, the sales and collective profits may be enormous'.[14] What he meant by this was that operations in India were too dispersed and profit margins were not adequate enough for large-scale corporations to seriously consider entering the business. By default, this segment came to be controlled by small but numerous operators, whose transactions were aligned to those of larger merchants in big cities. One could legitimately speculate that even traditionally in pre-modern India, the supply and brokerage business in textiles, sugar or indigo was channelled through a deep and wide-ranging network of intermediaries whose

reach went right up to the small producer. It was the depth of the
network of distribution and supply funnelled through advances
that made up the bazaar, which by the end of the nineteenth
century had grown exponentially in size. What is therefore
important to remember is that the bazaar was always a complex
and stratified world and commanded a huge turnover distributed
across various segments of the trading population. There were big
men who dominated the bazaar at its uppermost ends and those
who worked as commission agents for European firms, such as
Ghandshyamdas Birla, and smaller arhatiyas in the mandis that
emerged as nodal points of the distribution system. These men
had credit instruments at their disposal, railway bills of lading
that ensured the transportation of goods and store rooms to hold
goods and engage in forwards trading. Thus a host of instruments,
from hundis to railway bills, mediated the complex workings of
the bazaar, the intricacies of which Rajat Kanta Ray captures in
his work.[15]

The marketing of agricultural produce in India was
directed towards the large domestic market, with a small
proportion being allotted for export via colonial port cities. At
the top end of the system of trade and marketing, there were
international firms and exchange banks who played a major
role in importing bullion, distributing imports and financing
exports from the subcontinent. The firms relied on indigenous
up-country agents, and it was only occasionally that foreign
firms were able to bypass these agencies. These up-country
agents relied for finances on local hundis for purchases—hundis
that were drawn on the principals based in headquarters like
Calcutta and Bombay—occasionally on wire transfers from
exchange banks and, in some cases, even on local bankers who
were reimbursed by cheques. At the bottom of the system were

primary producers, peasants and agriculturists who produced
grain and other staples for their own consumption and for the
market. In between these two ends of the spectrum was the
bazaar that intervened to procure, finance the production and
marketing of goods for both exports (a small portion) and for
the home market. The business involved storage spaces, credit
for production, procurement, speculation and forwards trading.
The process went something like this: goods were traded at haats,
or local markets, mostly through cash transactions and sold to
the non-peasant sections of the population as well as traders who
were in charge of distributing them to the mandis. Mandis were
the nodal point of the great bazaar—of the distribution network
that connected the inland with coastal ports and export centres.
The key actors in the mandis were the arhatiyas, who procured
goods and sent them to railheads for further transportation.
These transactions ran on credit, with hundis the principal credit
instrument dominating the transactions. The hundi network
was in the hands of the sarrafs, or bankers, who were often also
the principal arhatiyas or commission agents as well. The density
of the bazaar's transactions cannot be estimated accurately, but
descriptive evidence indicates that it was staggering in its volume
and reach and that big bankers in Calcutta and Bombay oversaw
the enormous volume of financial transactions that entered
the financing of agriculture and marketing.[16] Ray illustrates
this point by quoting extensively from the Bihar and Orissa
Provincial Banking Enquiry Committee report (1929–30). It is
worthwhile to quote this extract as it brings the bazaar centre
stage and indicates how crucial it was in forging the integration
of trade flows. The report details the distribution of coconuts, a
key ingredient for sweetmeats. This ensured a thriving trade in
the nut and brought together a spectrum of players.[17]

According to the report that Ray refers to, coconuts were grown extensively in Puri district, which exported annually about 30,000 maunds (one maund is approximately 34 kilograms), almost *entirely to confectioners* in the Central Provinces (CP). The report identified four principal coconut dealers at the railhead, one Marwari and three Oriyas, who were known to have bought up the coconuts from the local Brahmin agriculturists who collected the produce of other ryots (peasants or tenant cultivators) and moved the coconuts by road to the railhead. The four coconut dealers financed one quarter of the nuts by advances, which carried no stipulation of exclusive right of purchase, and they paid cash down for the other three quarters. Once the nuts were received at the mandi, the merchant there filled an order from a CP confectioner by railing the ordered coconuts, telegraphing the buyer about the order. The buyer on his part wired back that he, i.e., the mandi merchant should draw a hundi on a particular merchant in Bombay or Calcutta. The coconut merchant drew a hundi accordingly and sold it locally in Puri to a merchant willing to remit money to either Calcutta or Bombay. He usually received a premium for a hundi drawn on Calcutta, to which plenty of merchants wished to remit. By contrast, he had to sell hundis at a discount in Bombay, where fewer merchants wanted to remit money. As the Bihar and Orissa Banking Enquiry Committee observed, this, 'seems to us to be a fairly typical account of business carried in a local product for which there is a distant sale, and there must be a great many similar enterprises going on throughout the province in other commodities'.

What this extract indicates is the circulation of and trade in hundis or credit instruments that underwrote inland trade transactions. Every part of the operation was done on credit, and credit notes or hundis were also traded in, which explains why they could be freely bought and sold. Normally, arhat and banking went on side-by-side—commission agents were also bankers who bought and sold goods for their principal and used hundis to finance the transactions. Ray's work brings out the magnitude of the bazaar's operations that were enabled by rail lines and credit networks and arhat (commission agencies) and hundi (bills of exchange) arrangements. Every conceivable agricultural crop was financed by arhatiyas and shroffs based in mandis. Grain arhatiyas in mandis bought 66 to 70 per cent of wheat purchases from peasants and were part of an integrated structure of credit and movement of goods. Thus, to use Ray again, the bazaar was an integrated system of inland business transactions between distant market towns moving through key financial exchanges that converged in major cities—Calcutta, Bombay, Ahmedabad, Madras and Kanpur.[18] The network of mandis and their nodal points was connected by infrastructures of information and transportation and by credit networks (hundi) and commission agencies (arhat), both of which feature prominently in indigenous business histories of the twentieth century. The world of the bazaar, in which hundreds of commercial communities participated, was marked by the ubiquity of commission agencies and sarrafi all over India.

Colonial officials were aware of the importance of the bazaar but did not accord formal recognition to the practices and protocols it adopted. The bazaar did not come under the formal economic sector and was seen as a domain of vernacular practices. This was especially true of the hundi or the bill of exchange, which did not enjoy legal status under the Negotiable Instruments Act of 1881. In fact, however, instruments like the hundi and other mechanisms that held the bazaar apparatus were impressive. For one, there was the *goladari*, which involved the business of storing and trading in a commodity. It was a risky business and required special skills. Essentially, the function of the *goladar* was to store grain for his client, or on his account, to sell grain on a commission basis (arhat) for his client and to make advances against the grain entrusted to the warehouse. Goladars therefore were traders and exported the produce by drawing hundis on commission agents based in the larger cities. Very often they were bankers as well and held agencies for imports. Ray mentions Khaliram Kedarnath, a leading goladar who held an agency of Esso for kerosene.[19] Storage facilities enabled active trade in futures or speculation; in fact, Ray calculates wheat trading in futures to about 70 million tons, although ten million tons was India's production figures. Actual buying and trading was undertaken by arhats, who were also bankers and used hundis for covering their transactions and raising credit. Arhat was an old and established practice, and we have references to this in the eighteenth century.[20] Buchanan Hamilton's survey in Bengal and Bihar referred to arhatiyas receiving goods from merchants and disposing of them by commission, assuming responsibility for the transaction. They were men of credit and were able to give this guarantee. Hamilton also identified small town bankers as arhatiyas, who had links with big mahajans, or bankers, in Patna and Benaras. They undertook sales and purchases for them on commission and realized their dues by approaching specific bankers for hundis, which they then sold to local merchants for cash. Local merchants, on their part, needed bills for sending remittances to Patna and Benaras. Evidently, in such a scenario, arhatiyas forged links between traders and bankers and 'formed the crucial link in the marketing chain from the producer in the village to the exporting firm in the port'.[21]

According to Ray, the system of arhat was a distinct form of commercial organization that took the place of wholesale trading.[22] It was an interlocking system of agency sustained by credit and owed its enduring vitality due to the inherent system of risk distribution. Under the system, losses in transit never fell on the consignor but were taken up by the consignee—only bad debts fell on the consignor. The system was supported by a system of market information, which was crucial when it came to the operations of hundis, or bills of exchange, the rates of which differed according to regional trade balances and which bankers had to remain abreast of.

The Hundi: The Driver of the Bazaar

Simply defined, the hundi was a bill of exchange that traders used to remit proceeds of trade and to finance their operations. Europeans were not unfamiliar with this instrument, which was seen as a marvellous example of trust and reciprocity on which pre-modern commerce depended. There were different categories of hundis: darshani (payable on sight), mudatti (payable after a specified period of time) and shahjogi (one that involved the guarantee of payment by a respectable merchant or shah).[23] Darshani hundis, according to Ray, were drawn by a seller of goods on the buyer, requesting him to pay on sight the banker or the merchant through whom the bill was negotiated. The mudatti hundis were used to borrow funds. *Hundiwals*, or holders of hundis, raised money from the bazaar by discounting it in the market with their own endorsement; hundis were bought and sold and could carry several endorsements. All arhatiyas drew and discounted hundis; some of them were bankers themselves. In other words, goods were bought and sold with credit raised and sent via hundis. Hundis and arhats were therefore inextricably connected. As Tirthankar Roy has demonstrated, the business of arhats, i.e., of facilitating the transaction between the producer and the final buyer, represented a new type of brokerage, for they guaranteed the hundis or credit instruments through which trade transactions were conducted between multiple levels of buyers and sellers.[24] Hundis did not operate in rural markets at the bottom of the chain, as peasants secured hard cash from arhats or forward traders in the market towns, then transported their produce to market towns and inland centres via the hundi and transportation network, which was operated by shroffs and arhats. A small proportion of the produce dispatched by rail was intended for export and entered, in the process, another world, leaving the bazaar far behind. Yet it was the bazaar and its men that ensured distribution of produce through the country and generated huge profits for men at the top and sufficient returns for those in the middle.

Commission agency and banking were thus closely allied activities—the arhat (commission agent) borrowed money from shroffs (bankers); the latter were seen to be more accommodating than formal banks because they only demanded a marginal amount of the goods pledged and were content having the keys to the warehouse, unlike banks, which insisted on putting their own locks on the warehouse doors. Arhats sent goods to other arhats in larger towns, and payments were made through darshani hundis supported by railway receipts. Thus, by the end of the nineteenth century, the railway network emerged as a major element in the distribution system serving the domestic and export markets—rail receipts along with hundi chittis were common mechanisms for the movement of inland trade. Ironically, but predictably, when there were breaches of agreement, we find information on how the system worked.[25] For instance, we have the case of Bansidhar Lakshminarayan vs Jwalaprasad Gayaprasad, wherein the former drew attention to several lapses and anomalies in the railway receipt that had accompanied hundis worth Rs 3000. It was pointed out that while Lakshminarayan had paid the amount of the shahjogi hundis, the railway receipt for the supply of linseed oil turned out to be a forgery and had never been issued. At this, the plaintiffs contended that their interests needed protection and demanded a reversal of the payment. They argued that according to well-established custom among shroffs, the shah who obtains payment of a hundi that turns out to be forged is required to refund the amount of the hundi with interest, unless he produces the actual drawer or the person who committed the fraud. Without going into details of the case and what the court ordained in terms of defining the shahjogi hundi, what is immediately obvious is how hundis and rail receipts constituted the nuts and bolts of the distribution system and how a huge volume of credit-supported transactions was in circulation.[26] We also have testimonies from bankers that hundis of different kinds were a protective and enabling mechanism to help the less successful merchants. *Maheshwari Jati ka Itihas*, a community history written in 1940, made this point explicitly when it said that hundis were key to the success of the community—that hundi transactions were conducted with great expertise,[27] that they even rented out hundis for insurance brokers (hundi bhada) and that family members who did not have adequate means to sustain their business were given mudatti hundis (payable after a designated period) as a resource for a start-up.

Yet the hundi, the classic instrument of the bazaar, extolled by British commentators at various times, did not enjoy the unreserved support of the imperial administration that refused to give it equivalence with other negotiable instruments. Although a key pillar of the bazaar, the hundi was unlike an English bill— namely that it was not unconditional. Under the English practice, a bill was drawn by an exporter upon a certain bank, which, acting under instructions from the importer's bank, accepted such bills provided they were drawn in accordance with the terms of the credit. These bills bore the evidence that they were drawn in good faith against actual goods duly dispatched from one trade centre to the other. In the case of hundis, there was nothing to show that they were drawn against commercial goods; they were more like cheques. To confound the situation further, there were many types of hundis, and here lay the difficulty. How were these to be reconciled when disputes had to be resolved? There were darshani hundis, mudatti hundis and shahjogi hundis. There were variations in form too. Hundis, like premodern letters, carried the names of gods and religious salutations, and the names of the drawer and drawee on the obverse and reverse, respectively. They could be discounted and re-discounted several times, and the endorser of the hundi was liable to the holder for its payment, though he could make a special endorsement called *sira* to the effect that if the hundi was not cashed by the drawee, it could be presented for payment to a specific person. This provision enabled its author to escape from liability, unless the payment was refused by both the drawee and the person intended to take the drawee's place. These variations and the recourse to custom made it difficult for the colonial state to treat the instrument at par with other bills under the Negotiable Instruments Act of 1881, which formalized the distinction between indigenous and formal banking.[28]

Apologists for indigenous banking maintained that hundis were key to the successful transactions of the bazaar and that these played a wider social role for the larger community. We have already noted how hundis and credit notes were used in the marketing of goods and how, along with rail receipts, featured as an important component in the marketing system. In the course of the depositions that marked the banking inquiry commissions in the 1930s, bankers maintained that their work was like a public good and insisted that their hundis be accorded the same status as that of cheques and other negotiable instruments. Many of them worked for reform from within and sponsored the standardization of hundi writing protocols and practices. This came around the first quarter of the twentieth century, by which time the bazaar had expanded and found it possible to stage itself as a key player in the economy of the interwar years.

Expansion of the Bazaar in the Interwar Period and the Great Leap Forward

The interwar years were crucial for the catapulting of Indian industry and manufacture. The extraordinary emergency situation characterizing the war when Britain was forced to focus on the war effort resulted in the introduction of measures that gave a fillip to Indian capital and industry. The decline of imports ensured Indian capital the advantages of a big domestic market, while the decision to go in for a measure of protective discrimination by the tariff board gave Indian industry a chance to expand and consolidate itself. It also impacted the bazaar at the top end with the Birla Brothers, who started out as jute suppliers to European companies, assuming charge for jute shipments on their own bat. Subsequently, they started exports of oil seeds, tea, rice and shellac and imported Burma rice and coal. Why this is worth mentioning is because the bazaar was now beginning to penetrate the formal domain of business so far held by multinationals and Europeans. The fact that the war and the interwar years loosened the grip of British capital on the economy released opportunities for those men of the bazaar who had started as arhats and sarrafs entering the formal business and even manufacturing sector. Besides, this increased speculation in the bazaar as more men speculated in grains, seed and jute. This is not to suggest that the Great Depression that intervened in the 1930s did not impact the Indian economy and agricultural sector, but ironically, it also undermined the efforts of the Europeans to penetrate the inland for their goods. Due to costs going up, several import–export firms went bankrupt and suspended their operations, and the ones that remained relied even more heavily on commission agents.[29]

It was not as though the bazaar had no potential for transformation or that it could not serve as a springboard for expansion. Not only did it support the colonial enclave and sustain India's international trade flows, it also served the needs of the domestic economy, whose operations generated low profit margins amid risks. It was here that the indigenous sector with its traditional devices stepped in and rendered its presence ubiquitous in all the middle-tier towns of northern, central and western India. These were part of the fraternity of what Ritu Birla describes as vernacular capitalists who were seen as 'outsiders to modern market ethics', and whose practices, especially *satta*, (betting or gambling) were seen as irrational and irresponsible by colonial authorities. As Birla points out, from 1914, when gambling came under scrutiny and was redefined, 'indigenous futures markets, which were wholly identified with risk-taking, were thought to promise fast windfall profits to an unsuspecting and ill-educated public'.[30] A hundred-and-forty-five surveys were conducted, but these did not end speculative practices. The same applied to hundi-related disputes, although by the first quarter of the twentieth century, indigenous bankers considered reforming the practice from within while insisting on its utility before banking inquiry commissions.

As an entity in the larger story of India's business, the bazaar at first sight may appear to be somewhat incongruous. Here was a space where a dense network of personalized connections and credit transfers fuelled and funded a gigantic flow of goods and commodities, some destined for global markets, others for domestic consumption. Thousands of transactions, innumerable goods mostly agriculturally produced, shipped and transported along railway lines, stocked and taken care of in godowns and warehouses, speculation and forwards trading in full spate all speak to a bustling and rugged business milieu. While it was not regulated in the same way as modern markets were and its chief instruments, the hundi, did not enjoy the equivalence that cheques did, it held its own and generated a huge turnover and provided the apprenticeship for several young men to go to the city, expand their operations, scale them up and diversify to emerge as major businessmen. An impressive and interesting anecdote retold by Narotam Sekhsaria speaks of Govindram Seksaria, born 1888 and not a relative of his, who used his skills in speculation to become an immensely successful cotton trader in Bombay, set up mills and deal in a variety of businesses.[31] This story was not exceptional, nor were bazaarmen impervious to the benefits of reform and improved regulation. They were conscious of their strengths and their strategies, which proved efficacious under the circumstances they operated in, and saw their services in funding the peasant cultivator and harnessing agricultural production as a major contribution. Distributing risks, speculating and taking calculated decisions on the basis of information flows and maintaining stocks were all part of rational business practices, which were the hallmarks of successful enterprise, or what we may wish to call vernacular capitalism. This involved catering to segmented demand, diversification of risks and working with relatively low profit margins but whose aggregation was impressive.

5

Engineering, Power and Transport:
Blazing New Trails

From steel and agricultural produce, we move to the automobile and power generation sector to engage with three major players: the house of T.V. Sundaram Iyengar (TVS), emblematic of the transport and automotive sector; the house of Bajaj, synonymous with the scooter; and finally, Kirloskar, a household name for pumps and diesel engines. In all three cases, the beginnings were humble but decidedly oriented towards public interest and welfare rather than just the pursuit of wealth. In each of these cases, the capital came from not just financial assets but from a passion for engineering and technical skills that held possibilities of capitalization and public benefit. Thus, if TVS pioneered public transport service almost 100 years ago in Madurai, Laxmanrao Kirloskar and his brothers started out with a small bicycle workshop and strongly believed that agricultural tools needed modernization and mechanization as pre-conditions to industrial growth. The choice of our protagonists is informed partly by considerations of location and partly by the nature of the enterprise they invested in; TVS did not come from a trading background, and in analysing his life and experience, we have the benefit of examining the milieu in southern India that is generally seen as a backwater as far as industrial expansion is concerned. On the other hand, we have the case of Jamnalal Bajaj, who was born in penury, adopted by a rich relative and expanded his business only to demonstrate an unusual approach to wealth and its management thanks to his long and deep association with Gandhi. With Laxmanrao Kirloskar too, we find a person starting his life as a schoolteacher but consumed with passion for mechanical drawing and a deep resolve to set up a small-scale engineering workshop. While Bajaj and TVS families invested in the automotive sector and introduced products in the market that enjoyed and continue to enjoy a near iconic status in modern India, the Kirloskars revolutionized agricultural tools and designed the pump drawing from the founder's lifelong interest in mechanical drawings. All of them were remarkable entrepreneurs; they were able to sustain their businesses intergenerationally and stand forward as makers of modern India. They exhibited extraordinary enthusiasm for new ideas and their implementation, enjoyed taking risks and above all, kept consumer satisfaction at the core of their activities. This was not fundamentally different from the experiences of Godrej, as we have seen in a previous chapter, but what is important about the comparison is to reiterate the entanglement of the emerging passion for science and technology with enterprise and manufacture that went far beyond the pursuit of wealth.

Early Beginnings: The Southern Context

While western India, for historical reasons, was the nucleus for trade and manufacture, southern India was markedly different, with industrialization experiencing a delayed start. It was not as though European agency houses and Indian commission businesses did not have roots in the Madras Presidency, but it wasn't until the swadeshi movement of 1905 that local groups began to seriously invest in manufacture. As Dwijendra Tripathi notes, apart from some local Muslim traders who acquired shares in the Binny & Co. cotton companies, most of the moneyed classes were reluctant to step forward. It was only during the swadeshi agitation that a spirit of enterprise gripped the imagination of individual families who entered the banking sector to begin with; the Canara Bank, the South Indian Bank, the Indian Bank and the Bank of Tanjore being important instances in point. There were also experiments in insurance and the shipping business.[1]

The relatively slow pace of indigenous industrial activity in the south was due to its specific configurations. For one, the influence of European capital was deep and pervasive. On the other hand, the region had several influential princely states whose intervention was not insignificant in helping articulate a clear economic agenda. Mysore, Hyderabad and even a small state like Ramnad came up with important contributions while aligning their activities to the larger mandate of the imperial authorities. At the same time, the region witnessed the expansion of cash crop cultivation[2]—groundnut, paddy and cotton—that helped dominant communities accumulate capital and contemplate a transition from trading and commerce to industry. There were infrastructural demands as well, as cash crop cultivation led to the establishment of small manufacturing units like dessicators, gins and presses on oil and rice mills, besides generating a demand for power. Not surprisingly, these persuaded enterprising individuals to step forward and capitalize on the emerging opportunities.

Interestingly, the communities coming forward were not from traditional trading backgrounds—agrarian communities (Kammas and Naidus) as well as Brahmin groups made their mark as entrepreneurs. For the latter, the excitement of using scientific and technical knowledge to initiate ventures that had a public profile seems to have worked as a catalyst. Take the case of the Seshayee brothers, who emerged as pioneers in the field of electrical lighting and automobile engineering. V. Seshayee and R. Seshayee were not real brothers but genuine partners, sharing an extraordinary passion for scientific learning and its application. Both were brothers in spirit and were consumed by their mutual interest in engineering. They went to St Joseph's High School in Trichy. V. Seshayee's aptitude and sincerity impressed the Jesuit fathers in the school who helped him with scholarships. The advent of new technologies after the war, namely electrical wiring and automobile engineering, appealed to their imagination. While R. Sehsayee was able to visit Singapore and formally improve his understanding, the other Seshayee worked presumably in the South Indian Railways, for we are told in virtually all the accounts that his wiring skills came to the notice of Mr Winter, the chief electrical and signals engineer. Seshayee was taken under his wing. He honed his skills so much so that he was able to design the 'block' system used by the railways. The passion for wiring and repair was such that with his friends he set up a small workshop that undertook repairs until the return of R. Seshayee from Singapore. Both of them were now determined to go beyond what they had learnt, and decided to invest in a business venture. The result was the formation of Seshayee Brothers Limited. There was now no turning back, and what followed was an impressive record of work that ranged from lighting palaces to repairing and running a lucrative passenger transport service. Known as Periyavar (the elder) and Chinnavar (the younger), their reputation in the business of oil engines, generation, automobile repairs and electrical wiring spread rapidly thanks to a couple of lucrative commissions coming from the states of Ramnad and Travancore. When the Raja of Ramnad got them to install a generator set for lighting up his palace, they did so with such gusto that temples (Madurai and Rameshwaram) and large, landed mansions in Chettinad came forward with similar orders. From here, the move to providing gensets to run movie halls or rice mills was a natural progression, and it was only a matter of time before the company would come to dominate the power generation and electrification industry.[3]

What this brief overview of an individual venture suggests is the changing mood of individuals and even groups towards business activity that was no longer seen as an exclusive prerogative of the trading community. It also indicates how, from within a middle-class professional group, the interest in converting expertise and service into a business venture was growing and how circumstances enabled this to materialize. This is clear with our protagonists, the TVS family as well. Inspired by a speech by Eardley Norton, a well-known lawyer on entrepreneurship, T.V. Sundaram Iyengar, a qualified lawyer who flirted with a small business in timber, failed and joined a bank as a clerk until his aborted promotion persuaded him to quit his job only to reinvest in timber with the small inheritance he got after his father's demise. The trade turned out to be profitable, giving him both capital and reputation and an appetite for profit. Collaborating with a local businessman and philanthropist, Bahadur Khan Nawaz Sahib, he started a bus service in 1912, which gained reputation as being punctual, fast and comfortable. It was also perhaps the first passenger bus service in the country, running between Madurai and Devakottai. The 102-km ride cost a princely Rs 4 but came with a free meal. It would seem that all that was required to start a bus service was permits from regional transport authorities and the Central Road Traffic Board.[4] Within a year, passenger bus rides had become so popular that several new operators rushed in and undercut fares to such an extent that TVS had to stop its operations and shift to a new route—Pudukottai to Thanjavur. Going by the anecdotal information we have on TVS, it would seem that he was open to any innovation for improving services; he took responsibility for maintaining bus routes and employed local boys to collect horseshoes and nails lying on the road until the system itself was modernized. Evidently nothing was trivial enough for him to oversee; every detail merited attention so as to guarantee the satisfaction of the customer. Also, the condition of the roads that did not really suit vehicular traffic warranted business diversification. To reduce maintenance costs, TVS had to double up as a road contractor and invest in the distribution of tyres and truck components. The slow and incremental gains that TVS made in terms of capital accumulation and expertise catapulted him to becoming a road king of sorts. In 1923, he became a subdealer for Chevrolet, and that was also the time when T.V. Sundaram Iyengar and Sons was established. In 1929, TVS & Sons was incorporated as a private company with his five sons joining the business. The same year saw the company acquire the General Motors dealership for Madurai, Ramnad, Tirunelveli and Pudukottai. Despite the depression, sales exceeded expectations, consolidating the reputation of the firm. This stood the family in good stead in later years too, as it opened doors to opportunities. In the pursuit of his business, TVS also fulfilled and gave expression to a vision of social empowerment; he is said to have taken barely literate farm boys and equipped them with some basic skills, such as reading mechanical drawings, training to be drivers, fitters and conductors, performing to time, entering logbooks and transitioning to a professional existence without formal degrees and certificates.[5] This was a case of business and stewardship oriented to a larger social mandate.

Expansion From the Interwar Years to Free India: Fathers and Sons

As we have noted in previous chapters, the war years were especially significant in providing a boost to Indian industrialization. Whether it was the import substitution drive or the growing demand that Indian products enjoyed in the world market enabling major industrial houses (Tata and Birla) to capture a huge segment of the manufacturing sector, the fact was that the interwar years spurred young men to try their hand in business. For those like TVS, who did not come from a traditional trading background, the excitement was in engaging with engineering as a practice and turning a profit from it. Just as we saw with the Seshayee brothers, the potential for turning a passion for scientific and technical knowledge into a lucrative business was apparent in the case of TVS and his sons, who responded to the needs the war years threw up. Thus, scarcity of petrol during the war years led to the designing of a gas plant to help run vehicles with charcoal gas. Similarly, to overcome the rubber shortage and trim the tyre bills of its fleet, TVS opened a re-treading factory in Pudukottai that made belts for Ford and Chevrolet. Thus, by the end of the war, the firm had established its reputation as a major transport player, dealing with the purchase and sale of cars, spares and accessories, and as the managing agent of several allied transport companies. In the succeeding decades before and after Independence, the business was expanded and organized around Sundaram Motors Division and Madras Auto Service division, with the shares of TVS and Sons being held by the four sons of Iyengar and their family members.[6]

The development of the automobile industry after Independence guaranteed a measure of business for the group. An emerging automotive market attested by the establishment and expansion of Hindustan Motors, Tata Motors, Ashok Leyland (formerly Ashok Motors) and The Premier Automobiles Limited meant that an ancillary industry came into being as spare parts and automotive accessories and auto-components grew in demand. This did not, however, automatically translate into opportunities for doing business thanks to the restrictive regime under which enterprises operated in the years of the Licence Raj referred to earlier. In the 1960s, the group embarked on a rapid expansion of the auto component sector and even made a bid to acquire land (in Padi) to house new units, namely Wheels India Limited and Brakes India Limited. These companies emerged as a strong bulwark to the emerging automobile industry.[7] In 1963, one of the sons, T.S. Santhanam, moved to Madras and spearheaded the group's entry into the automobiles spare parts trade in the form of the Madras Auto Service and India Motor Parts and Accessories. The exponential growth of the business rested on the financial support the family seems to have marshalled—Wheels India was set up with an investment of Rs 20 crore with promoters TVS & Sons and the British collaborator Dunlop contributing

Rs 25 lakh to the equity and with financial institutions making good the remaining balance.[8]

The success of TVS and sons relied on individual talent and expertise built over the years, as well as an imagination that saw India and Indians on the move and wanted aspiring young people to acquire vehicles easily. From here came Sundaram Finance Ltd. (SFL), the brainchild of T.S. Santhanam, which offered easy financing options and helped broaden the demand for automobiles and two-wheelers. In fact, his expertise, as well as that of the family, was acknowledged by the government as it drafted policies on transport development.[9] Even when nationalization policies were implemented and that directly impacted the running of services associated with the firm, we find T.S. Santhanam at the forefront of negotiations in 1968. He made a fervent plea on behalf of transport operators who had worked to develop the industry not to speak of his family enterprise, the Southern Roadways bus service in Madurai. The terms of nationalization that followed were reasonable, and one could also say that the foundations for bus transport in Tamil Nadu were laid by private operators such as TVS & Sons.

The operative word in the success of TVS and its various concerns was 'Sons'. Each one of T.V.S. Iyengar's children demonstrated his mettle to create an empire. Santhanam paved the way for setting up the Madras Auto Service and India Motor Parts and Accessories for the distribution of auto spare parts, accessories and garage equipment. T.S. Krishna (1910–75) was responsible for inventing a gas plant that generated charcoal gas for use in automobiles, while his son Suresh Krishna set up the Sundaram Fasteners and Sundaram Brake Linings company, the former undertaking the manufacture of high-tensile fasteners, cold-formed/extruded parts for auto and non-auto applications and automotive powder metal parts. The family mantle was effectively held by sons and grandsons who were in charge of the four main subsidiaries: Southern Roadways Limited, Sundaram Industries Private Limited, Sundaram Fasteners Limited and Sundaram Textiles Limited.

Besides the contributions made by individual family members in blazing the industrial trail and in maintaining excellent relations with the state government, there was the organizational factor as well that stood the company in good stead until the 1990s and was even identified as a major factor in the success of the enterprise. What gave the company its cohesiveness was its organizational structure. The parent company held the reins as it promoted virtually all the other companies in the group, especially the public limited companies. TVS & Sons, along with two of its subsidiaries, Sundaram Industries Pvt. Ltd (SIPL) and Southern Roadways Pvt. Ltd (SRPL), held a considerable proportion of the share capital of the rest of the group companies, the exceptions being Sundaram Ltd and Sundaram Finance Ltd. Hence, these three companies were the holding companies of the group. Until 1973, only male lineal descendants (meaning male descendants in the male line only) could hold shares and be members of the company. After 1973, the word 'male' was deleted, and the clause read as 'only lineal descendants of T.V. Sundaram Iyengar shall be members'. In 1979, this clause was also deleted to remove the restriction and conform to the requirements of a public company. A special resolution was passed defining a 'family' and laying down conditions under which decisions could be undertaken in a board meeting. According to this resolution, the 'family' strictly comprised the four sons of T.V. Sundaram Iyengar and their spouses. Even though the company document filed with the Registrar of Companies classified the holding of shares among three components, namely, bodies corporate, directors and their relatives, and other top fifty shareholders, in fact the corporate bodies are nothing but small private limited companies promoted by one or other of the four families with shares held by the family members themselves.[10]

The success and pre-eminence of the group may then be ascribed to both the context in which they started and consolidated their ventures and the imagination they collectively embraced. Based in Tamil Nadu, the group responded to the industrial policies of successive governments, which according to several scholars, have successfully worked with business groups to secure economic growth. This did not mean that business groups were able to wield political power, but only that they responded to industry-friendly state governments. We could also infer that business houses like TVS were committed to the idea of industrial growth as a tool to social upliftment and to improvements via research and development. Until the second generation, the group companies worked together almost as a single unit with multiple transactions among them as they were part of the auto-ancillary value chain. They managed the group companies and passed them on to their successors. With the third generation, there were some disputes and disagreements leading to litigation. Where the family showed a real degree of statesmanship was not allowing the disagreements to degenerate into an open split. One of the reasons why this did not happen was because there were complex cross-holdings between the group companies run by different family members. Additionally, the group companies were part of the value chain of the auto-ancillary industry and had plenty of business transactions between them. Economist Padmini Swaminathan suggests that the group was able to hold a semi-monopolistic position with its goods thanks to an excellent system of distributorship .[11]

Thus, even when disputes and litigation threatened the family and its unity in the 1990s, the members appreciated the importance of concentrating on the opportunities for growth that the decade saw. The growth of foreign investment in India post liberalization meant that family members had to set aside disputes and strategize to be able to capitalize on exports by leveraging their brand value. On the other hand, there was enough space for successors to set up their own companies; however, it was only in 2020 that the TVS group decided to formally divide the empire among fourth-generation family members. The group, as mentioned before, has been well served with successors, each of them investing in education and cultivating an open and inclusive attitude to risk-taking and innovation. Take, for instance, the case of Suresh Krishna, the founder of Sundaram Fasteners, who confronted major challenges in building the business, especially when it came to acquiring foreign technology in a highly restrictive business environment. He coped with this largely by adopting a transparency in transactions that helped deflect labour agitation and in winning the confidence of foreign investors and subsequently going on to receive the 'Best Supplier Award' from General Motors. He carried the spirit of enterprise that TVS was known for, began like his forbears in a small shed in Ambattur to make fasteners and learnt painstakingly what customers wanted and what quality levels were required at international levels. It is worth remembering that businessmen like Krishna have straddled two worlds in their lifetime: the world of restrictive enterprise that was focused on import substitution based on an artificially pegged value of the rupee, which had no bearing to its market value that was hampered by bureaucratic roadblocks, and the world of liberalization and opening of the economy. Yet he persevered, and his curiosity about how things worked stood to his advantage. In an interview, he pointed out, how during his travels, he would actually learn from 'the nuts and bolts people', who, in his own words, 'gave technology out of kindness . . . whether it was Lamson & Sessions Co. in Cleveland, Republic Steel or Canada Steel'. The process helped the company grow organically and at its own pace; its strength derived from this and the fact that it was 'completely Indian in terms of management, and it was completely Indian in terms of where it wanted to go not only in the Indian economy but also in the international economy'.[12]

Accessing Suresh Krishna's experiences, thanks to an interview he gave for the Harvard Business School 'Creating Emerging Markets' project (19 December 2012),[13] gives us graphic details of the difficulties that he and all other businessmen encountered and how they pulled off their business under extremely difficult conditions and how the family name helped open doors a little bit even though it was an uphill struggle thereafter. Reflecting on how he started his stint with Sundaram Fasteners, he mentions how penetrating the supply market was difficult even after initial access. His first meeting with a surly development manager at Tata Motors in Jamshedpur was a disaster, but he stuck to his mission and met the general manager, who took a shine to him and asked him to manufacture a special fastener. What followed was an exhilarating experience in the workshop, where working at breakneck speed enabled the manufacture of a special fastener in just four days. He took this back to Jamshedpur, the manager was impressed and allowed him to choose a bulk order. Predictably, Suresh Krishna chose an order for Tata Motors, which immediately alienated his competitor, who baulked and threatened to withdraw all supplies, forcing Tata Motors to reduce the order given to Sundaram Fasteners. This came as a disappointment but did not deter the young entrepreneur, for he found through this transaction a firm entry point for sales of his product. Given the massive constraints he faced in terms of undercapitalization, a non-existent customer base, and a restrictive business regime because of government controls and policies regarding what was to be categorized as a product for small scale, any opportunity was a heaven send, which he made full use of.

Reading the interview retrospectively brings out the extraordinary acumen and perseverance businessmen demonstrated at a time when doing business was not easy. For Suresh Krishna, the challenge was compounded by the fact that he had no joint venture partner; he was manufacturing a product and then hawking it and doing so without the 'advantages' small-scale units had. As he points out,

> I had to get an exemption from the government to make a small-scale industry product. Added to that was the fact that I belonged to an MRTP (Monopolies and Restrictive Trade Practices act) house. And finally, it was a major undertaking, because of TVS. Everything went against me. Every strike was against me.[14]

As a result, when he urged for expansion, the government refused, as they did not appreciate the fundamental difference between fasteners used for windows, which were manufactured by small-scale people, and high-tensile, high-alloy fasteners meant for automotive engineering. Finally, it was only by agreeing to offload a certain percentage of shares to the public that he made headway, and the rest was history! It helped that because of labour issues faced by several competitors, Sundaram Fasteners grew steadily and then, after 1991, exponentially.

In reviewing the lives and labour of the founder and one of his successors, the abiding impression is one of extraordinary commitment to a cause, the ability to persevere despite odds and to maintain an impeccable reputation for ensuing quality. The group had an excellent track record of industrial relations, virtually no strikes and a culture of transparency and honesty. In many ways, the group like that of Godrej, whom we have studied earlier, participated in enterprise as a social project that appreciated the importance of honouring artisanal activity and expertise and of seeking advanced technology, while maintaining a uniquely Indian business culture. This did not necessarily mean it was predisposed to conservatism (an accusation often levelled against the group) but merely that it was cautious and prudent in husbanding its resources and committed to taking all its stakeholders together in a collective mission. This culture was not born in a day but cultivated consistently despite the odds of an interventionist state, capital constraints and intergenerational tensions that surfaced. Like the other stalwart business families we have looked at, this family too participated in a real project of social commitment and responsibility, making business more than just the pursuit of wealth.

The Gandhian Capitalist: Jamnalal Bajaj and His Legacy

Jamnalal Bajaj (1889–1942), self-styled as an uneducated Jat and extolled as a true Gandhian for living life according to principles of integrity and honesty, is not an easy figure to reconstruct. Adopted twice in his life, first by Seth Bachhraj and then by Mahatma Gandhi, his life and sensibility reflect unusual hues. He was a true Gandhian committed to truth and charity, believed in the idea of trusteeship, ran his business strictly on ethical principles, refusing to compromise on any occasion, maintained a circle of close associations with prominent westernized businessmen in Bombay, and till the end of his life showed very little interest in money as a personal asset. Born to a poor family in Sirohi in Japiur state, he was adopted by a wealthy relative, Seth Bachhraj. Legend has it that to mark the adoption of the child, the seth agreed to bore a well for the village, an act of altruism that was prescient of the child's future. The child had only a rudimentary formal education but turned out to be an autodidact and capable of absorbing knowledge. Sensitive to a fault, young Jamnalal reacted badly to his father's remonstrances and allusions to the fortune he had inherited. On one occasion, he ran away from home, leaving behind a letter where he expressed his utter detachment with money and worldly possessions, which he said distorted human personality.[15]

How did such a child turn out to be a big businessman, turning his inheritance into a massive enterprise that exceeded what he had inherited? As T.V. Parvate, one of his biographers, points out, 'Jamnalal had inherited an estate worth only five or six lakhs of rupees, but on account of his ability, foresight, honesty and integrity, he increased his business to such an extent that he could spend more than Rs 25 lakh in charity'.[16] While we cannot trace every step he took and the mechanics of his business dealings, we can identify the dynamics of the context in which he operated and how he cultivated consciously values of integrity and responsibility that his subordinates had to respect and eventually absorb. These certainly helped Jamnalal establish a reputation and accumulate huge capital reserves that subsequently his able sons were able to invest in manufacture. Jamnalal remained not just an enterprising trader, cutting his teeth in the cotton trade and sarrafi business, but eventually setting up sugar mills and acquiring steel mills, like the Mukand Iron and Steel Engineering Works. What is especially remarkable about Jamnalal Bajaj's life and work is how he busted all stereotypes about businessmen and actively translated Gandhian ideals into management and business principles that helped him steer and steward a competitive trade like that in cotton in the twentieth century. Each of these principles was an affirmation of the principle of honesty that would guide every act, from saying no to a potential customer when you could not meet your obligation to maintaining a scrupulous record of accounts that were not intended to obfuscate but reveal the exact situation and to maintaining quality control even if it was not profitable.[17]

The traditional business of the Bachhraj family appears to have been cotton and banking. Its antecedents lay in the demand for Indian raw cotton that Britain needed during the years of the American Civil War that disrupted cotton supplies to Lancashire. The brief window that the disruption offered was enough for Indian trading groups to invest in cotton and participate in its extensive distribution all across western and central India. Seth Bachhraj's family was part of the migrating Marwari network. Bachhraj's father Sevakram had migrated to Nagpur and started trading and moneylending; his son Bachhraj diversified the business and turned to the purchase and sale of cotton bales. Establishing branches in Hinganghat, Arvi, Sindi, Pulgaon and other places around Wardha, he established his reputation as a senior trader. Being a childless couple, he and his wife made a trip to their ancestral village, where they adopted Jamnalal. As Bachhraj passed away when Jamnalal was barely sixteen, the young man had to shoulder his extensive business—no easy task for someone who wasn't predisposed to commercial pursuits. But he was an astute young man and decided to play the game on a fair wicket, bringing to the table what seemed perfectly sensible and virtuous ideas but which struck most as outlandish and stupid. For one, young Jamnalal abhorred duplicity and dishonesty and came down heavily on adulteration practices that involved the deliberate wetting of cotton to add to its weight but compromising its quality in the long run. He insisted on his bales being stamped with his signature 'Water Free' with excellent results. Buyers, especially foreign buyers, bought their supplies from him even at higher prices. An equally impressive, even if quixotic, innovation was his refusal to sell cotton samples that he even received for sampling in his storage space, which involved huge amounts of labour in classifying, storing and accounting for. By this time Jamnalal had moved to Bombay where he had his office that worked as an agency for other people's goods.[18]

These small acts of innovation helped establish Jamnalal's reputation as an unusual, honest and forthright businessman in Bombay. By this time, roughly after the years of the swadeshi movement, Bombay had emerged as an influential nucleus of industrial capital, with major players like the Tatas floating and acquiring companies and inviting subscriptions in the capital market. Impressed by his principles, the house of Tata offered 5000 shares of the Sassoon Group of Textiles at the face value of Rs 10, whereas the market share was Rs 14. Jamnalal politely declined the offer and chose to buy at the market price. This made such an impression on the Tatas that when Jamnalal supported the project of an Indian insurance company, the Tatas were willing to back this unequivocally.

If honesty and probity marked Jamnalal's business philosophy, efficiency and management were the hallmarks of his venture. His head office remained in Wardha. He made routine and regular visits to cotton mandis, travelled to Bombay and Calcutta, and developed a reputation for being a smart businessman, ready to transition from being an upcountry trader and entrepreneur to a modern businessman. It would also seem that he valued western education and learning just as he was deeply moved by his encounter with Gandhi and the Mahatma's philosophy. But before that, we must mention an unusual friendship that blossomed with Shrikrishna Jajoo and acted as a catalyst for Jamnalal. A Marwari from a Maheshwari background with an exemplary academic record, Jajoo moved to Wardha to practise as a lawyer and brought with him radical ideas of change and social reform. The association that sprang between the two men saw the materialization of social service projects (such as flood relief) and small-scale social reform and education for the community. He floated the idea of a Marwari college in Bombay and, in the course of his consultations, met with several influential men, including senior British officials who looked at him with favour and appreciation.[19]

By 1913–14, Jamnalal had travelled a far way, from being a diffident, awkward and sensitive young man to one with poise and membership in a social circle that thought on progressive lines. It was in this year that he also faced a family crisis with his business partner, who insisted on the dissolution of the partnership. In the division of assets that followed, Jamnalal was left with house property and stocks of unsold cotton bales, which were hardly guaranteed to generate profits given the crash of cotton prices in the wake of the outbreak of the First World War. The situation gave him sleepless nights and even panic attacks until he drew himself to reaffirming his basic sympathy with the imperial government against Germany. He divided his time between Wardha and Bombay, where he devoted time to philanthropy and re-entering the cotton market, which saw an upswing.[20] Jamnalal's patience, unswerving commitment to integrity, a real passion for social work and openness to liberal influences had stood him in good stead and provided him with a strong foundation for later efforts. What strikes us retrospectively about Jamnalal was his genuine conviction that business ethics had to be reformulated, emphasized and taken seriously, as well as his commitment to supporting scientific and educational projects. The entwining of business and scientific and social projects is what makes our protagonists similar in many ways.

Meeting the Mahatma: Changing Course

Meeting Gandhi and taking up politics changed Jamnalal's life entirely. We do not have many details about when exactly Jamnalal met Gandhi or when he was persuaded by his views and actions on his return from South Africa. However, what is clear is that Jamnalal, like many enterprising businessmen, had benefited from opportunities generated by the war in terms of import substitution and was already part of a political circuit providing donations to the Indian National Congress without entirely severing connections with the British imperial set-up. The impact of Gandhi and his philosophy and politics, however, was transformational and we find Jamnalal almost entirely focused on satyagraha, swadeshi, boycott and social reconstruction. This meant that his business took a back seat, and it was entirely due to the efforts of his staff and managers that the concerns (banking and cotton) continued to do well. In 1920, Bachhraj and company was transformed into a private company limited where influential business partners were roped in. This was in fact an important strategy that not only enabled Jamnalal to enlist the financial support of seniors but also to recruit efficient and competent managers to run his companies. These links proved especially useful when he faced disputes and litigation suits from within the family. His son-in-law, Rameshwar Prasad Nevatia, was particularly astute and enterprising as he took charge of the Karachi branch of the company in 1930. Around the same time, Jamnalal made a major move into manufacturing as he set up the Hindustan Sugar Mills with a capital of Rs 5 lakh and with shares being held by prominent businessmen such as the Birlas and the Ruias. The choice of sugar was both important and challenging; it reflected Jamnalal's accurate reading of the economic situation that was marked by agricultural depression and agrarian discontent, against which the government of India adopted protectionist measures. The recommendations of the tariff board to impose duties on imported sugar meant that exports dwindled and generated opportunities for those who entered the manufacture of sugar, and Jamnalal and his able lieutenants were no exception. In fact, it was as much Rameshwar Prasad's initiative as Jamnalal's that the factory made its mark.[21]

Just as Jamnalal had understood the mechanics of cotton production and imposed stringent measures to prevent adulteration, Rameshwar too familiarized himself with sugar cultivation. For example, he realized that growers preferred to retain their cane for gur, or jaggery, and were reluctant to sell it to factories, partly due to middlemen pocketing the greater part of the proceeds. Rameshwar solved the problem by opting for direct purchases and even persuaded neighbouring factories to demarcate a specific area from which they would draw their cane directly. Not only did this improve logistics related to haulage and cost, it also incentivized the production of better varieties of cane. The factory itself was run in accordance with Jamnalal's principles of fair play.[22]

The 1930s saw the firm acquire more assets. In 1937, having given up the idea of buying a textile mill that went against Gandhi's principles of abiding by handloom, Jamnalal acquired an interest in Mukand Iron and Steel Works Limited. Between 1937 and the end of the war, Jamnalal seems to have lost interest. We hear of his ennui and dejection. He resigned as chairman and director of three big businesses—steel, sugar and real estate—and preferred to leave these affairs to his son and son-in-law Rameshwar Das Birla. Partition was another major blow as the family lost considerable assets. How were these dealt with? We must remember that Jamnalal was an activist dedicated to the nationalist cause, that his time was divided and that he was an activist and philanthropist first and a businessman later. But this did not mean that he had neglected to train his sons and family members or that his ethical values did not stand them in good stead in the future. In fact, if anything stands out in both the lives of Jamnalal and his son and grandson, it is the seriousness of intent, commitment to values and the ability to absorb from circumstances they found themselves in. Whether it was exposure to the Gandhian ashram in Sevagram or to the rough and tumble of nationalist politics in which Jamnalal and his son Kamalnayan participated wholeheartedly or indeed from foreign travel and exposure, the Bajaj men were quick to learn and absorb skills and deploy them whenever it was required.

Sons and Successors: The Vision of Bajaj

On 11 February 1942, Jamnalal Bajaj died, leaving his affairs to be taken up by his son and loyal family members. Kamalnayan, his son, was more than equipped to deal with a challenging situation thanks to the support he had from his uncle and extended family and father's business circle. He was still involved in the nationalist struggle, but by no means was he without initiative; in fact, he was known to speak his mind, referred to as a Gandhian rebel and known to take risks, an absolutely essential prerequisite for being a businessman. He tried his hand at launching a number of small industries but without much success, except perhaps in the case of the Radio Lamps Works, which he acquired in 1954 and which was merged with Bajaj Electricals Ltd in 1960. By this time, Kamalnayan had decided to enter the transport sector and expand Bajaj Auto Ltd, which had been set up in 1945. In 1959, it obtained a licence from the government of India to manufacture two-wheelers and three-wheelers and also a licence from Piaggio to manufacture Vespa scooters in India.

Two questions crop up here, both of which are relevant to the vision of Bajaj and of its subsequent success. Why did Kamalnayan go for the humble scooter? And how did the Italian connection happen, and how did this help the fledgling business? For Kamalnayan, the humble scooter was the vehicle that the common man wanted. In fact, he was so committed to the requirements of the average customer that he resisted price augmentation. Given the low spending power of his consumer base, he kept prices low, something that the Bajaj ads of the 1970s reflect quite clearly. The Italian connection derived from the fact that in his father's lifetime, the firm had imported scooters for Enrico Piaggio and that from the 1960s, there was a technical partnership between the two, as a result of which Bajaj Auto became the licensee for the Vespa brand of scooter. This was sold and assembled in India by licensees such as the Bajaj group.

It was during the 1960s that Indian business began to cut its teeth effectively and respond to new developments that presaged the licence quota system mentioned earlier. In the first decade after Independence, business houses felt encouraged by industrialization plans under the second five-year plan, only to be thwarted by the changing scenario under former prime minister Indira Gandhi, whose agenda was to exercise greater control over the economy and thereby ensure better distribution of wealth. In order to facilitate the funding of populist programmes, a slew of reforms began with the nationalization of banks, followed by the establishment of the Monopolies and Restrictive Trade Practices Commission (MRTC) in 1969, which mandated business groups with assets over Rs 200 crore to undergo scrutiny and apply for permission for further expansion. We will see how these created challenges for Rahul Bajaj, but for now, let us stay with Kamalnayan.[23]

In 1960, Bajaj Auto became a public company when subscriptions to Bajaj Auto started with the Controller of Capital Issues giving his consent on 21 October 1960. Kamalnayan's advantages lay with his access to a solid and reliable network of associates and financiers, and, as the day approached, the directors, Kamalnayan Bajaj, Rameshwar Prasad Nevatia, Viren Shah, Madanmohan R. Ruia, Ramnath Podar, Shantanu L. Kirloskar and M.K. Firodia, had their ears close to the ground of the Bombay Stock Exchange. Bajaj Auto had ten brokers selling the issue: six in Bombay, two in Delhi and one each in Madras and Calcutta. The results were impressive. The Rs 60.10 lakh issue was one of the biggest to hit the market, and soon the issue was oversubscribed. The shares of the company were first listed on the Bombay Stock Exchange in April 1961, and from then on, there was no turning back.[24] The money that was generated was allotted for new machinery to be installed at the Akurdi plant designated for manufacture. There was a lot of catching up to do in terms of innovation in manufacturing and in training his workers and managers. Even before this in 1957, he had started training programmes for workers, managers and engineers. He set store by technical collaboration and innovation. Whether it was in the field of electric equipment or automotive sectors, joint ventures gave him a firm basis to consider expansion and consolidation.

Fighting Odds, Gaining Strides

The 1960s were not an easy period for doing business. There were many vicissitudes, largely on account of the foreign exchange situation, that made imports and technical collaboration difficult. We have already noted how the MRTP Commission mandated business groups with assets worth more than Rs 200 crore having to undergo scrutiny and clearance. Furthermore, there was the Industrial Licensing Act of 1970, which categorized industries on the basis of their assets into core, middle, non-core heavy investment and de-licensed sectors, requiring private industries to be scrutinized and obtain licences to continue their operations. The number of licences needed for big industries, starting from importing supplies to exporting products, was often large, which led to major constraints in their operating potential. Unhealthy competition among companies for licences and corruption ensued. It was under these circumstances that the Bajaj men had to navigate amidst foreign exchange constraints. As a result of the Foreign Exchange Regulation Act (FERA) passed in 1973, multinational investors were required to dilute their share in their Indian subsidiaries to 40 per cent. It also imposed severe restrictions on the exchange of foreign currency among individuals as well as industries.

How did Kamalnayan and his successor Rahul Bajaj deal with the situation? Without compromising their basic ethical stand and abiding by the needs of the customer, they threw themselves into production and used every rule in the book to secure permission to do so. Licences were hard to come by and were exceedingly slow; starting with a modest trickle of licences to make 1000 scooters and autorickshaws a month, in 1962 it increased to 30,000 scooters and 6000 autorickshaws. Requests for further expansion became a recurrent feature until, in 1971, the government approved an increase of capacity to 48,000 scooters although this remained a dead letter. The company continued to press their case even while they developed three models—Bajaj 150, Bajaj Chetak and Bajaj Super—that replaced the Italian Vespa.[25] Demand for the scooter grew exponentially—the joke was that the waiting period for a vehicle was ten years! Rahul himself seems to have had a personal affinity for the scooter, riding it in Bombay in his youth.

What seems to have worked for Rahul Bajaj (1938–2022), as he admitted in a 2014 interview to Harvard Business School professor Srikant M. Datar, was his commitment to price levels, the availability of a loyal and efficient management team and the openness to technical innovation and improvement. In the interview, he mentions a rear-engine three-wheeler, which was a radical move. He also refers to the success in exporting scooters especially Sri Lanka, which became a 'Bajaj country'.[26] Behind this banter was an extraordinary appreciation for the individual consumer and his requirements. Legend has it that he despaired the growing obesity of middle-class Indians who would no longer be able to sit on his scooters—the aloo paratha demographic![27] The ability to appreciate the pulse of the consumer and the preparedness to go in for innovation and research and development seems to have been the most important factor in the phenomenal success of Bajaj and its scooters after the challenges of the 1970s. From being a scooter licensee to becoming a lead manufacturer of motorcyles, Bajaj Auto became the ultimate roadrunner.

The success story continues today as Bajaj ranks as one of the major players in the Indian market and among the top ten companies in India, with its footprint extended over major sectors that include automobiles and home appliances.[28] In its fiftieth year of operations, it sold ten million vehicles. From licensing the Vespa 150 to launching the Chetak and subsequently the Bajaj M50 and KB100, it has been a singular story of vision, research and the will to reach out to millions of aspirational Indians. Bajaj family members prided themselves on their commitment to the nation and on the cohesiveness of the family firm and the effectiveness of group companies that were important factors in the success of Bajaj.[29] It is also worthwhile remembering that succession disputes were not so marked. Rahul Bajaj mentions how he began very consciously to delegate business power and authority to his sons and whose understanding of the market, especially the trend in favour of motorcycles over scooters, helped. It was not as though there were no disagreements but the overall confidence that the family reposed in the head of the family proved to be decisive. This was by no means exceptional to the Bajaj family, but it is a trait that we will have occasion to elaborate on, especially in the context of splits and breakaways, which happened in virtually every family and which were tided over, each in their own ways. What is striking, whether it was Bajaj or TVS, was the absolute clarity of vision, the passion to pursue a dream and the determination to battle against odds. The extent to which the struggle against the political impacted business ethics and attitudes in the long run is not something we can assess immediately but it is an issue that cannot be overlooked either. Can we actually see the same commitment to social projects by younger business icons compared to their grandfathers or even fathers? Is it even realistic to expect this given the rapid transformation that has occurred in society and societal values and in the social and educational profile of the younger lot?

Of Bicycles, Chaff Cutters and Pumps: The Brothers Kirloskar

We now turn our attention to a very different kind of business enterprise spearheaded not by a business family and not rooted in trade and commercial operations but in a consummate passion for machines and their design and application in agricultural activity. While there are some convergences with the experience of T.V.S. Iyengar and Sons, the specificities of the local context and the Marathi Brahmin business experience are also striking and worthy of attention. Two things are especially important in relation to the emerging discourse on technology and modernization. One was the growing traction for the idea of mechanization and the projection of the technological Indian, and the second was the growing and committed interest in developing the agricultural sector through mechanization. It is useful to remember that from the 1880s there were in Maharashtra the beginnings of an active promotion of the idea of mechanization by middle-class Hindus and of improved agricultural activity. Ross Bassett elaborates this in his work,

The Technological Indian, pointing out how in 1884, M.M. Kunte, the headmaster of Poona High School, addressed a group of middle-class Indians, urging them to embrace mechanization and become blacksmiths. With great rhetorical flourish, he said,

> For eradicating the undesirable and establishing the desirable in society, there is no option but to follow and spread widely the art of mechanization. If you want to eat, be a machinist. If you want to win freedom, you have to learn to be a machinist. If you want to live as luxuriously as our rulers, you have to run the machines. If you want this country to progress like that of England, all of you have to become blacksmiths.[30]

Notwithstanding the unrealism and naivete behind Kunte's speech that Bassett decodes, there is some truth in the fact that middle-class western educated Indians began to imagine a technological India of whom men like Laxman Rao and his son Shantanu were important instances. Both men again worked within a network of local and global connections and contacts that set up a basis for a truly successful entrepreneurial venture.

The attention to agriculture and agricultural reform was thus entirely consistent with the family background that Laxman Rao Kirloskar, a Belgaum-based Karhade Brahmin, belonged to. His family connections enabled him to tap an informal network of contacts that would be of immense value in popularizing his early manufactured products that, in Bassett's words, 'were able to tap into a larger movement for improved scientific agriculture in the Bombay presidency'.[31] Like several service families, Laxman Rao's father was a supervisor under the Bombay Presidency government and had connections with local officials and with the small state of

Aundh, whose ruler would, at a later stage, help out Laxman Rao with money and estate in housing his industrial workshed. From his youth, Laxman Rao demonstrated great talent in mechanical drawings and craft and was allowed to pursue his interests in the J.J. School of Art in Bombay. His partial colour blindness precluded a career in painting, so he turned to a formal study of mechanical design. Subsequently, he took admission in the Victoria Jubilee Technical Institute on a small monthly salary, but where he found an opportunity to make full use of the opportunity to devour publications such as *American Machinist* and *Scientific American*. Passed over for a promotion on apparently racial grounds, he came back to Belgaum to start up with his brother, a small business of selling bicycles and repairing them. The passion for machines took the brothers to new pastures; designing and manufacturing a variety of simple, even rudimentary machine tools like ploughs followed with great energy and enthusiasm.

Why did the brothers turn to the manufacture of ploughs and farm equipment? Here the immediate context was important. It was not as though there was a clearly identifiable market for small machine tools that could facilitate agricultural operations. In fact, we only come across small artisanal initiatives in Punjab, where there were workshops pioneering the manufacture of basic tools such as deep gap cone pulley lathes and deep throat drilling machines that were used for the fabrication of chaff cutters and cane crushers.[32] However, given the emergence of a scientific agricultural movement, Laxman Rao may well have sensed an opportunity and the potential for simple equipment. We are told how, on one occasion, on his return from Aundh, he was approached by a local farmer for repair of agricultural equipment, especially ploughs. His curiosity and obsession with machines took over, and he set out correcting the basic weakness in the equipment. The result was a newly designed plough that became hugely popular encouraging him to think of chaff cutters, sugar cane cutters and pumps. Some of these he was able to exhibit; some were picked up by agricultural enthusiasts. For instance, in 1909, at the inaugural session of the Deccan Agricultural Association, his ploughs and cutters found mention. In the following year, Harold Mann, a leading advocate of scientific agriculture in India, delivered a lecture in the Deccan Agricultural Society and mentioned Kirloskar's ploughs with some approbation. But, just as things seemed to be settling down nicely, Laxman Rao faced challenges when the local municipality forced him to move his workshop. Fortunately for him, his connections with the prince regent of Aundh, who also happened to be a fellow student in Bombay, intervened, gave him land and loaned him capital to set up what became known as Kirloskarvadi. The rest was history as the factory in Kirloskarwadi set out manufacturing pulleys and windlasses (*pavanchakki*), sugar cane crushers and pumps.[33]

The factory in Kirloskarwadi steadily grew even amidst the years of the First World War. These were mixed years, for while there was a demand for ploughs, there were also constraints in the form of the availability of iron. His son, in his autobiography, refers to the perennial shortages that his father and factory faced—pig iron and steel were in short supply, not to speak of the shortage of cash. The brothers persevered, carefully preserving their reputation and their connections with the government. The latter's support was necessary, especially when machinery had to be imported. By 1920, the Kirloskar Brothers went public as a registered company. The initial years were exciting, even heady as it set out making drilling machines, machines making nuts and bolts and paying its shareholders a dividend of 6 per cent. In 1924, it imported a 350-hp gas engine from the United States. Meanwhile, the KK plough was perfected and even sent as an exhibit to the British Empire Exhibition at Wembley Park in London in 1924. Two years down the line, the company came up with its centrifugal pump, a testimony to the boundless passion and energy of Laxman Rao. He seems to have communicated this spirit to his son and family members, who were undaunted and undeterred by the challenges of the cash crunch and uncertain demand during the Depression years and took pride in India's homespun machine revolution.[34]

Laxman Rao was a family man and took pains to encourage talent when he saw it. He spared no efforts in giving them a decent education and a leg up. His was a deeply scientific temperament, something he shared with some publicists like Balaji Prabhakar Modak, who were engaged at this time with the dissemination of science to a larger public through lecture demonstrations and exhibitions.[35] Modak's efforts were directed at creating a scientific temperament through public lectures and demonstrations. It is very likely that Laxman Rao was a product of these times and therefore valued scientific training even if he had been an intuitive learner. His son Shantanu Rao studied in the United States and came back to take the mantle; his other brothers studied at Cornell and MIT and demonstrated the same drive and energy that characterized Laxman Rao. What thus stands out in the family saga of Kirloskar is the fidelity to the idea of scientific progress, technological design and innovation, the pursuit of which would not brook any compromise. It was in part a nationalist dream, in part a love for machines and for using them to help out large sections of the population. Shantanu Kirloskar mentions in his autobiography how, in an altercation with Gandhi, his father was adamant about the need for machines and their benefits for the population. He overrode all arguments that the Mahatma put up and said he was and would remain a machine man.

The years of the Second World War generated new challenges and opportunities. Indian industry enjoyed a degree of government sanction and support as part of the war effort. This meant that the demand for machine tools went up, that licensing agreements to purchase machine tools were made and that technicians from the UK were invited to give Indians assistance. All these worked to the advantage of the company, and it expanded its operations, setting up Kirloskar Oil Engines Limited (KOEL) in Poona and Kirloskar Electric Company Limited (KECL) in Bangalore. These were spearheaded by Shantanurao Laxmanrao Kirloskar (1903–94) under whom the company registered a massive increase.

A Worthy Son and An Outspoken Industrialist

Shantanurao Laxmanrao Kirloskar (SLK) was aware of the responsibilities he had to shoulder and an enthusiastic champion of industry that he believed was vital for the emancipation of the country. In every way, he was touched by the enthusiasm of his father, while his training overseas in engineering gave him a new vision for planning the future of his father's enterprise. His life and labour spanned several crucial decades after Independence, and amid grave challenges, he took the company to great heights, achieving an extraordinary growth rate. Not only did he establish new ventures, such as KOEL in Poona and KECL in Bangalore, but he also opted for an export strategy with remarkable success. In several countries, especially in the Middle East, the very name

Kirloskar stood for engine! He also initiated major international collaborations at a time when bureaucratic red-tapism, foreign exchange controls and the Licence Raj were at their height. Aiding him and his agenda were an indomitable spirit and passion that he had inherited from his father, contacts with international players and the ability to leverage the government.

For the sake of convenience, we will look at SLK's career in several phases, one in the 1950s and 1960s, then after 1965 and leading up to the opening of the Indian economy and finally under conditions of liberalization. We will not go into technical details about what he produced and manufactured; simply highlight the major achievements and the strategies undertaken to realize them. We will pay special attention to the context in which this happened and the nature of the legacy that he left behind. It is useful to remember that SLK was an outspoken critic of the planned economy and import substitution model that was put in place over the 1950s and that directly interfered with his plans of exporting his manufacture.[36] His autobiography, albeit florid in its critique, gives us a good idea of the challenges that he faced, especially in exporting his engineering products. It also suggests the kind of strategies that he adopted, namely actively seeking out foreign collaboration to bridge the technological gap between Indian and international manufacture, relying on innovation to expand capacity and developing talent within his own organization. As he once famously put it, 'factories have a longer life than human' and with that mantra, went about expanding his father's ventures and fulfilling several of his dreams.

In 1947, KOEL began producing small vertical diesel engines for farm irrigation, and in 1949, the first batch of engines (5HP Kirloskar Petter AVI) rolled out, and by 1951, maiden dividends were made available. The next few years saw positive trends, but soon, thanks to the miscalculations of the Planning Commission that had overestimated demand and encouraged imports, the market was glutted, leading to massive losses for the company. It was therefore no surprise that SLK's opinion about the government and its controls was negative. It was sheer grit that saw the company and its proprietor through—first came the decision to sell the engines to farmers through cooperatives, then came the decision to set up the Indian Diesel Engineering Manufacturers Association to put pressure on the government and to relax its policies. A second strategy lay in devising international collaboration, and here his connections helped. An agreement with MAN (Augsburg, Germany) and a collaboration with Cummins, and Ricardo helped in expanding the range of manufacture. Exports were key to the success of the company; between 1950 and 1965, exports expanded to the Middle East and parts of Southeast Asia. SLK was constantly on the lookout for collaboration, exchange of technical knowhow, scouting talent, and setting up assembly plants. These years were one of cautious optimism, and while SLK was outspoken about his reservations against the mixed model economy of the governing regime, he was able to leverage his position and operationalize his export drives. Fundamentally, there was a contradiction; SLK had no confidence in import substitution policies and believed that they simply delayed India's manufacturing potential. According to him, if his company made any profits at all, it was despite the presence of the government.[37]

The optimism of the 1960s turned into bitter disappointment, and as SLK writes in his autobiography, the period after 1965 was a dark age of confused planning, legal restrictions, switching of government interest from large to small industries and the infighting among politicians culminating in the splitting of the once monolithic Congress party. Yet, amid these difficulties, SLK remained resolute and, through sheer grit and foresight, built his empire, diversifying and expanding global manufacturing strategy. He trained his family members, treated workers well and organized a space where industrial management was like a trusteeship but run on sophisticated and modern lines. He had an astute understanding of the macro-context of industrial development and wealth generation. He made the most of his contacts in Europe and supplied labour-intensive items for German companies (such as Schuler) and endeavoured to give Indian products a finish that they normally lacked. His candour and outspoken criticism of government policies, especially the handling of licences for imports and foreign collaborations, was grounded in a deep understanding of the situation on the ground that enabled him to live up to his promises. This was evident in the case of the tractor deals with Klöckner Humboldt Deutz AG when, after delays and controversies, the licences were granted in 1972, enabling Kirloskar to surge ahead.[38] However, it must be noted that, even as he was critical of the controlled economy of the 1960s and 1970s, he was no blind champion of liberalization and believed that its modalities hurt several industries like that of machine tools. Way ahead of his times, he played a key role in developing India's industries, a huge growth in assets and a vision for future development, something that was transmitted to the family. It is no wonder then that the various lines of the family have taken the initiative forward and diversified in many directions and retained their eminence as a leading player in pump and valve manufacture. In this connection, mention must be made, as Bassett's work suggests, of the importance of SLK's initiative in developing Pune as a major industrial hub and in the area's industrialization. Committed to developing local skills, he worked for both artisans and small local entrepreneurs, working like a facilitator for small start-ups; among these, mention may be made of Bharat Forge, which provided forgings for Kirloskar and registered impressive sales.[39]

Like so many business families, the Kirloskars were not immune to family disputes, which have occasionally turned public and resulted in the depletion and fragmentation of assets. This has not, however, undermined the performance of the group, as we find younger members assuming lead roles and operating within a globalized environment. Women of the family too (Geetanjali and Manasi Kirloskar for example) have come forward as entrepreneurs in their own right, and this too speaks of the extraordinary liberality of the family that distinguished itself with its love for machines and design and an uncompromising commitment to modern education.

Families and Business in India

What do the stories of our protagonists tell us about family and business, of families in business? These are individual stories, each marked by their own eccentric drive and impulse, and yet they carry certain broad patterns that could be generalized. In every case, we have a deep commitment to industry and manufacture as a public good and how essential this is for the country's future. We also have the effective dissemination of the ideology by the founder to his immediate successor (son, nephew or another family member), who in virtually all cases turned out to be effective captains of industry and successful stewards of enterprise. Whether it was T.S. Krishna, Kamalnayan Bajaj or Shantanurao Kirloskar, the hunger for growth and success was intense, and the drive to fight odds was impressive. All these men also happened to share the general optimism of Independence, and reposed faith in a model and vision of a free India where industry would partner government to lead the country into growth and prosperity. It was with the next generation that signs of caution and even disenchantment emerged as the Licence Raj was distorted beyond redemption, and doing business required nerves of steel and enormous patience to overcome bureaucratic tangles. Yet the groups survived, thrived even, and here we must consider the enormous premium that business families put on education and technical expertise. Gone was the image of the tight-fisted sethia who sat on his money bags and espoused an orthodoxy that was evident in the private domain and in the public one. This, in addition to certain values that were anchored within a family structure, ensured the vitality of manufacture and enterprise in independent and post-liberalization India. A judicious mix of paternalism and professionalization created a modern entrepreneurial culture that helped families survive feuds and wrangles, overcome problems of capitalization and safeguard reputations in the market.

6

Business in the Age of Licences: Dhirubhai Ambani and the Rise of Reliance

'The most important external environment is the government of India. You have to sell your ideas to the government. Selling the idea is the most important thing and for that I would meet anybody in the government. I am willing to salaam anyone. One thing you won't find in me is an ego.'

—Dhirubhai Ambani[1]

'I did not just like him; I liked him very, very much.'

—Former union finance minister and senior Congress leader Pranab Mukherjee[2]

Both confessions are telling; the first speaks of an unusual confidence and of an unflinching commitment to the pursuit of success, the preconditions of which Dhirubhai Ambani had unerringly identified, while the other suggests an intimacy between businessman and minister. In many ways, the rise of Dhirubhai Ambani (1932–2002) and the Reliance empire that he began and built was predicated on his ability to leverage the

197

regulatory regime of the government of India and to capitalize on
the shifts in the global textile trade, which was structured around
synthetic fabrics, polyester in particular, and which found new
markets and production centres in Asia, including India. It is
therefore not far-fetched to suggest, as Surajit Mazumdar does,
that the run-away success of Dhirubhai and Reliance was 'very
much a product of the pre-1991 regime of Indian capitalism'.[3]
What was distinctive about the nature of Indian capitalism in
this period, and how the personality of Ambani was able to cut
several Gordian knots to create a new business and a new model
of financing it, creating in the process an altogether new equity
culture, will constitute the principal themes of this chapter. It will
navigate the life story of Dhirubhai, aligning it to the specificities
of the context in which he operated with full understanding of
the challenges that lay ahead and the enormous potentialities that
could be tapped. And tap he did, and as Gita Piramal mentions,
he founded an upstart company that challenged existing ways of
doing business, aggressively acquired export or replenishment
licences from the government to dominate the yarn market
and subsequently went in for updated textile mills and huge
petrochemical complexes.[4] In his own words, he was a pathfinder,
'excavating the jungle and making the road for others to walk.
I like to be the first in everything I do. Making money does not
excite me, though I have to make it for my shareholders. What
excites me is achievement; I could never do a normal job'.[5] Even
if one discounts the hyperbole in this admission, there is no doubt
that his life story is the stuff of thrillers, much more than the rags
to riches story, embodying an altogether new spirit that came to
dominate the Indian market. It is not as though the market in
India had not witnessed speculation and share mania, but with

Dhirubhai and Reliance, the scale of investment and speculation was unprecedented, just as the factories and mills that were put in place aspired to be top-class in terms of technology, equipment and professional management. A new era of enterprise was unleashed as the entrant seemingly an outsider gave expression to a new imagination, dressing up new Indian customers with 'Only Vimal' and bringing small retail investors into capital markets. How did all this happen?

Early Beginnings

Born in a Modh Bania family in 1932, Dhirubhai's father Hirachand was the village schoolteacher in Chorwad—Hirachand Ambani was known for being a good teacher and a disciplinarian. The family, like most Bania families, was commercially oriented; Hirachand himself had dabbled in retailing ghee but without much success. What was important were the connections and the networks that the family enjoyed, which would come in handy for his son. Further, like most Gujarati families of the times, sons apprenticed with some establishment or the other in West Asia and East Africa, where older networks fashioned by trade contacts and the imperial regime encouraged young men to find employment as clerks in commercial firms and sharpen their own business understanding and skills. Thus, it was not coincidental that Dhirubhai's brother worked in Yemen and served as a point of contact for his younger sibling. Dhirubhai completed his school education from Bahadur Kanji school, where he flirted briefly with Gandhian politics and befriended Krishna Kant Shah, a fellow student demonstrating his powers of persuasion when he intervened to get his friend released from the police.

After graduation, he immediately sought employment and went to Aden, where he briefly worked at a petrol station as attendant, and then found a job in the French firm A. Besse & Co., which held agencies for several companies, most notably that of Shell. Retrospectively, it seems that Ambani, in working for A. Besse & Co., had found in its owner, Antonin Besse, a kindred spirit, a go-getter who acquired factories, built dhows and showed his skills in local and international currency trading. A. Besse & Co., like many others in Aden, employed Gujaratis as clerks. Dhirubhai was assigned to market Shell products, an activity that he not only carried out competently but one that gave him a deep understanding of the networks in which he operated and which in the future would give him unexpected advantages. At the same time, he saw first-hand the building of the British Petroleum oil refinery that must have left an indelible impression on the salience that oil and petroleum commanded. The city's growth, the massive advances in infrastructure, the access to commodities and the potential for trading in currency were critical elements in firing young Ambani's ambition, and unlike his counterparts, who preferred to play it safe, Dhirubhai showed no such restraint. Story has it that he bought reals at the souk of Aden, melted them down and sold them as ingots to bullion dealers in London, making small money but gaining huge experience in 'knowing the market', as he would call it. This also involved trading in small commodities like rice and sugar. These small deals that Dhirubhai performed outside regular hours of work, were not always spectacularly successful, but they highlighted his ability to take bold decisions, learn to read the situation and stay ahead of the curve. His apparent nonchalance and fearlessness made him an enigma of sorts, an impression that was only partly attenuated by the deep friendships he cultivated and remained loyal to. Hamish McDonald refers to his relationship with Jamnadas Sakerchand Depala, whose instructions and reprimands Dhirubahai was supposed to defer to without demur.[6] Close associations turned out, as we shall see, to be an important feature of Ambani's business and personal style; he valued his contacts and was mindful of safeguarding them, not only because it was strategic.

In 1958, Dhirubhai returned from Aden to Bombay with a small saving of $3000 and decided to go in for trading. He mobilized funds from friends and relatives and set up the Reliance Commercial Corporation in Bombay, which undertook trading in spices (ginger, cardamom, pepper and turmeric), betel nut, cotton and nylon textiles to Ethiopia, Somalia and Kenya. This was a network that he was familiar with thanks to his stint at A. Besse & Co. His long-term objective, however, was to experiment with trading in synthetic yarn, the commodity of the future, and set it up as a springboard for his plans. These plans, in turn, were informed by the emerging trends in the global economy of textiles and in the national planning scenario. By the early 1960s, two things were evident. One, that the Indian market was getting ready for man-made fibre and that the ruling government was in favour of exporting artificial silk made by power loom industries. Dhirubhai undertook the export of nylon as a means of securing export, or replenishment, licences that he could use for importing polyester fibre. Supplies of fibre were hard to come by; Hamish McDonald mentions how yarn dealers in Bombay faced conditions of uncertainty and shortage and that smugglers had a field day providing the necessary material.[7] The Japanese supplied sari-length material, and the only other source for procurement was the import licence given by the government to

registered exporters of textiles. The latter were allowed to import
raw materials worth a certain percentage of their export earnings.
Dhirubhai realized very early on that securing and cashing in on
the export licences was the route to success and thus became a
player in the licences market.

The issue and acquisition of export licences were part of the
regulatory system initiated by the post-Independence government
to ensure planned growth, reduce poverty, support small industries,
promote import substitution and achieve agricultural self-
sufficiency. The regulatory system evolved over time; between 1947
and 1951, when its overall structure was put in place, the idea was
to ensure agricultural self-sufficiency, help small-scale industries
and regulate private enterprise. Thus, under the Industries Act of
1951, private firms had to apply for licences for every conceivable
aspect—setting up new factories or expanding their capacity and
even for their change in location. More importantly, they required
permission to import foreign technology, consumer goods, as
well as requisite raw materials, capital and intermediate goods.
To import raw materials, manufacturers had to demonstrate one,
proof of necessity, i.e., that the goods required were essential and
two that these were not locally available. The import licences were
not easy to acquire in view of chronic red-tapism, files moving
slowly from desk to desk, creating inordinate delays. These
inconveniences worsened in the second phase of the regulatory
system (1951–69)[8] when mechanisms were put in place to control
monopolies and prevent concentration of economic powers and
foreign nationals. These restrictions coincided with rising costs of
election campaigns and with major changes in the overall political
scenario that Dhirubhai was later to exploit.

In the second phase of the operation of the regulatory
system, which essentially involved the acquisition of licences to

invest, trade, export and import, a quid pro quo relationship emerged between the government and the private interests, who made substantial donations and contributions in return for benefits. This was aggravated by massive political turmoil in the wake of divisions within the Congress forcing Indira Gandhi (elected in 1965) to attack those leaders (the Syndicate) who had relations with prominent businessmen. A spate of hard decisions such as bank nationalization, monopoly controls, bans on company donations and abolition of privy purses followed with major consequences.[9]

These circumstances in which traders found themselves were hardly conducive. Smuggling, black marketing was rife and to be able to import polyester fibre, Dhirubhai had to improvise, and in the process, build connections with people in power, and renew old ones with friends and business associates including bankers who had initially funded Reliance Commercial Corporation. This came in handy as he was able to bypass controls in a way that he was ahead of his competitors and was able to even persuade the government to initiate schemes that benefited him directly. As a trader in yarn, his priority was to secure import licences that in turn required him to export nylon. In achieving this quid pro quo arrangement, he is supposed to have persuaded his old-time friend T.A. Pai, minister of industries to authorize imports of filament yarn for nylon exports. This found expression in the High Unit Value Scheme of the government of India in 1971 and of which Dhirubhai turned out to be the biggest beneficiary. Reliance Commercial Corporation accounted for nearly 60 per cent of exports under the scheme which enabled Ambani to get massive import entitlements that became the basis of his future plans.[10]

These early successes earned Dhirubhai both fame and notoriety. His detractors pointed out that the export business that

Ambani ran was bogus, while Dhirubhai himself defended his
stance, saying that he was fleet-footed while his competitors were
not, and that they failed to react to state schemes and incentives
with alacrity. It is also likely that Ambani projected himself to be
an outsider, an upstart without the social capital of established
business families and the government of the day was happy to
prefer him over his competitors. This is a point that Pranab
Mukherjee in an interview referred to:

> You must remember that his is a rags-to-riches story. In
> the Indian corporate world, you will not find a parallel to
> him. He started from scratch and built this giant industrial
> house . . . In Dhirubhai, I saw a man who grew before my
> own eyes, by the sheer dint of his determination, sharp business
> sense, focus and vision.[11]

What was moot was the intimacy that Dhirubhai enjoyed with
key people in the inner circle of the Licence Raj that gave him
an insider's advantage. On the part of the government, it was
obvious that it saw the licence permit quota system as a useful
lever for extracting donations and contributions. For example,
Stanley Kochanek in his article mentions how minister for trade
L.N. Mishra found the system useful to pressurize businessmen.
Under the circumstances, it is not surprising that Dhirubhai
found it essential, even critical, to keep the government on
his side and build up connections from the humblest security
guard to the top bureaucrat to get his work done. This became
even more pronounced when he went in for manufacturing and
industrial licensing.

The yarn business earned huge profits, and with these,
Dhirubhai turned to actual manufacture. In 1966, he decided to

go in for textile manufacture for the domestic market and, with his second cousin, Champaklal Damani, set up the Reliance Textile Mill in Naroda. With a small investment of Rs 28 lakh, he took the plunge to produce yarn, which he saw as the commodity of the future.[12] With two circular and two warp knitting machines, the mill was ready to go to manufacture apparel for a domestic market. In setting this up and overseeing the operations, Dhirubhai showed enormous energy. He selected a committee team, sent them overseas for training and soon was able to record an impressive growth in sales and profits. He subsequently established a new brand name, Vimal, and thanks to an advertisement blitzkrieg with the 'Only Vimal' tagline, oversaw massive manufacturing growth. The Naroda factory proved to be the first of many watersheds in Dhirubhai's life, transforming him from a canny yarn trader to an ambitious industrialist who seemed to know how to leverage the political establishment. Reliance sales went up steadily, and by 1976–77, Reliance had an annual turnover of Rs 70 crore that went up even more spectacularly at the time of Dhirubhai's demise.[13] According to Piramal, fixed assets rose 'from Rs 2,80,000 in 1966 to Rs 145 million in 1977, more than doubling to Rs 370 million in 1979'.[14] It was an incredible saga that could only be explained by Dhirubhai's shrewd calculation of demand for new polyester apparel and his ability to take risks and negotiate with the power establishment to get preferential treatment for licences. He insisted that his success did not come on a platter and that it was only because he foresaw what was coming, made full use of his personal contacts and never baulked at restrictions. As Hamish McDonald reiterates in his biography of the 'Polyester Prince', he never did anything illegal but was creative with his interpretation of regulation. What seems to have really worked was his proximity to bureaucrats, bank officials and leaders who mattered. He was unceasing in keeping up his contacts, a trait that we have already identified since his childhood. Whether it was looking after an old school friend or a business associate, Dhirubhai valued people, and this helped in both managing his staff and management and in bargaining with the politicians who mattered.

Only Vimal: Clothing for New India?

By the 1970s, Dhirubhai Ambani's sights were firmly set on the domestic market for synthetic textiles. While he definitely benefited from the export scheme of nylons in return for polyester fibre, getting there early and cornering the import business, he did not overlook the Naroda factory, which was built and run on international standards. He trained personnel by sending them overseas and ensured top-of-the-line equipment working on the maxim that he was after the best and was prepared to put in what it needed. His team was fired up by Dhirubhai's enthusiasm; one of his staff who was sent overseas for training had this to say of his boss: 'It was only his talk that made us mad for success, mad to be the best, to be number one. We felt elevated. We had a physical sense of being uplifted in the air. He was a tremendous leader who transforms his men from clay into steel.'[15] With this grit and frenzied commitment, profits poured in and were systematically ploughed back and the result was a huge expansion of sales. The factory manufactured yarn and textiles at a dizzy pace; Dhirubhai went in for a brand and the result was 'Only Vimal'. Aggressive marketing and advertising made Vimal a household name, creating a new taste for excellence and fashion. 'Only Vimal' embodied a new register of aspiration and taste of the middle class—the advertisements featuring cricket icons and glamorous models presaged the coming of age of the consuming middle class, something that Dhirubhai had managed to tap into.

How do we account for this prescience—the ability to know and gauge what the market wanted and how best to fulfil it? Was it a reflection of Dhirubhai's own understanding of what a good life was meant to be and how it was to be achieved? It is likely that having cut his teeth in Aden and witnessed a cosmopolitan consumer culture that valued imported fabric and accessories, he was mindful of their appeal and was determined to make it a mass product. It is also likely that he was not tutored in the traditional style of business that families like the Tatas and Birlas were used to and was therefore free of the constraints imposed by tradition. As Pranab Mukherjee put it, he did not inherit a mantle; he worked for it in a way akin to Napolean Bonaparte, saw what was coming, assessed his skills and went for the chase. He was canny and shrewd and understood that the day belonged to the bureaucrat who held the powers to move files, issue licences, revoke the same and therefore, any businessman wishing to succeed would have to take care of the system. It is interesting to contrast the nonchalance of Ambani about government intervention with the exasperation of Rahul Bajaj, for instance, and deduce from it the multiple ways in which businessmen calibrated the relationship between business and politics, especially in and after the 1970s.

The emergence of the middle-class consumer in India was a factor that Dhirubhai could not have overlooked. While we do not have accurate figures and statistics for consumption, especially of the middle class, qualitative data suggests how middle classes were consuming differently, whether it was household appliances and storage equipment or new kinds of apparel. The economist Omkar Goswami, using data from the issues of the Consumer Purchase of Textiles (1973–84), suggests that there was a marked fall in the per capita consumption of cotton textiles, including in rural areas, and a simultaneous growth in non-cotton consumption in urban and rural areas. Admittedly, Reliance targeted middle-class consumers with disposable income who were willing to spend on fancy clothes and offered them a premium product at a premium price. The ads extolled Reliance's commitment to world standards and to updated facilities that enabled them to turn out products that were excellent. The messaging was all about Reliance owning the best factories and the best technology and thus feeding into the nascent middle class enamoured by fashion, glamour and sport. In a way, Dhirubhai, himself quite unprepossessing, was selling a dream product and making it accessible to a wide swathe of the population by organizing independent and exclusive showrooms, creating in the process, a massive retail network. Before the retail network materialized, legend has it that he would go to retailers with his cloth and request that they sell it. The following extract from Prateeksha Tiwari's biography, *Corporate Guru: Dhirubhai Ambani*, reveals the essentials of the strategy adopted by Dhirubhai, working on trust and on a shared dream of wealth creation:

> My name is Dhirubhai Ambani. I am a *sadakchhap* but I want to be big one day. I want *you to grow with me*, though at this moment I have nothing big to offer you. My brothers, some friends and I have just set up a factory at Naroda. We make knitted fabric there. The wholesalers are boycotting our material for fear of the big millowners. I offer this material to you. I don't want any money. You sell it. If you make money by selling our material, give me whatever and whenever you want to. Now will you offer me a cup of tea before I go?[16]

The extract may be apocryphal but is telling in many ways. It reveals the absolute confidence that Dhirubhai had in his product and in his ability to sell his ideas to people who were coopted into his project. Retailers came forward enthusiastically to see his fabrics. Dhirubhai himself undertook extensive tours in the country to build hundreds of showrooms, exposing non-metropolitan populations to the new fabric.[17] Tiwari mentions how between 1977 and 1980, new and exclusive retail outlets selling Vimal fabrics came forward, and by 1980, Reliance apparel was available all over India and managed by an extensive chain of retailers, franchised outlets and regular retail stores.[18]

Going Public, Juggling Enterprises

By 1977, Dhirubhai seemed to have arrived in the world of manufacturing and big industry. He was no longer a trader but a manufacturer and was soon to add to his repertoire through new operations. The ability to juggle several balls and keep them in the air was most likely due to his exceptional interpersonal skills that endeared him to his staff, persuaded bureaucrats and functionaries to defer to his requests and opened vital lines of communication with the government. Indeed, the post-1976 phase of Dhirubhai's career reveals this facet acutely even as he confronted a particularly challenging set of political circumstances.

The year 1977 was a watershed moment for Dhirubhai Ambani, Reliance and India in more ways than one. This was the year when Indira Gandhi went in for elections after the suspension of the Emergency. The elections brought the opposition bloc, the Janata party to power, and it was a tricky situation for Dhirubhai who had remained close to Mrs Gandhi. At this time, the Reliance group comprised Reliance Exports, Vimal and three companies, wherein Ambani family members were partners.[19] Why Dhirubhai chose this point to go public with his company is not clear. Was it because he was experimenting with a new mode of financing his ventures? Or was he genuinely keen on selling the cult of equity to a capital-starved market? What seems apparent is his decision to go big, but after safeguarding his family interests. For what he did before he went with a public offer for equity shares and listing in the Bombay and Ahmedabad stock exchange, was amalgamating Reliance Textiles with another company christened Mynylon Limited with no business, a shell company in other words. According to Surajit Mazumdar, this was a strategy to maximize, 'the increase in the family holding in Reliance Industries',[20] as a result of which, the number of shares increased from a mere 17 to a whopping 59.5 lakh. From this new pool, Reliance offered 28.2 lakh shares for sale to the public in 1977.

Two features stand out in the transformation of Reliance Industries into a public company. One was the induction of first-time, small and middle-class retail investors largely from middle-tiered towns into the company by floating an initial public offer of 2.8 million equity shares valued at Rs 10 each at par. The offer met with a resounding reception as Dhirubhai was able to convince small-time investors to come forward in anticipation of handsome returns. Dhirubhai would appear to have kept his word to the shareholders who became part of a large, loyal Ambani shareholder family. In 1986, there was a spectacular shareholders meeting held at the Cross Maidan in South Bombay—30,000 of them meeting together to pay allegiance to the company that had earned them substantial amounts of money. The personalized nature of Ambani's business ethos and dealings was never concealed; the entrepreneur took pride in the fact that he knew people and valued them, and it was this trust that enabled him to play with innovative devices to raise money. Later, observers, including businessmen, pointed out that there was nothing altruistic about Dhirubhai's policies and that it was a calculated strategy. In the words of Seksaria, 'In the unregulated pre-SEBI era, it ensured that no speculator could corner large chunks of shares on the stock market and conspire to beat down the share price or mount a takeover bid'.[21] Dhirubhai did not compromise his family holdings, and this brings us to the second feature of the Reliance venture. Dhirubhai safeguarded family interests by every possible means. On this occasion, he took the measure of increasing the number of trading and investment companies under Reliance so that the shareholding of Reliance Industries that the family could control would also correspondingly increase.

Once the company went public, there was an acceleration in the stage of expansion. The number of installed looms went up and the spinning of yarn was also experimented with on the setting up of a new unit. This was done by acquisition as well— specifically that of Sidhpur Mills. Expansion was conceived of in terms of forward and backward integration into other sectors but notably ordered around petrochemicals and oil. In 1982, the company, i.e., Reliance Industries Ltd (RIL) launched the first phase of its polyester filament yarn on its site in Pataganga and, by 1991, commissioned the first phase of the petrochemicals complex. Dhirubhai employed a judicious mix of innovative financing strategies and of capitalizing on government schemes to be able to undertake massive expansion of capacity, especially of Reliance Petrochemicals Ltd (RPL), which was a natural extension of the textile business. All this happened notwithstanding the political turbulence in the country in the wake of Indira Gandhi's loss in the elections of 1977, her return in 1980, the slow but growing presence of Rajiv Gandhi in politics and the developments following Mrs Gandhi's assassination. Dhirubhai was undeterred and was able to maintain his own, call the shots and manage to expand and diversify.[22]

Where did Dhirubhai find his reserves? How was he able to persuade investors to trust him and work around regulations to get the best deal? Critics and detractors would argue that the proximity to the political establishment helped him get approvals that others could not. Apologists would say that Ambani knew how to get along with people and how to devise apparently incongruous strategies to mobilize funds, thanks to the equity culture he had fostered in the first place. The answer perhaps lies in between, but mostly in the farsightedness of Dhirubhai to strike early and to maintain personal connections studiously. For example, setting up RPL in Hazira in Gujarat in 1987–88 was calculated to take advantage of the fact that Hajira was in a backward area, something that would give him access to government incentives.[23] At the same time, Dhirubhai relied upon retail investors to generate funds for the project. This was done by the issue of fully convertible debentures expected to generate Rs 590 crore for the company. The fact that Dhirubhai and Reliance were able to persuade millions of investors to do their bidding indicated the level of trust that the company has achieved in what was a very short time. It proudly projected itself as a people's company (see annual report) made possible by an obliging government. Thus, the timing of government decisions seemed especially to favour Dhirubhai, who had wind of these even before they were notified and implemented. For example, the government announced a new policy to enable companies with lower capacities to enhance their scale to achieve the new minimum economic capacity. Dhirubhai took advantage of this and furthermore was able to tap funds from state financial institutions; his company was allowed to 'convert its parts B and C of the convertible debentures to equity shares that could remove the burden of payment of interest. Further, the conversion of debt to equity was also accepted at par and not at the premium that Reliance had promised at the time of the issue'.[24]

The manipulation of financial arrangements did not stop here. Escalating costs and servicing equity and debt were big challenges that Dhirubhai had to overcome. He took the option of mergers; RPL was merged with RIL in order to buy assets and capital of RPL at a cheap price. The decision disadvantaged non-promoter shareholders of RPL but added a huge amount to RIL's reserves. Further, in 1988, he took control of Larsen and Toubro (L&T), the company in charge of supplying equipment to the RPL project. This was done with the help of institutions such as the Life Insurance Corporation of India and the Unit Trust of India that had sold 7 per cent of L&T shares to a newly created investment entity, the Bank of Baroda Fiscal Services. Subsequently, as chairman of the company, he floated a public offer of 8.2 billion convertible debentures.[25] These acts were not conventional measures, but Dhirubhai was anything but a conformist who played by the rules of the game that others drafted. He was very much a man of his times—aware of one, the loopholes in a regulatory system staffed by bureaucrats and functionaries who were not above persuasion and two of the mechanisms of state-owned enterprises that he could leverage effectively and finally of the immense potential of the Indian capital market. The audacity of his moves was representative of changing times, wherein businessmen were prepared to play with high risks and innovate.

Kochanek suggests that the innovations were not always lawful; there were allegations that Dhirubhai set up plants with capacity that exceeded their licences, that he made false custom declarations to claim favourable duties suggested that this was not business as usual. On his part, Dhirubhai continued to enjoy the favour of the state. The catalogue of benefits was impressive. On 7 May 1987, the government reduced the tax on purified terephthalic acid (PTA), a crucial ingredient in the making of polyester fibre. As a major consumer of this component, Reliance benefited from the concession. Kochanek mentions how, in fact, the tax reduction saved the company Rs 22.5 crore per year.[26] This concession was followed by the re-designation of the Patalganga complex as a refinery that allowed RIL to pay lower domestic excise duty for raw materials like Naphta. Additionally, several financing schemes and alterations, such as the permission to convert debentures into equity, were approved and rapidly passed through. There was a variety of special tax collections as well, all of which gave Dhirubhai a huge head-start to forge ahead of his competitors. On the debit side, there were allegations and accusations, especially from the Wadia group, at a time when the government was seriously considering an overhaul of the system and addressing 'corruption' frontally.

Messiah or Manipulator? The Stock Market Crisis of 1982

The cultivation of the bureaucracy and the state machinery for concessions was matched by Dhirubhai's uncanny appreciation of the stock market and his ability to use his trusted shareholders to play the market and augment the value of his company's shares. This came to play in the Bombay Stock Exchange Crisis of 1982, referred to as a great 'financial thriller' whose protagonist, the audacious Dhirubhai, demonstrated his ability to ward off the powerful Marwari bear syndicate of Calcutta. It is instructive to read contemporary reportage on this to get a clear sense of how the businessman had consolidated his pre-eminence as a people's person and a trader who could not be intimidated. Less than five years after the company went public with shares being offered, we find Dhirubhai battling the syndicate of Marwari brokers—'bear speculators' who were bent on bringing down the value of the Reliance shares. They used the technique of short selling, to sell 11 lakh Reliance shares, valued at Rs 16 crore, hoping to bottom out the market but were pre-empted by Ambani's brokers, who went about buying every share possible. The buying spree went on to create a huge and artificial spiral wherein the already overinflated Reliance stock rose to very steep heights from about Rs 125 in March to about Rs 202 in April. Amid this, Dhirubhai decided to deliver the sucker punch when, on the clearing day of 30 April, all transactions had to be squared and adjusted, Ambani's brokers refused any postponement in delivery, knowing fully well that the bears had no shares to actually sell. As the *India Today* report of 31 May 1982 put it, 'Knowing that the sellers would not have the shares to offer for delivery since they had indulged in massive short selling, Ambani's brokers refused any postponements except at a staggering Rs 50 per share (involving the paying out of Rs 5.50 crore).[27] This was obviously a penal rate meant to teach the bears a lesson, since *badla* charges rarely cross into double digits'. What followed thereafter was total bedlam at the Stock Exchange, which had to be closed for two days to salvage operations and a degree of respectability. As it became clear that Ambani and his brokers would not yield, the bears bought every conceivable share in the market. Reliance shares disappeared and prices skyrocketed; Ambani's men bought up every share in the market, notwithstanding that this was not entirely legal. Detractors pointed this out repeatedly, but admitted that the fiasco unmistakably demonstrated Ambani's shrewdness and ruthlessness in defending his issues (debenture), which was the principal means to financing his ventures. Subsequent investigations by the government revealed that a non-resident Indian had invested nearly Rs 22 crore in Reliance in 1982–88; all of this had been channelled through companies registered in the tax haven of Isle of Man and under a single ownership that went by the name of Shah. The investigations could not prove any major rule violations. For the moment, Dhirubhai's coup brought him an extraordinary aura of invincibility and built up his reputation as the ultimate stock messiah, the king of the share market, an image that appealed to thousands of Indians who were beginning to appreciate and participate in the culture of equity. The offers of Dhirubhai resonated with the desire of Indians to believe in what he said and to trust savings into his hands in the anticipation of handsome dividends. Just as his Vimal apparel resonated with the dreams of many Indian users, his shares became a valued asset to be invested in. It was a new class of Indians whom Dhirubhai appealed to—a new middle class who were not interested in small returns from unit trusts and post office savings but who were prepared to watch a new market in equity take shape and become willing participants in it. Dhirubhai was able to sense the growing aspiration of the middle class and make use of it, and in remaining committed to his shareholders, prepared to run the last mile. It was not as though he did not have to face his share of troubles, especially after the change of guard in the regime and when V.P. Singh became finance minister under Rajiv Gandhi and got a clean chit from him to launch a vigorous anti-corruption drive. This coincided with media interest in Dhirubhai's dealings, which happened to engage the attention of the media industrialist R.P. Goenka, who went ahead with exposés to unravel the complex linkages between business and politics. More than anything, the media coverage initiated by journalists like S. Gurumurthy illustrated the conditions under which a very distinct, even distorted business milieu had emerged, one that Dhirubhai represented and was even partly responsible for.

Battling the State and the Fourth Pillar

The growth of Reliance from its first mill in Naroda to the Patalganga refinery, the creation of an equity market, a spate of successful debenture issues to help support worsted mills, modernization projects, and the financing of polyester filament yarn (PFY) manufacture were marks of extraordinary success and dynamism. This, however, did not happen in a vacuum. Without detracting the intrepid energy and ambition of Dhirubhai, it is nonetheless important to place his success in perspective and in relation to a political establishment that went far beyond its remit to favour him. Whether we wish to see this as an expression of Dhirubhai's sagacity and personal affability or as a mark of the rot that lay behind the licence permit quota system is a matter of interpretation. For his competitors, there was no question that Dhirubhai was ruthless and took advantage of his political proximity to the government and was singularly responsible for nursing a culture of ruthless ambition and cutthroat competition, which, in the end, gave way to a major crisis and controversy. Resentment against Dhirubhai's success and his dealings surfaced, which both the media and the government took up in right earnest. Dhirubhai weathered the storm, but not before the nature and progression of the calamity brought home to the investor and the public the gravity of the situation.

The crisis began to unravel sometime in 1985, by which time Rajiv Gandhi as the elected prime minister attempted to foster better conditions for business, restrain the excesses of the licence permit quota system, reduce corruption and address the issue of black market and illegal donations. Even though, in the long run, he was unable to maintain his Mr Clean image and walk the talk, the processes that he set in motion with the appointment of V.P. Singh as finance minister were decisive in upsetting the applecart. The vigorous anti-corruption drive that Singh embarked upon targeted, among others, Ambani and Reliance, whose tactics came under scrutiny. The timing was the result of a major corporate war that had broken out between Dhirubhai Ambani and Nusli Wadia of Bombay Dyeing, arguably the biggest textile mill in India.[28] Wadia claimed that Dhirubhai was obsessed with his own success so much so that he could not stand others succeeding and even pointed out that he sabotaged one of his projects, the DMT project. It must be mentioned that Wadia, like Ambani, happened to be in the business of manufacturing certain polyester intermediates that required the purchase of certain components like paraxylene and held very divergent views about the level of import duties to be charged on this item. But Nusli seemed to be operating in a not-so-level playing field and alleged that his

licence applications were always delayed and denied, whereas
Reliance seemed to get approval even when norms were flouted.
He made a point of mentioning the anomalies that characterized
Reliance businesses, including the installation of plants with
capacities that they did not have licences for. Some of these issues
made their way into the press and the result was a war of words
in the *Economic Times* that brought yet another player, Ramnath
Goenka, into the fray.[29]

In October 1985, the *Economic Times* published a story about
an inquiry instituted by the CBI into the dealings of Reliance.
These involved the issue of backdated letters of credit by Reliance
worth Rs 100 crore.[30] Ambani refuted the charges and instead
took the offensive to say that the inquiry was motivated and
manufactured by a DMT-producing company (i.e., Bombay
Dyeing), which was unable to produce quality DMT and was in
financial stress. This was a way of diverting public attention from
its own condition, and Ambani went on as far as to press for an
apology from the chairman of the PTI, Ramnath Goenka. The
latter issued an apology but was determined to get to the bottom
of the matter and began a serious investigation. The result was a
series of reports by the journalist, S. Gurumurthy, appointed by
Goenka to pursue the matter. The finance minister meanwhile
applied the brakes on Ambani's juggernaut; Dhirubhai's access
to the ministry was reduced while his requests came under
greater scrutiny.[31] At the same time the government decided to
bring imports of PTA from the open general licence to limited
permissible lists—a change that required more clearance and hence
more time, which was not good news for Ambani's new plant that
required the product. Dhirubhai appeared unfazed and responded
by getting letters of credit worth a billion rupees (mentioned by

the *Indian Express*), but the government struck back with the levy of an import duty of 50 per cent upsetting Dhirubhai's cost calculations. Soon a second blow came when the government withheld permission to convert non-convertible debentures into convertible ones. It is likely that V.P. Singh was responding to the reports in the *Indian Express* that gave bad press to Dhirubhai and questioned his access to capital, pointing to the anomaly of the excessive overdrafts that sixty investment companies enjoyed without any security record. The newspaper claimed that these companies actually belonged to Reliance and that they borrowed money to buy debentures cheaply to convert them into overpriced shares. In October 1986, when the government appointed Fairfax, a private investigation agency, to look into the overseas finances of wealthy Indians, Dhirubhai too came under the scanner. In the end, Singh's initiative was questioned, resulting in his resignation and sullying the reputation of the prime minister, who had not been able to practise what he had preached.[32]

But what of Dhirubhai and his ventures? Controversy did not cease to dog him, nor did troubles, especially after the new national front government was voted in with all his opponents back in power.[33] A number of cases against Reliance were revived—mostly to do with questionable imports of spinning line plants whose capacity did not match the licences.[34] The most serious assault came with removing Dhirubhai as chairman of L&T and the decision taken by the new chairman to sell off Reliance shares, leaving Dhirubhai with a huge deficit in financing his projects at Hazira. His fortunes revived with the dismantling of the government, enabling Dhirubhai to resume his connections. After 1991–92, with the beginning of the reforms under P.V. Narasimha Rao, Dhirubhai and his projects would settle down to a new regime where licences did not have to be bargained for and connections did not have to be blatantly flaunted. Dhirubhai went all out for more internationalization and set the company on clear waters.

We will not go into the career of Dhirubhai in the last decade of his life that coincided with the opening up of the Indian economy. Our focus has been on Dhirubhai's exploits during the 1970s and 1980s to highlight both his appetite for business and his entrepreneurial practices, as well as the context in which he operated. In a sense, Dhirubhai's life and career in the years that we have reviewed mark the potential of Indian entrepreneurship in extraordinary times. The innovative aspect of Dhirubhai's approach lay in sensing the readiness of the Indian public to go in for investment and equity and in playing the system of licences and regulations to suit his interests. In the process, however, Ambani had built up an enormous business with substantial assets and continued to command the confidence of the investing public. All this went a long way in helping the company transition to a new regime. Suffice to say that Reliance responded with imagination, went in for diversification, moving into the oil and gas sector, and in less than a decade between 1997 and 2008, expanded its assets from Rs 20,000 crores to Rs 1,50,000 crores—no mean achievement for the poor son of a village school teacher.[35] Our focus in tracking the story of the pre-1991 period is to make the point that Dhirubhai's success was due to his astute handling of a very particular and distinct political situation that facilitated a very specific kind of state-business nexus. Dhirubhai and his family benefited from the opening of the economy in terms of business expansion, to be sure, but even before that, they were able to find their way through the labyrinth of power and bureaucracy to strike when it was right. Negotiations with the state could not be avoided, and in this aspect, we can draw a linear continuity between early modern merchant princes and the contemporary 'Polyester Prince' with the caveat that the pre-modern Mughal state was much more hands-off in its policies towards the merchants. Dhirubhai made no bones about the need to enlist state support, but this was not his only resource; he was innovative in his mobilization of financial resources and in effectively using the tax regime.[36] That said, there is no doubt that Dhirubhai embodied a very different entrepreneurial spirit than that exhibited by his immediate predecessors, whose approach was more conservative and who looked at the business of wealth generation differently. This is not to make a value judgement but merely to discern the difference and understand it in context. The trajectory of state power in India in and after the mid-1960s called for a new nexus between capital and politics, and Dhirubhai was prescient enough to participate in it.

What was the nature of the legacy that Dhirubhai left behind when he succumbed to a massive heart attack in 2002? It was the realization that dreams could be realized and that determination and foresight could combat odds that came in the way. To this could be added efficient project management and developing capital markets. By seeding the equity cult and converting debts into equity, he cut his capital costs and thought along global lines. His sons, who were closely involved in the ventures that their father had started, combined their inhouse experiences with high-level education (in this respect, the family displayed common values as Bajaj and Kirloskar) and have continued to develop the Reliance empire whose shares enjoy currency to this day.

Retrospective Reflections

To reflect on Dhirubhai and the qualities that he possessed is akin to a rollercoaster ride without an idea of where the bumps, the highs and the lows lie. The resources that he brought to the table were many, the successes that he enjoyed were immense and the controversies that he courted were spectacular. His modest background proved to be an asset; for one, he did not belong to an established business family caught up in the throes of tradition and habit. He was driven by ambition to do something big, and nothing stopped him in his tracks. One may argue that there was a cynicism in his approach to negotiations with the government and that he was sanguine that he could persuade the bureaucracy and establishment to extend him favours that were discriminatory. The practical side of his business persona asserted itself when he was forced to contend with the regulatory regime that did not seem to care about the needs of business and its escalating costs created by delays. But beyond this, there was the grit and determination to see his empire grow, which meant the willingness to learn the nuts and bolts of business and aim for the absolute best. The fact that he was determined to make first-rate factories that met international standards is testimony to his ambition that was not just about making money. This was achieved by fearlessness, the ability to take risks and by adopting a professional attitude towards factory and product management. Even as a young person, he was a daredevil, not intimidated by a challenge. He kept an open mind, absorbed information and observed the nitty-gritty of business very acutely, which gave him a perspective to see far beyond the obvious. He had a knack for sensing a good deal and backed this up with careful reading and observation. He is supposed to have recognized his animal instinct about trading, which had to be carefully steered, and as he put it,

> but there was a lot of reading and understanding behind that animal instinct of mine. I read every bit of paper I could lay my hands on about what was happening around the world, I listened carefully to every word uttered in the market, picked every bit of gossip in the shopping circles and pondered long through the night in the bed about the pros and cons of every deal I wanted to make.[37]

The ability to make deliberative decisions and be one step ahead of competitors and to read the market astutely marked all his subsequent deals. For instance, the very choice of polyester that he wanted to trade in and manufacture is telling; while partly the choice of the material was to do with his stint in the oil business and to do with growing up in cosmopolitan Yemen with its markets of fancy cloth and transistor radios, it was also to do with his understanding of consumption trends. There was a definite shift in the demand curve for artificial fabric in India, and Dhirubhai was determined to exploit the opportunity without wasting any time. Moving to Bombay after his return saw him scour its streets, getting to know the intricacies of the textile and yarn business, calculating investments wisely and spending money when it was essential. This was on full display when he built the plant in Naroda that matched any in the world. He was not averse to spending when it was essential. As Gita Piramal puts it, he saw the future in the present and this lay at the core of his success and vision—the average Indian had a role to play in the future that he envisaged. In his scheme of things, India in terms of manpower had immense potential, which had to be harnessed; it was perhaps this conviction that persuaded him to turn the ordinary investor into his ardent supporter. The belief that everyone had the right to dream of a better life and that he or she could be a partner in his enterprise made Ambani and his Reliance Industries genuinely original. As *India Today* journalist Sumit Mitra put it, Dhirubhai put into 'the psyche of his people a new and welcoming attitude to wealth, not as inheritance but as something worth earning'.[38] Mitra also pointed out correctly how Dhirubhai's success could not be explained only by an indulgent government, for after the opening up of the Indian economy, he was still able to retain an edge and diversify his ventures. He was a consummate businessman who knew how to sell his ideas to the government and convince them that his schemes worked in the national interest. He was one step ahead all the time, whether it was identifying the right technology or working out new ways of marketing yarn and finally forecasting the advantages of convertible debentures.[39] In the words of Prateeksha Tiwari,

> Without Dhirubhai, we would not have learnt how to think big, not in terms of a small factory here and there, but in terms of giant plants as big as anywhere in the world and as modern as they come. Dhirubhai taught India to think big, and he usually said, 'ours is a big country and if we do not think big, we should never be able to attain our potential'.[40]

There is some truth in the accolade that Tiwari extends to the corporate guru. There is something larger than life about his grit and determination, a never-say-die attitude to his ventures. He is also an enigma in that he did not publicly subscribe to an ennobling ideology of business. Unlike some of our other protagonists, for whom business was a trusteeship that had a clear social function, Dhirubhai was driven by an inexorable will to succeed. Yet as a student and practitioner of history, one must also read Dhirubhai and his life and labours in context. Individual agency is also shaped by the milieu in which it can express itself. There is no doubt that a pre-existing network of trade and commercial connections linking Gujarat with West Asia was what in the first place enabled young, enterprising Gujaratis to try their hand in commercial establishments, Dhirubhai being no exception. It is equally true that he was able to dip into the existing and established bazaar networks in yarn and cloth in Bombay and that community connections and personal friendships stood young Ambani in good stead. That said, it was his individual drive and determination to succeed and strike out in original ways that cast him in a different mould and enabled him to battle difficult years during the late 1960s and 1970s. He was quick to appreciate the overarching power of the state and the government, whose goodwill and cooperation he sought at any cost and to turn it to his advantage. He did this while daring to dabble in the stock market and acquaint the average person with the possibilities of playing the stock market. It was a move that radically altered the perception of business and enterprise and helped India to move in step within a larger global market. To that extent Dhirubhai was a man ahead of his times, embodying the emerging change and shifts in business culture that were being prepared for the future to come.

How do we compare Dhirubhai with his counterparts? Corporate gossip is replete with details of the rivalry between Nusli Wadia and Dhirubhai Ambani, who were as different in temperament and sensibility as one could imagine. The comparison is not intended to make a value judgement over business practices but to underscore the native intelligence of Dhirubhai, who honed his skills in the marketplace, whether in Aden or in Bombay. What was impressive was the rapidity with which he moved into industry and manufacture and learnt the ropes to emerge as a big player in a global market, notwithstanding the peculiarities of the contemporary industrial situation. The emphasis on excellence also made him a product-conscious entrepreneur, whether it was in apparel or his shares that retail investors were so ready to buy. Ironically, he is remembered as a manipulator of the system, unlike his Parsi counterparts, Nusli Wadia and Ratan Tata, who admittedly worked in a different sector. Both of them were candid in their resistance to manipulating the system and spoke of values that distinguished them from Dhirubhai Ambani. However, all of them admitted that he was a master of the game and showed an entrepreneurial genius that was unmatched.[41] For us interested in identifying key moments and protagonists in the changing landscape of Indian business, his life and exploits presage a distinct shift in popular attitudes towards wealth acquisition, an important precondition in driving manufacturing growth.

Epilogue

Choosing my protagonists was not easy. My choice was informed
by several considerations. I wanted to capture regional variations
of business behaviour; how different, for example, was the
Bengali gentry's approach to enterprise than that of Parsi traders
was a question that dogged me. There was also the question of
technology and its reception at a particular historical moment and
the fascination this held for some who embarked on a project of
translating their passion into a business venture. In factoring these
concerns, I was aware that I did not have a long list of men to choose
from—not because India did not have enterprising entrepreneurs
but because they were not always adequately represented. I also
wanted to focus on those individuals whose work corresponded
to the peculiarities of a given situation that generated very specific
opportunities that they could take advantage of and capitalize on
them to generate wealth. Each of our protagonists, therefore, was
very much an entity of his times and carried with him the values of
the age and foresaw where his business activities could take him.
Thus being rooted in one's context with the ability to see into the
future was a trait common to all of them across time and space,
whether it was Arjunji Nathji, the Gujarati banker who bankrolled
the English company's wars and expansion projects, or J.N. Tata,
whose ideas and aspirations were in perfect sync with those of the

enterprising free merchants and private traders, or Dwarkanath Tagore, who followed European commercial methods closely to revisit the very idea of trade and entrepreneurship as a public good.

As the process of industrial growth matured into the second half of the nineteenth century, when Indian capital came to appreciate the potential of large-scale industrial enterprise within the context of a colonial state and its regulations and to simultaneously think of swadeshi projects, a new set of actors came on the scene. While many of them, or at least their ancestors, had cut their teeth as collaborators and participants in the imperial and colonial economies, they were moved by the idea of wanting to do something on their own—this was especially true of Godrej, whose self-image was predicated on swadeshi ideals. These ideas were not just ritual invocations but were an actual basis for thinking about industrial manufacture and carried through right down to Independence and thereafter. The period between the wars and the decades leading to Independence was a crucial one for the assertion of industrial capital that found expression in a range of significant and innovative practices that the book has tracked through the lives of men like T.V.S. Iyengar, Jamnalal Bajal and Laxmanrao Kirloskar. The book also takes up the case of some of their sons and successors to highlight the changes in the overall milieu that came with Independence and thereafter, necessitating particular styles of strategy and decision-making. The last actor in our cast of characters is Dhirubhai Ambani, who broke the mould and set the stage for a different kind of vision, value and aspiration.

Keeping in line with the standard convention of an epilogue, we could well ask what happened to these families, what the sons and successors of our protagonists did and what that says of Indian business, in structural terms as well as in its global rankings. Barring the case of eighteenth-century bankers and businessmen and the case of Bengali enterprise championed by Dwarkanath Tagore, the rest can claim to have success stories—the firms they oversaw have not suffered inter-generational instability. This is despite succession struggles and family fallouts. In the case of our eighteenth- and nineteenth-century pioneers, Arjunji Nathji's family lapsed into oblivion and survived only as part of the city of Bombay's business mythology. We come across an interesting letter written by Jeverilal Yajnik to the Bombay Gazette (6 September 1881) about the exploits of the banker, how he was reputed to be among the richest merchants of Surat city and how he made advances to the company when others did not. He also mentioned that the banker's descendants had been reduced to penury and were starving and urged his city men to do something for the family. With Dwarkanath Tagore and his concerns, the challenges were different. The failure of the Union Bank that he floated was accompanied, as we saw, by a shocking loss of confidence in business among middle-class investors, who turned their backs on enterprise and found comfort in landed income and government service. It was only much later in the twentieth century, when ideas of swadeshi and self-pride persuaded the Bengali gentry to go in for business, that we find a shift in the milieu and collective ethos. Circumstances were very different in western India, where indigenous capital was robust and resilient and found it profitable to invest in industry, in textile mills mostly. It is from this region and sector that we encounter Gujarati and Parsi entrepreneurs such as the house of Tata that subsequently went on to invest in iron and steel and emerge as the steel makers of the nation. Today, Tata Steel is comparable with any of the largest integrated steel mills in the world with enormous assets. Steel stood for modernization and both the houses of Tata and Godrej specialized in this material to give India an important legacy of manufacture.

A key actor to emerge in our study has been the state. Economic and business history scholars have long debated the relationship between business and markets and the state, arguing that the two entities were not compatible. Ironically, the pre-Mughal state had a hands-off approach to business and individual instances of extraction were more an aberration than a norm. Merchants were left to their devices and could count upon the benefits of political security and infrastructure. Subsequently, the situation got complicated, especially in the colonial centuries, when the colonial/imperial state regulated the economy in a manner that benefited the metropolitan core at the expense of the colonized periphery. It was only during the interwar years, when the colonial state adopted a policy of protection to foster Indian industry that would help them in the war effort, benefited Indian industry and gave them a new sense of self-confidence and ambition to further their agenda. It was therefore understandable that Indian business would get used to a protectionist regime, which they upheld even after Independence. It was only when the regulatory apparatus degenerated into a licence permit quota system that business groups began to chafe at the restrictions and strove to question it. Out of skilful negotiation and occasional confrontation, a robust business and entrepreneurial culture emerged in India that was eventually able to successfully weather storms and overcome technological lags to carve a rightful place for itself under the sun.

Notes

Introduction

1 Debby Applegate, 'From Academic Historian to Popular Biographer: Musings on the Practical Poetics of Biography', in *The Biographical Turn Lives in History*, eds Hans Renders, Binne de Haan and Jonne Haramsma (London and New York: Routledge, 2017), p. 193.

2 Mira Wilkins, 'Chandler and Global Business History', *The Business History Review*, Vol. 82, No. 2, 2008, pp. 251–256.

3 'Debating methodology in business history', (Published online by Cambridge University Press, 10 October 2017), pp. 444, 447, 450.

4 Arthur Cole, 'What is Business History?', *The Business History Review*, Vol. 35, No. 1, 1962, pp. 98–106.

5 Ibid, pp. 102.

6 Per Hansen, 'Business History: A Cultural and Narrative Approach', *The Business History Review* Vol. 86, No.4, 2012, pp. 693–717.

7 Ibid, p. 708.

8 Geoffrey Jones and R. Daniel Wadhwani, 'Entrepreneurship and Business History: Reviewing the Research Agenda', Working paper, 2006, https://www.hbs.edu/ris/Publication%20Files/07-007.pdf Accessed 20 June 2024.

9 Irfan Habib, 'Potentialities of Capitalist Development in the Economy of Mughal India', *The Journal of Economic History*,

Vol. 29, Issue 1, 1969, pp. 32–78. Also see Irfan Habib, *Indian Economy Under Early British Rule 1757–1857* (New Delhi: Tulika Books, 2022)

10 A.D.D. Gordon, *Businessmen and Politics – Rising nationalism and a modernising economy in Bombay, 1918–1933* (Bombay: Manohar, 1978)

11 Claude Markovits, *Indian Business and Nationalist Politics 1931–1939* (Cambridge: Cambridge University Press, 1985)

12 Amiya Bagchi, *Private Investment in India 1900–1939* (Cambridge: Cambridge University Press, 1972), p. 91.

13 Tirthankar Roy, *The Economic History of India 1857–1947* (New Delhi: Oxford University Press, 2011)

14 Dwijendra Tripathi, *The Oxford History of Indian Business* (New Delhi: Oxford University Press, 2004), *The Dynamics of a Tradition Kasturbhai Lalbhai and his Entrepreneurship* (New Delhi: Manohar, 1981)

15 Douglas Haynes, *Small Town Capitalism in Western India, Artisans, Merchants and the Making of the Informal Economy* (Cambridge: Cambridge University Press, 2012)

16 Medha Kudaisya, *The Life and Times of G.D. Birla* (Oxford University Press, 2006) and Medha Kudaisya, ed., *The Oxford India Anthology of Indian Business* (New Delhi: Oxford University Press, 2011)

17 Christophe Jaffrelot, Atul Kohli and Kanta Murali, eds., *Business and Politics in India* (New York: Oxford University Press, 2019)

18 Hamish McDonald, *The Polyester Prince: The Rise of Dhirubhai Ambani* (St Leonards, NSW: Allen & Unwin, 1998), Gita Piramal, *Business Maharajas* (New Delhi: Penguin India, 2011) and *Rahul Bajaj An extraordinary life* (New Delhi: Penguin Portfolio, 2022)

19 See Hans Renders, Binne de Haan and Jonne Harmsma, eds., *The Biographical Turn Lives in History* (London: Routledge, 2017) pp. 48 and 192–93.

# #

20 S.L. Kirloskar, *Cactus and Roses: An Autobiography* (Pune: Macmillan: 2003); Also see T.V. Parvate, *Jamnalal Bajaj: A Brief Study of his Life and Character* (Ahmedabad: Navajiban Publishing House,1960) and B.R. Nanda, *In Gandhi's Footsteps: The Life and Times of Jamnalal Bajaj* (New Delhi: Oxford University Press, 1990)

1. Pre-Modern Business in the Age of Empire: Trade, Capital and Markets in Late Mughal India

1 John F. Richards, *The Mughal Empire (The New Cambridge History of India)* (Cambridge: Cambridge University Press, 1995).

2 Quoted in B.G. Gokhale, *Surat in the Seventeenth Century* (Bombay: Popular Prakashan, 1979), pp. 39–40.

3 *Travels of Fray Sebastien Manrique* (London: Printed for the Hakluyt Society, 1927), Vol. 2, pp. 155–156.

4 Jean Baptiste Tavernier, *Travels in India,* Vol. 1 (London: Oxford University Press, 1925), p. 82.

5 Ibid, p. 31.

6 Ibid, p. 6.

7 Ashin Das Gupta, *Indian Merchants and the Decline of Surat c.1700–1750* (Wiesbaden: Franz Steiner Werlag, 1979).

8 Lakshmi Subramanian, *Indigenous Capital and Imperial Expansion: Bombay, Surat and the West Coast* (New Delhi: Oxford University Press, 1996).

9 Jawaid Akhtar, 'A Reappraisal of the Political Influence and Assets of Mulla Abdul Ghafur, a Merchant of Surat', *Proceedings of the Indian History Congress,* Vol. 77: 2016, pp. 226–230.

10 Ibid, p. 226.

11 Ron Harris, 'The Institutional Dynamics of Early Modern Eurasian Trade: The Commenda and the Corporation',

November 2008 (SSRN: https://ssrn.com/abstract=1294095 or http://dx.doi.org/10.2139/ssrn.1294095)

12   Ibid, pp. 10.

13   Ghulam Nadiri, 'The Maritime Merchants of Surat: A long-term perspective', *Journal of the Economic and Social History of the Orient*, Vol. 50, Nos. 2–3, 2007, pp. 243–244.

14   These instances of confrontation are captured elegantly by Ashin Das Gupta in his monograph on Surat (1979).

15   Ron Harris, 'Family Firms in Three Regions', in *Going the Distance: Eurasian Trade and the rise of the Business Corporation 1400–1700* (Princeton: Princeton University Press, 2020), p. 176. https://doi.org/10.23943/princeton/9780691150772.003.0007)

16   Ashin Das Gupta, 'The Maritime Merchant of India', in *The World of the Indian Ocean Merchant 1500–1800 Collected essays of Ashin Das Gupta*, compiled by Uma Das Gupta (New Delhi: Oxford University Press, 2001), pp. 98–99.

17   Ashin Das Gupta, *Indian Merchants and the Decline of Surat c.1700–1750*, pp. 718–19.

18   Sudev Sheth, *Bankrolling Empire: Family Fortunes and Political Transformation in Mughal India* (Cambridge: Cambridge University Press, 2024), p. 329

19   William Foster, *The English Factories in India 1637–1641: A calendar of documents in the India Office and British Museum*, Vol. 6 (Oxford: Clarendon Press, 1912), p. 125.

20   Quoted in Sudev Sheth, *Bankrolling Empire: Family Fortunes and Political Transformation in Mughal India* (Published online, Cambridge University Press, 2024), p. 90. These observations by English factors are important in demonstrating Shantidas' clout and their bias against the Mughal governor.

21   Ibid, p. 28.

22 Ghulam Nadiri, 'The Maritime Merchants of Surat: A long-Term Perspective', *Journal of the Economic and Social History of the Orient*, Vol. 50, Nos. 2–3, 2007, pp. 243–244.

23 Lakshmi Subramanian (1996), pp. 176–95, 332–34.

24 Quoted in Introduction of J.H. Little, *House of Jagat Seth*, with introduction by N.K. Sinha (Calcutta: Calcutta Historical Society, 1960), p. xvii.

25 Sushil Chaudhuri, 'The Banking and Mercantile House of the Jagat Seths of Bengal', *Studies in people's History*, Vol. 2, No. 1, 2015, p. 86.

26 Lakshmi Subramanian, 'Banias and the British: Role of Indigenous Credit in the Process of Imperial Expansion in Western India in the Second Half of the 18th century', *Modern Asian Studies*, Vol.21, No.3, 1987, pp. 473–510.

27 Samira Sheikh, 'Reaching Across Land and Sea: The Trans-Regional Networks of a Local Man' in *Trans-Regional Trade and Traders: Situating Gujarat in the Indian Ocean from Early Times to 1900*, eds. Edward Alpers and Chhaya Goswami (New Delhi: Oxford University Press, 2019)

28 Michelguglielmo Torri, 'Trapped Inside the Colonial Order: The Hindu Bankers of Surat and their Business World During the Second Half of the Eighteenth Century', in *Trade and Politics in the Indian Ocean; Historical and Contemporary Perspectives*, ed. Giorgio Borsa (New Delhi: Manohar, 1990), p. 52.

29 Lakshmi Subramanian (1996), pp. 290–294.

30 Govind Narayan Tembe, *Mumbai: An Urban Biography From 1863*, ed. and trans. by Murali Ranganathan (London: Anthem, 2008), pp. 57

31 Ibid, pp. 57.

32 R.A. Wadia, *The Bombay Dockyard and the Wadia Master Builders* (Bombay, Published by R.A. Wadia,1955)

33 Ibid, p. 216.

2. New Merchants, New Cities and New Imaginings: Jamsetjee Jeejeebhoy and Dwarkanath Tagore

1 Tembe (2008), p. 51.
2 Jaleh Tajaldini, 'Bombay in the Early Nineteenth Century: From the (almost) lost diaries of Abdul Latif Shustari', *South Asia Research*, Vol. 41, Issue 1, 2020.
3 Peter Marshall, *East Indian Fortunes: The British in Bengal in the Eighteenth Century* (Oxford: Clarendon Press, 1976), pp. 97–101.
4 Ibid, pp. 129–33.
5 Michael Aldous, 'Partners, Servants or Entrepreneurs? Banians in the Nineteenth-Century Bengal Economy', https://web.archive.org/web/20210226180651id_/https://www.cambridge.org/core/services/aop-cambridge-core/content/view/6A0EF39B96309CAFD48DD062828B4CBA/S0007680520000689a.pdf/div-class-title-partners-servants-or-entrepreneurs-banians-in-the-nineteenth-century-bengal-economy-div.pdf Accessed on 1 July 2024.
6 Blair Kling, *Partner in Empire: Dwarkanath Tagore and the Age of Enterprise in Eastern India* (Berkeley: University of California Press, 1976), pp. 6.
7 S.B. Singh, *European Agency Houses in Bengal 1783–1833* (Calcutta: Firma K.L. Mukhopadhyay, 1966), pp. 21 ff.
8 Subramanian (1996), pp. 187–194, 199–206.
9 Pamela Nightingale, *Trade and Empire in Western India 1784–1806* (Cambridge: Cambridge University Press, 1970), pp. 178–9, 189.
10 Jesse Palsetia, *Jamsetjee Jeejeebhoy of Bombay: Partnership and Public Culture in Empire* (New Delhi: Oxford University Press, 2015)
    Also see Lakshmi Subramanian, *Three Merchants of Bombay* (Portfolio Penguin, 2012) and Asiya Siddiqi, 'The Business World of Jamsetjee Jeejeebhoy', *The Indian Economic and Social History Review*, Vol.19, Nos. 3–4, 1982, p. 308

11 Siddiqi (1982), pp. 301–324, p. 304.

12 Ibid, p. 306.

13 Amalendu Guha, 'Parsi Seths as Entrepreneurs', *Economic and Political Weekly*, Vol. 5, No. 3, 5 August 1970.

14 The best and most detailed treatment of opium cultivation, sales and trade can be found in Amar Farooqui, *Smuggling as Subversion: Colonialism, Indian Merchants and the Politics of Opium* (Lanham: Lexington Books, 2005), pp. 77, 84, 88, 101–105

15 Siddiqi (1982), pp. 309–313.

16 Ibid, pp. 309–310.

17 Quoted in Subramanian (2012), p. 121.

18 Quoted in Subramanian (2012), p. 119.

19 Siddiqi (1982), p. 320.

20 Ibid, p. 321.

21 Quoted in Subramanian (2012), p. 137.

22 Ibid, p. 137.

23 Krishna Kripalani, *A Forgotten Pioneer: A Life* (New Delhi: National Book Trust, 1980), pp. 51–52.

24 Kling (1976), pp. 54–55 for expansion of Indigo cultivation and commercial agriculture; pp. 30–35 for the early career path of Dwarkanath.

25 Kling (1976), p. 44.

26 Blair Kling, 'The Origin of the Managing Agency System in India' (Downloaded from https://www.cambridge.org/core. INSEAD, on 14 July 2018 at 08:49:05, subject to the Cambridge Core terms of use, available at https://www.cambridge.org/core/terms. https://doi.org/10.2307/2051830)

27 Kling (1976), p. 95.

28 Kripalani (1980), p. 83.

29 Kling (1976), p. 200.

30 Ibid, pp. 200–01.

31 Blair Kling, *Partner in Empire*, p. 165

3. Powering Industrial Enterprise: Parsi Business Families in Late Colonial and Early Independent India

1 Mircea Raianu, 'The Incorporation of India: The Tata Business Firm Between Empire and Nation ca. 1860–1970', *Enterprise and* Society, Vol. 19, No. 4, 2018, p. 817.

2 Dwijendra Tripathi and Makrand Mehta, *Business Houses in Western India: A Study in Entrepreneurial Response 1850–1950* (New Delhi: Manohar Publications, 1990), pp. 40–45

3 Claude Markovits, 'Bombay as a business centre in the colonial period: A comparison with Calcutta', in *Merchants, Traders, Entrepreneurs Indian Business in the Colonial Era* (Basingstoke: Palgrave Macmillan, 2008), p. 121

4 Tripathi, *The Oxford History of Indian* Business, p. 112.

5 Quoted in Verrier Elwin, *The Story of Tata Steel* (Bombay: Commercial Printing Press, 1958), p. 15

6 Fredrick James, 'The House of Tata: Sixty Years of Industrial Development in India', *Journal of the Royal Asiatic Society of the Arts*, Vol. 96, No. 4776, 1948, pp. 612–622, p. 614.

7 Elwin (1958), p .25.

8 Tripathi (2004), pp. 114–115.

9 Elwin (1958), p. 36.

10 Tripathi (2004), pp. 121–124. Also see Tripathi & Mehta (1990), pp. 55–63.

11 R.M. Lala, *Beyond the Last Blue Mountain: A Life of J.R.D. Tata* (India: Penguin Books, 1991), p. 221

12 A. Sinha and J. Singh, 'Jamshedpur', *Journal of Planning History*, Vol. 10, No. 4, 2011, pp. 263–81, p. 266.

13 Lala (1991).

14 Godrej Archives, Mumbai, see Centenary Collection files MS06-01-94 ('The Man Who Makes the Godrej Safes', *Times of India*, 27 April 1927).

15 B.K. Karanjia, *Godrej: A Hundred Years 1897–1997* Vol. 1 (N.P. Viking Penguin Books, 1997)

16 Karanjia (1997), p. 102.

17 Jahnvi Dameron Nandan, *Pukka Indian: 100 Objects That Define India* (New Delhi: Roli Books, 2017), pp. 42.

18 Harini Alladi, 'Cultural Branding in India: The Case of Godrej "Storwel" cupboards (1944–1991), *Journal of Historical Research in Marketing*, pp. 5–19.

19 Godrej Archives, Mumbai *Times of India* (Proquest collection) 'Best Office Equipment from Godrej', *Times of India*, 17 March 1955, p. 30.

20 Godrej Archives, Mumbai, See Acc. No. NDS/Cir/29145, 4 September 1951, Part 2 of 5.

21 'Steel Shortage', *Times of India,* 1 July 1958, p. 6.

22 Circular collection, Godrej Archives, Mumbai. (MS 08-01-419-212) Letter dated 27 March 1958.

23 Godrej Archives, Mumbai. See PER-14-01-322-238, *Industrial India*, Vol. 8, No. 11, November 1958.

24 Karanjia (1997), pp. 120–124.

25 Karanjia (1997), pp. 89–90.

26 Godrej Archives, Mumbai. See Centenary collection files, MS06-01-94-30. Written sketch of Mr Sohrab Pirojsha Godrej and family compiled by Dr Viraf Minocher Dhalla.

27 *Times of India*, 24 September 1955 'When security became too secure', by M.D. Japeth (Proquest Historical newspapers, accessed in Godrej Archives, Mumbai)

28 Godrej Archives, Oral History (OH006014) Interview of Johnny Fernandes, 4 December 2006.

29 Godrej Archives, Oral History (OH 09043) Interview of T.V.V.S. Chowdhary.

30 Godrej Archives, Oral History (OH 08009) Interview of Ananthswamy, p. 8 of 14.

4. Money in the Bazaar: A Story of Indigenous Credit

1 Anand Yang, *Bazaar India: Markets, Society and the Colonial State in Gangetic Bihar* (Berkeley: University of California Press, 1999).

2 C.A. Bayly, *Rulers, Townsmen and Bazaars: North Indian Society in the Age of British Expansion, 1770–1870* (Cambridge: Cambridge University Press, 1983)

3 Subramanian (1996), pp. 176–78.

4 Maharashtra State Archives, Mumbai. See Revenue Department Diary of the Bombay government, 1791. Minutes of Council, 10 May 1791.

5 Amar Farooqui, 'Opium Enterprise and Colonial Intervention in Malwa and Western India, 1800–1824', *The Indian Economic and Social History Review*, Vol. 32, No. 4, 1995.

6 C.A. Bayly, 'Patrons and Politics in Northern India', *Modern Asian Studies*, Vol. 7, No. 3, 1973 (Published online, 2008), pp. 353–355.

7 Rajat Kanta Ray, 'Asian Capital in the Age of European Domination: The Rise of the Bazaar 1800–1914', *Modern Asian Studies*, Vol. 29, No. 3, 1995, p. 493.

8 L.D. Satya, 'British Imperial Railways in Nineteenth-Century South Asia', *Economic and Political Weekly*, Vol. 43, No. 47, 2008, p. 69.

9 Ray (1995), pp. 493–494.

10 Mohanlal Badjatya, *Bhartiya Vyapariyon Ka Parichay* (Bhanpura, Indore: Commercial Publishing House, VS 1985, 1928), pp. 382, 467.

11 Thomas A. Timberg, *The Marwaris: From Traders to Industrialists* (New Delhi: Vikas Publishing House, 1978), pp. 52–53.

12 A. Calangutcar, 'Marwaris in the Cotton Trade of Bombay: Collaboration and Conflict (ca. 1850–1950)', *Proceedings of the Indian History Congress*, Vol. 73, 2012, pp. 658–677.

13 Rajat Kanta Ray, 'The Bazaar Changing Structural Characteristics of the Indigenous Section of the Indian Economy Before and After the Great Depression', *The Indian Economic and Social History Review* 25, 3, 1988, p. 268.

14 Ibid, p. 269.

15 Ray 1988.

16 Ibid.

17 Ibid, p. 288.

18 Ray 1998, pp. 293–94.

19 Ibid, p. 294.

20 Referred to (1995) by Ray in 'Asian Capital in the Age of European Domination: The Rise of the Bazaar, 1800–1914', p. 494.

21 Ray (1988), p. 299.

22 Ray (1995), p. 494.

23 Ray (1988), p. 307.

24 Tirthankar Roy, 'The Monsoon and the market for money in late colonial India', *Enterprise and Society*, Vol.17, No.2, 2016, pp. 328–330.

25 Lakshmi Subramanian, 'Settling Accounts: Indigenous Bankers in Search of New Histories in the Twentieth Century', *The Indian Economic and Social History Review*, Vol. 60, No. 2, 2023, pp. 125–157, pp. 140–42

26 Ibid, pp. 140–142.

27 *Maheshwari Jati ka Itihas* (Bhanpur: Maheshwari History Office, 1940).

28 Ibid.

29 Ibid.

30 Ritu Birla, *Stages of Capital Law, Culture and Market Governance in Late-Colonial India* (Durham: Duke University Press, 2009), p. 145.

31 Narotam Sekhsaria, *The Ambuja Story* (India: Harper Collins, 2021), p. 231.

5. Engineering, Power and Transport: Blazing
New Trails

1   Tripathi (2004), pp. 160–161 ff.

2   N. Tyabji, 'Industrial Development in South India
    1880–1947', Working Paper No. 98, Madras Institute of
    Development Studies, pp. 15–16.

3   'Switching on Innovation', *The Hindu*, 5 August 2016 (https://
    www.thehindu.com/features/metroplus/Switching-on-
    innovation/article14553242.ece) Accessed 1 March 2024.

4   T.R. Vivek, 'T.V. Sundaram Iyengar: A Business Leader
    With a Socialist Vision', *The Hindu Business Online*, updated
    13 December 2020, https://www.thehindubusinessline.com/
    companies/tvs-sundaram-iyengar-a-business-leader-with-a-
    socialist-vision/article33309990.ece Accessed 29 August 2024.

5   Sangeetha Kandavel, 'When T.V. Sundaram Iyengar operated
    the first bus service in Tamil Nadu', The Hindu, updated 17
    February 2023 https://www.thehindu.com/news/national/
    tamil-nadu/when-tv-sundaram-iyengar-operated-the-first-
    bus-service-in-tamil-nadu/article66518061.ece

6   Harish Damodaran, *India's New Capitalists: Caste, Business
    and Industry in a Modern Nation* (Basingstoke: Palgrave
    Macmillan, 2008). Also see Sangeetha Kandavel, 'When T.V.
    Sundaram Iyengar Operated the First Bus Service in Tamil
    Nadu', *The Hindu*, updated 17 February 2023 (https://
    www.thehindu.com/news/national/tamil-nadu/when-tv-
    sundaram-iyengar-operated-the-first-bus-service-in-tamil-
    nadu/article66518061.ece) Accessed 1 March 2024. Also see
    S. Subramanian, 'Splitting the Century-Old TVS Group', *The
    Hindu Business Online*, 22 August 2022, https://bloncampus.
    thehindubusinessline.com/case-studies/splitting-the-
    century-old-tvs-group-case-study/article65798962.
    ece#:~:text=They%20decided%20to%20restructure%20

the,crossholdings%20to%20avoid%20future%20discontent. Accessed 29 August 2024.

7 'Three pioneers of industrialisation', Madras Musings, 17 September 2024, https://madrasmusings.com/Vol%2022%20 No%2018/three-pioneers-of-industrialisation.html

8 S. Viswanathan, 'TVS Group Restructured', *Industrial Economist*, 5 September 2022, https://industrialeconomist. com/6310-2/ Accessed 1 March 2024.

9 https://madrasmusings.com/Vol%2022%20No%2018/ three-pioneers-of-industrialisation.html

10 Subramanian (2022).

11 Padmini Swaminathan, 'A Study of the TVS Group of Companies', *Economic and Political Weekly*, Vol. 23, No. 20, May 1988.

12 Suresh Krishna interview, *Harvard Business School*, https:// www.hbs.edu/creating-emerging-markets/interviews/Pages/ profile.aspx?profile=skrishna Accessed 5 September 2024.

13 Ibid.

14 Ibid.

15 B.R. Nanda, *In Gandhi's Footsteps: The Life and Times of Jamnalal Bajaj* (New Delhi: Oxford University Press, 1990), p. 10.

16 T.V. Parvate, *Jamnalal Bajaj: A Brief Study of His Life and Character* (Ahmedabad: Navjivan Publishing House, 1962.), p. 95.

17 Ibid, p. 79.

18 B.R. Nanda, 'The Merchant Prince', in *In Gandhi's Footsteps: The Life and Times of Jamnalal Bajaj* (New Delhi: Oxford University Press, 1990), pp. 13–14.

19 Nanda (1990), pp. 17–18.

20 Parvate (1962), p. 86.

21 Nanda (1990), p. 306 ff.

22 Ibid, pp. 309–310.

23 The section on Kamalnayan Bajaj draws from Gita Piramal, *Kamalnayan Bajaj: Architect of the Bajaj Group* (Hyderabad: Kamalnayan Charitable Trust, 2015)

24 Piramal (2015), p. 33.

25 Ibid, pp. 35, 43.

26 'Creating Emerging Markets—Oral History Collection', Rahul Bajaj interview by Srikant M. Datar, *Harvard Business School*, 8 July 2014, https://www.hbs.edu/creating-emerging-markets/Documents/transcripts/Bajaj_Rahul_Web%20Transcript.pdf Accessed 6 September 2024.

27 'Rahul Bajaj: The King of Mobility and His Two-Wheel Revolution', *The Wire*, 13 February 2022.

28 'Bajaj Group', iloveindia.com https://www.iloveindia.com/economy-of-india/top-50-companies/bajaj-group.html Accessed 6 September 2024.

29 Datar (2014).

30 Ross Bassett, *The Technological Indian* (Cambridge Mass: Harvard University Press, 2016), p. 1

31 Ibid, p. 62.

32 Ron Mathews, 'Development of India's Machine Tool Industry', *Economic and Political Weekly*, Vol. 23, No. 40, 1988, pp. 2061–68.

33 Bassett (2016), pp. 224–225. Also see by S.L. Kirloskar, *Cactus and Roses: An Autobiography* (Pune: Macmillan, 2003), pp. 11–30

34 Kirloskar (2003), p. 62.

35 Abhidha Dhumatkar, 'Forgotten Propagator of Science: Kolhapur's Balaji Prabhakar Modak', *Economic and Political Weekly*, Vol. 37, No. 48, 2002, pp. 4807–16.

36 Bassett (2016), p. 227 ff.

37 Ibid, p. 228.

38 Ibid, pp. 298–99.

39 Ibid, p. 230.

6. Business in the Age of Licences: Dhirubhai Ambani and the Rise of Reliance

1 In an interview to Prabhu Chawla, *India Today*, 30 June 1985.

2 In an interview to Sheela Bhat, Rediff, 7 July 2002, https://m. rediff.com/money/2002/jul/07pranab.htm Accessed 9 September 2024.

3 Surajit Mazumdar, 'From Outsider to Insider: The Case of Reliance', *South Asia Multidisciplinary Journal*, Vol. 15, 2017, (electronic version, URL: http://journals.openedition.org/ samaj/4278 DOI: 10.4000/samaj.4278)

4 Gita Piramal, *Business Maharajas* (Gurgaon: Penguin Books, 1997)

5 'Dhirubhai Ambani's words of wisdom', Rediff, last updated 3 June 2010, https://www.rediff.com/money/slide-show/slide-show-1-dhirubhai-ambanis-words-of-wisdom/20100603. htm Accessed on 29 August 2024.

6 Hamish McDonald, *The Polyester Prince* (New South Wales: Allen & Unwin, 1998), p. 21

7 Ibid, p. 25.

8 Stanley Kochanek, 'Briefcase Politics in India: The Congress Party and the Business Elite', *Asian Survey*, Vol. 27, No. 12, 1987, pp. 1278–1301.

9 Kochanek (1987).

10 McDonald (1998), pp. 38–39.

11 Sheela Bhatt, 'I liked him very, very much', Rediff, 7 July 2002, https://m.rediff.com/money/2002/jul/07pranab.htm Accessed 9 September 2024.

12 Mazumdar (2017).

13 '40 years ago . . . and now: Dhirubhai Ambani changed the idiom of doing business', *Business Standard*, 14 January 2015, https://www.

business-standard.com/article/companies/40-years-ago-and-now-he-changed-the-idiom-of-doing-business-115011400005_1. html Accessed 9 September 2024.

14 Piramal (1996), Chapter 1 (Location 545 in Kindle edition).

15 Prateeksha Tiwari, *Corporate Guru: Dhirubhai Ambani* (New Delhi: Diamond Books, 2011), p. 46.

16 Ibid, p. 43.

17 Piramal (1996).

18 Tiwari (2011), p. 44.

19 Mazumdar (2017).

20 Mazumdar (2017).

21 Sekhsaria (2021), p. 94.

22 Piramal (1996).

23 Amar K.J.R. Nayak, *Indian Multinationals: The Dynamics of Explosive Growth in a Developing Country Context* (Basingstoke; New York, Palgrave Macmillan, 2011), p. 212

24 Ibid, p. 215.

25 Ibid, p. 215–216.

26 Kochanek (1987), p. 1295 ff.

27 Chander Uday Singh, 'Bear speculators fails to bring down price of Reliance shares through large-scale selling', *India Today*, 31 May 1982, updated 7 August 2014, https://www.indiatoday.in/magazine/economy/story/19820531-bear-speculators-fails-to-bring-down-price-of-reliance-shares-through-large-scale-selling-771843-2013-10-12 Accessed 10 September 2024.

28 'Ambani vs Wadia: The most celebrated battle in Indian corporate history', *India Today*, 31 August 1989, updated 30 October 2013, https://www.indiatoday.in/magazine/cover-story/story/19890831-ambani-vs-wadia-the-most-celebrated-

battle-in-indian-corporate-history-816467-1989-08-30
Accessed 10 September 2024.

29 Jagannath Dubashi and Prabhu Chawla, 'Dhirubhai
    Ambani of Reliance and Nusli Wadia of Bombay Dyeing
    spar over PTA, DMT', *India Today*, 15 December
    1985, updated 3 April 2014, https://www.indiatoday.in/
    magazine/economy/story/19851215-dhirubhai-ambani-of-
    reliance-and-nusli-wadia-of-bombay-dyeing-spar-over-pta-
    dmt-802256-2014-01-26. Accessed 10 September 2024. Also
    see Piramal (1996), Kindle Location 1033.

30 T.N. Ninan, 'Dhirubhai Ambani's gambit to net Rs 60 crore
    in cost savings comes a cropper', *India Today*, 31 October
    1985, updated 28 March 2014, https://www.indiatoday.in/
    magazine/economy/story/19851031-dhirubhai-ambanis-
    gambit-to-net-rs-60-crore-in-cost-savings-comes-a-
    cropper-802107-2014-01-14 Accessed 10 September 2024.

31 Kochanek (1987), p. 1296.

32 Sumit Mitrae, 'From the archives: Dhirubhai Ambani, the
    futurist', *India Today*, updated 27 December 2021, https://
    www.indiatoday.in/india-today-insight/story/from-the-archives-
    dhirubhai-ambani-the-futurist-1892875-2021-12-27   Accessed
    10 September 2024.

33 McDonald (1998), pp. 64–68.

34 Nayak (2011), p. 216.

35 Nayak (2011), p. 243.

36 Mazumdar (2017), FN44 p. 20.

37 Tiwari (2011), p. 21.

38 Mitre (2021).

39 T.N. Ninan and Jagannath Dubashi, 'Dhirubhai Ambani
    emerges as India's most outstanding businessman of the
    last two decades', *India Today*, 30 June 1985, updated

2 June 2014, https://www.indiatoday.in/magazine/cover-story/story/19850630-dhirubhai-ambani-emerges-as-indias-most-outstanding-businessman-of-the-last-two-decades-770192-1999-11-29 Accessed 10 September 2024.

40 Tiwari (2011), see introduction.

41 'Nusli Wadia explains his loss to Ambani in polyester war', Firstpost, 4 December 2012, https://www.firstpost.com/business/nusli-wadia-explains-his-loss-to-ambani-in-polyester-war-514427.html

Scan QR code to access the
Penguin Random House India website